ECONOMICS OF SPORT

Other Titles in the Sport Management Library

— • —

ECONOMICS OF SPORT
Second Edition

Mark J. Eschenfelder
ROBERT MORRIS UNIVERSITY

Ming Li
OHIO UNIVERSITY

Fitness Information Technology
a Division of the International Center
for Performance Excellence
262 Coliseum, WVU-PE, PO Box 6116
Morgantown, WV 26506-6116

Library of Congress Card Catalog Number: 2006929899

ISBN: 978-1-885693-72-3

Copyeditor: Corey Madsen
Cover Design: Bellerophon Productions
Production Editors: Corey Madsen, Matt Brann
Typesetter: Bellerophon Productions
Proofreader: Maria E. denBoer
Indexer: Maria E. denBoer
Printed by Sheridan Books
Cover photos: Jackson $20.00 bill courtesy of iStockphoto, baseball game and race track courtesy of stock.xchng iv

10 9 8 7 6 5 4 3

Fitness Information Technology
A Division of the International Center for Performance Excellence
262 Coliseum, WVU-PE
PO Box 6116
Morgantown, WV 26506-6116
800.477.4348 toll free
304.293.6888 phone
304.293.6658 fax
Email: fitcustomerservice@mail.wvu.edu
Website: www.fitinfotech.com

Acknowledgments

The first edition of this book was the work of Ming Li, Susan Hofacre, and Dan Mahony. The present volume is built upon their work. The book follows their original organization and contains much of their writing. Susan Hofacre planned to be involved in revising and updating the book for this edition. Her involvement ended with her untimely death in January of 2005. She is sadly missed by her friends and colleagues. Due to the constant increase in his administrative responsibilities, Dan Mahony decided not to participate in the revision. We owe a debt to both Susan and Dan for their prior involvement with the book and contributions.

We thank many people for their support of this project. Colleagues past and present encouraged us in our interest in the economics of sports. Scott Branvold provided helpful feedback on revised chapters as well as insight from teaching a course on the Economics of Sport. Kongting Yeh reviewed the draft of Chapter 12 and provided insightful comments of how to revise the chapter. Our students in Economics of Sport classes helped us through their questions, interests, and enthusiasm. Our spouses Cora Eschenfelder and Wan Chen provided encouragement and understanding.

Thanks also to Corey Madsen and Matt Brann, Production Editors at Fitness Information Technology (FIT), who handled the production of the second edition of this book. Finally, our gratitude goes to all the other people at FIT for their work and for making the writing of this second edition a positive and rewarding experience.

Contents

Detailed Contents

Preface

Sport is a very visible part of our business and cultural environment. A wide variety of people follow spectator sports through reading newspapers, watching sports on television, attending games, buying sport merchandise, and other activities. People follow spectator sports for different reasons, including allegiances to communities, schools, and individuals; an interest in sports gaming; and enjoyment of the excitement that the uncertainty of outcomes in sports generates. Millions of people also participate in sports, fitness, and recreation activities daily. This interest in sports generates curiosity about the business side of the sport industry. This text on the economics of sport attempts to answer some of the questions people have about the business of the sport industry.

The following are some of the questions we hope to answer in this text. Why do some professional athletes earn million-dollar salaries? Why can professional sports leagues operate as monopolies in the sale of broadcast rights? How does competition affect the behavior of firms in the sport industry? Why do private firms (for-profit and not-for-profit) provide some sport activities and the government others? Broadly speaking, this text is about decision making in the sport industry. Understanding decision making in the sport industry can help people answer many of the questions they have about the nature of the business of sport.

Research on the economics of sports has been a growth industry in economics for over fifty years. Much of the work by economists has focused on the economics of spectator sports in the United States, in particular Major League Baseball. While this text explores the economics of spectator sports, its focus is the broader sport industry. In this text issues in youth sport, recreational sport, the sporting goods industry, and many other segments of the sport industry are explored.

The primary audience for the text is upper-level undergraduates studying in sport management programs. Much of the material has been used in undergraduate sport economics courses taught by the authors. In writing the text, we assumed students have had some exposure to economic concepts and analysis, perhaps an introductory course in economics. Most economic concepts are reviewed before they are applied to the sport industry. The text could be used in a lower division economics course for economics majors or in a course for students in a master's degree program in sport management. The text may also serve as a reference for people curious about the economics of sport.

The book is organized into thirteen chapters. After the key concepts and main topics of the chapter are presented, a brief summary is included. There are chapter questions at the end of each chapter, as well as learning activities for those chapters whose concepts can be put into practice. The chapter questions provide students with the opportunity to reflect on the topics that have been covered in the chapter.

Chapter 1, *An Overview of the Sport Industry in North America*, is designed to give students an overview of the sport industry in the United States. A two-sector sport industry model developed by Li, Hofacre, and Mahony (2001) is explained. This chapter is one of the unique features of this book. The authors of the book strongly believe that it is important for students in sport management to have a clear understanding of what constitutes the sport industry before they can truly grasp the economic phenomena that occur within it.

Chapters 2 through 5 examine fundamental economic concepts and principles and how they can be applied in explaining events in the sport industry. Chapter 2, *Basics of Economic Analysis*, introduces students to economic analysis in the sport industry. It reviews models economists use to explain decisions and the behavior of firms. Chapter 3, *Demand, Supply, and Pricing in the Sport Industry*, explains and applies demand, supply, pricing, and revenue in the sport industry. Elasticity of demand and supply are covered in terms of decisions sport managers must make. In addition, the factors that influence supply and demand are also examined.

In Chapter 4, *Markets and the Sport Industry*, the behavior of firms in the sport industry is linked to the type of market in which they compete. Markets are characterized by attributes (such as barriers to entry) that influence the types of decisions firms must make. Models for competitive, monopolistic, and monopolistically competitive markets are presented in the chapter.

Examples of oligopoly in the sport industry are presented in Chapter 5, *Oligopoly and the Sport Industry*. The difficulty of analyzing the behavior of firms in oligopoly is explored. The behavior of firms in oligopolistic markets is tied to their beliefs about the likely reactions of rival firms. Several models of oligopoly are described in the chapter.

Several sport delivery structures in the United States are analyzed in Chapter 6, *Sport Industry Delivery*. The philosophy, objectives, leadership, and finance of the three common sport delivery structures—government, community-based organizations, and private enterprise—are presented.

Chapter 7, *The Sport Industry: A Critical Center of Economy*, answers the question of how big the sport industry is in the United States. Specifically, it provides students with a detailed review of the issues related to determining and measuring the size of the sport industry so that they will gain a better understanding of how important the sport industry is to the national economy.

Chapter 8, *Economic Impact of Sport*, reviews the concept of economic impact and addresses how to properly conduct an economic impact study. The theoretical foundation of economic impact studies, procedural steps to execute an economic impact study, and common errors committed in conducting economic impact research are explained.

Chapter 9, *Labor Markets and Sport*, explores labor market issues in the sport industry. The operation of competitive labor markets is explained. The demand for labor is related to the productivity of workers and product demand. The bilateral monopolies that characterize the labor markets for many professional athletes are described. Particular attention is paid to the role of collective bargaining in professional sports to increase competition in the labor market for players.

Economic issues and theories of both government and industry self-regulation in the sport industry are examined in Chapter 10, *Regulation of Sports*. Specifically, this chapter discusses why and how government regulates industry, and why an industry regulates itself and how it can do it effectively.

Chapter 11, *Antitrust Issues in Sport*, begins with an overview of the antitrust laws and exemptions to the laws that are significant in the sport industry. The role of the court in interpreting the antitrust laws is stressed as the application of the antitrust laws in the sport industry is explored.

Chapter 12, *International Issues*, helps students understand several important issues concerning internationalization. The issues include why the economic system of a country affects the sport governance in the country, what the theoretical foundations for globalization of sport from an economic perspective are, and how sport organizations expand internationally.

The last chapter, *Future Direction of the Sport Industry: An Economic Perspective*, explains challenges facing the sport industry in the United States and North America in the 21st century. The growth of the sport industry, the changes in demographics of the population, the impact of competition, and changes in technology are some of the factors generating challenges for the industry.

Chapter One

AN OVERVIEW OF THE SPORT INDUSTRY IN NORTH AMERICA

Introduction

What is the sport industry? This is a question that has never been answered clearly by either scholars in sport management or practitioners in the industry that we call "sport." Numerous attempts were made in the past, but no indisputable answer to the question was found. In other words, concerned scholars in sport management have not yet reached a consensus in terms of how to define the sport industry. People in the industry have literally used the term at their own discretion. For example, organized sports has been used as an equivalent term while calculating the size of the sport industry (Broughton, Lee, & Nethery, 1999). Accordingly, defining the sport industry in North America becomes an important task for the sport management professional. An understanding of the sport industry in North America will provide the student with an analytical foundation for further examinations of various economic issues in sport.

Definition of an Industry

An industry can be defined according to one of two criteria: similarity of products and similarity of economic activities. Defined with the first criterion, an industry refers to a group of firms that provide similar, well-defined products and services (Lipsey, 1999; Shim & Siegel, 1995). Most of the industries in the United States are labeled in this way, such as the automobile industry. An industry can also be defined by the similarities of firms in economic activities/production. This is the method utilized by the U.S. Census Bureau in the development of the North American Industrial Classification System (NAICS). The Census Bureau in the United States used to utilize a system called the Standard Industrial Classification (SIC) codes to classify the industries in the country. In 1997, NAICS was adopted and replaced the SIC codes in industry classifications. NAICS was developed jointly by the three nations in North America to provide new comparability in statistics about business activity across the United States, Canada, and Mexico. Based on a production-oriented conceptual framework, NAICS groups industries according to their similarities in the process of goods or service production (Office of Management and Budget, 1997).

> **An Overview of the Sport Industry in North America**
>
> XYZ International is an international oriented firm specializing in sport marketing and facility management. The company was recently contacted and hired by the Sports Bureau of the People's Republic of China to provide consultation services to the Chinese sport leadership in terms of how to possibly model the sport industry in China after the U.S. model. At the first meeting between the Chief of the Sports Bureau and the general manager of the firm, the former asked the latter this question: "Can you give me a detailed description of the sport industry in the United States?" Assume you were the general manager. What is your answer?

As mentioned above, NAICS defines an industry as a grouping of economic activities. So, industries are grouped by the similarity of their economic activities, not by their products. The producing units within a particular industry share a basic production process and use a similar technology in production (Office of Management and Budget, 1997). Using the definition as a guideline, NAICS groups all economic activities into a 20-sector structure and it

> uses a six-digit coding system to identify particular industries and their placement in this hierarchical structure of the classification system. The first two digits of the code designate the sector, the third designates the subsector, the fourth digit designates the industry group, the fifth digit designates the NAICS industry, and the sixth digit designates the national industry (Office of Management and Budget, 1997, p. 15).

Table 1-1. The 20 Sectors or Major Economic Activities That Are Categorized by NAICS

Two-Digit Code	Industry Categories
11	Agriculture, forestry, fishing, and hunting
21	Mining
22	Utilities
23	Construction
31–33	Manufacturing
41–43	Wholesale trade
44–46	Retail trade
48–49	Transportation and warehousing
51	Information
52	Finance and insurance
53	Real estate and rental and leasing
54	Professional, scientific, and technical services
55	Management of companies and enterprises
56	Administration and support and waste management and remediation services
61	Education services
62	Health care and social assistance
71	Arts, entertainment, and recreation
72	Accommodation and food services
81	Other services (except public administration)
91-91	Public administration

Source: Meek, A. (1997). An estimate of the size and supported economic activity of the sports industry in the United States. *Sport Marketing Quarterly, 6*(4), 15–21.

The Sport Industry in North America

Table 1-1 shows the 20 sectors or major economic activities that are categorized by NAICS. NAICS does not consider sport a major economic activity and, therefore, does not treat the sport industry as a stand-alone industrial sector or industry. The industrial activities related to sport are placed into several of the major sectors, such as manufacturing, arts, entertainment, and recreation (see Table 1-2 for details).

Table 1-2. The 20 NAICS Sectors or Major Economic Activities and Placement of Sport-Related Economic Activities

Two-Digit Code	Industry Categories
11	Agriculture, forestry, fishing, and hunting
21	Mining
22	Utilities
23	Construction
	234990 . . Athletic field construction
31–33	Manufacturing
315	Sport/athletic apparel, sports clothing
	316219 . . Athletic footwear manufacturing
	33992 . . . Sporting goods manufacturing
41–43	Wholesale trade
42191	Sporting and recreational goods and suppliers, and wholesalers
44–46	Retail trade
	451110 . . . Sporting goods stores, sports gear stores
	453310 . . Sporting goods stores, used
48–49	Transportation and warehousing
51	Information
52	Finance and insurance
53	Real estate and rental and leasing
	532292 . . Sporting goods rental
54	Professional, scientific, and technical services
55	Management of companies and enterprises
56	Administration and support and waste management and remediation services
61	Education services
	61162. . . . Sports and recreation instructions
62	Health care and social assistance
71	Arts, entertainment, and recreation
	71121. . . . Spectator sports
	711211. . . Professional or semiprofessional sports teams and clubs
	711212. . . Racetracks
	711219. . . Independent professional or semiprofessional athletes (race car drivers, golfers, boxers), owners of racing participants (e.g., cars), and independent trainers
	711310. . . Sports arena and stadium operators, sports event managers, organizers, and promoters
	71131. . . . Promoters of sports events
	711320. . . Sports event managers, organizers, and promoters without facilities
	71132. . . . Promoters of sports events without facilities
	712110. . . Sports halls of fame
	71391 . . . Golf courses and country clubs
	71392 . . . Skiing facilities
	71394 . . . Fitness and recreational sports centers
	71395 . . . Bowling centers
	713990 . . Recreational or youth sports teams and leagues
	711410. . . Sports figures' agents or managers
72	Accommodation and food services
81	Other services (except public administration)
	81149. . . . Sport equipment repair and maintenance
	81391 . . . Municipal sports authorities and councils
	81399 . . . Administrative or regulatory athletic associations (e.g., leagues)
91-91	Public administration

Source: Office of Management and Budget (1997). *North American Industry Classification System (NAICS)—1997*. U.S. Department of Commerce, Washington, DC.

The contents of NAICS provide sport management professionals with a useful reference in terms of what activities are considered sport-related by the government. Nevertheless, since NAICS groups the economic activities based on their similarity in production, the sport-producing units are scattered across eight NAICS sectors. It is very difficult, if not impossible, to conceptualize the industry we call "sport." In addition, many traditional sport-producing units, such as sport television and radio networks, are not specifically classified. Thus, a conceptual framework that includes and links together all the sport-producing units in a systematic matter must be constructed. As mentioned above, previous attempts have been made to define and outline the sport industry.

Meek (1997) uses a three-sector model to describe the sport industry in North America. The three main sectors are (1) sports entertainments and recreation, (2) sports products and services, and (2) sports support organizations. The first sector, sports entertainment and recreation, includes professional and amateur sport teams, sport events, sport media, and sport tourism-related businesses. The sport-producing units related to sporting goods design, manufacturing, and distribution, as well as to provision of sport services, are included in the sports products and services sector. The sport support organizations, the third sector of the sport industry, include all professional and amateur organizations, such as leagues, marketing organizations, and law firms (see Figure 1-1 for details). Meek's model presents a broad operational definition of the sport industry because it "includes not only the economy activity of sports teams and recreational sports but also the

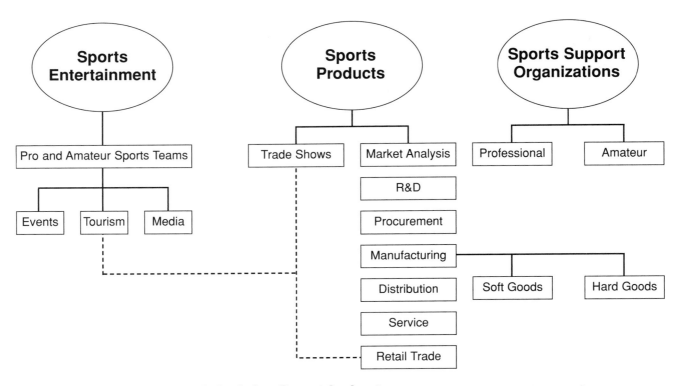

Figure 1-1. Meek's Model of the Sport Industry

Source: Meek, A. (1997). An estimate of the size and supported economic activity of the sports industry in the United States. *Sport Marketing Quarterly, 6*(4), 15–21.

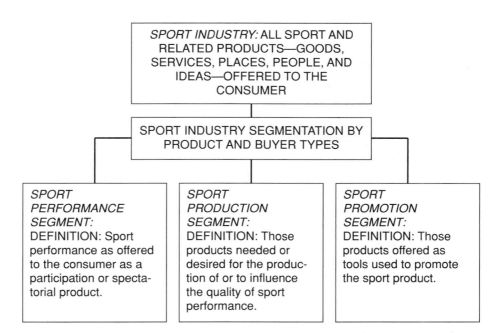

```
┌─────────────────────────────────────┐
│  SPORT INDUSTRY: ALL SPORT AND       │
│  RELATED PRODUCTS—GOODS,             │
│  SERVICES, PLACES, PEOPLE, AND       │
│  IDEAS—OFFERED TO THE                │
│  CONSUMER                            │
└─────────────────────────────────────┘
        ┌─────────────────────────────┐
        │ SPORT INDUSTRY SEGMENTATION BY │
        │ PRODUCT AND BUYER TYPES        │
        └─────────────────────────────┘
```

| SPORT PERFORMANCE SEGMENT: DEFINITION: Sport performance as offered to the consumer as a participation or spectatorial product. | SPORT PRODUCTION SEGMENT: DEFINITION: Those products needed or desired for the production of or to influence the quality of sport performance. | SPORT PROMOTION SEGMENT: DEFINITION: Those products offered as tools used to promote the sport product. |

Figure 1-2. The Sport Industry Segment Model Proposed by Pitts, Fielding, and Miller

Source: From Pitts, B. G., Fielding, L. W., & Miller, L. K. (1994). Industry segmentation theory and the sport industry: Developing a sport industry segment model. *Sport Marketing Quarterly, 3*(1), 15–24.

spending of participants, spectators, and sponsors in connection with sports events" (Meek, 1997, p. 16). So, the foundation of his model is spending, not just the economic activity engaged in by sport-related firms and organizations. This may be a limitation of his model. In addition, the three sectors are parallel, and they are not entirely separate from one another. Such a structure has caused some confusion as it does not clearly delineate the defined products or services of the sport industry.

Pitts, Fielding, and Miller (1994) also attempted to depict the sport industry with another three-sector model. In their model, the sport industry is defined as "a market in which the products offered to its buyers are sport, fitness, recreation, or leisure-related and may be activities, goods, services, people, places, or ideas" (p. 3). The industry is divided into three segments: (a) the sport performance industry segment, (b) the sport production industry segment, and (c) the sport promotion industry segment. The sport performance industry segment refers to those sports firms that offer sport performance to the consumer either as a participation or spectatorial product. The sport production industry segment includes those firms whose products are needed or desired for the production of or to influence the quality of sport performance, such as sporting goods manufacturers. The sport promotion industry segment includes those firms whose products offered as tools used to promote the sport product. Figure 1-2 shows the three segments and their respective descriptions. The separation of the three industry segments is based on the benefits of a product to a consumer. As Pitts and Stotlar (1996) maintain, "this type of categorization, called industry segmentation, is helpful to the sport marketing professional in planning marketing strategies"

(p. 19). This model does not, however, outline the relationship among sport-producing units of the sport industry. In addition, the separation of the three segments seems to imply that sport firms and organizations included in one segment are not related to those in another segment.

Li, Hofacre, and Mahony (2001) believe that sport competitions and events are one thing that all the firms and organizations in the sport industry can relate to. In other words, sport activities are the center around which many other products and services are produced in the sport industry. The sport activities are what make the industry different from other entertainment counterparts. With this perception in mind, they define the sport industry as the cluster of (1) the firms and organizations that produce sport activities, (2) the firms and organizations that provide products and services to support the production of sport activities, and (3) the firms and organizations that sell and trade products related to sport activities. Conceptualized under this definition, a sport industry model is constructed.

Li, Hofacre, and Mahony's Sport Industry Model

The model has two main sectors. The first sector is the sport activity producing sector. The firms and organizations that produce such activities as sport competitions, sport events, and sport services are included in this sector. Professional and semiprofessional teams, intercollegiate and interscholastic athletic departments, municipal and county recreation departments, sports and fitness clubs, independent professional athletes, sports trainers and instructors, and owners of racing participants (e.g., race cars and horses) are examples of the sport activity producers. The sport activity producing sector is the core of the sport industry. Sport activities are the main line of operations of all the firms and organizations in this sector. They can distinguish their line of operations clearly from those of other industries.

The second sector is labeled as the sport supporting sector. The firms and organizations that make up this sector are in the role of either providing products and services to support the production of sport activities or selling and trading products that are related to sport activities. There are six sport supporting subsectors: administrative and regulatory athletic associations (e.g., USOC, NCAA, and NFL), sporting goods manufacturers, wholesalers and retailers, sports facilities and buildings, sport media, sport management firms, and municipal and county sports councils and authorities. Detailed descriptions of firms and organizations that are composed of these two sectors are given later in the section, and Figure 1-3 illustrates the conceptual framework of the sport industry and the relationship between the two sectors.

It must be noted that all the sport supporting subsectors overlap somewhat with the sport activity producing sector, since sometimes firms and organizations in the sport supporting sector also sponsor and organize sport events. A good example is the recent creation of the Great Outdoor Games by ESPN, which makes the sport-supporting television company also a sport event producer. This phenomenon is reflected by the shaped areas between the big circle and the six smaller ones shown in Figure 1-3. However, since the primary role of firms and organizations in the

Figure 1-3. The Two-Sector Model of the Sport Industry

Source: Li, M., Hofacre, S., & Mahony, D. (2001). *Economics of sport.* Morgantown, WV: Fitness Information Technology.

sport supporting sector is to facilitate the production of sport activities or to sell sport-related products, it would be appropriate to label them as sport supporting subsectors. For example, sporting goods manufacturers, through their various wholesale channels, furnish athletic and sport equipment, such as baseball helmets, balls, and bats, to the municipal park and recreation departments all over the country. They are not in a position to produce sport activities but to supply athletic and sport equipment, and other sporting goods (e.g., athletic shoes and apparels) to firms and organizations in the sport activity producing sector. This explains why sporting goods manufacturers, wholesalers, and retailers are classified as a sport-supporting subsector. The relationship between firms and organizations in the sport activity producing sector and sport media is another appropriate example to explain why the latter is a sport-supporting subsector. The games produced by and existence of professional sports teams provide the sport media with sources of information, such as news, statistics, and player stories. This is what the sport media depends on and what it tries to sell to the general public. It is logical, therefore, to regard them as one of the important constituents of the sport-supporting sector.

As mentioned above, the sport activity producing sector comprises several types of firms and organizations that are primarily engaged in producing sport competitions, events, programs, and services. They represent what the industry that we call "sport" is all about.

PROFESSIONAL AND SEMIPROFESSIONAL SPORT TEAMS

The Sport Activity-Producing Sector

Professional sport teams refer to those firms that are "primarily engaged in participating in live sporting events . . . before a pay audience" (Office of Management and Budget, 1997, pp. 659–660). According to the United States 2002 Economic Census (U.S. Census Bureau, 2002), there were about 819 professional sport teams or clubs affiliated with various leagues at both the major and minor league levels at that time. As firms in the sport-producing sector, individual professional sports teams or "franchises" are responsible for producing games to satisfy the needs and interest of consumers for sport entertainment. Each team usually has an exclusive right to market and operate in a designated area. Gate receipts, sales of premier seats and luxury suites, parking and concession, corporate sponsorships, and sales of local broadcast and telecast rights are the revenue sources the teams receive to sustain their operations. In the United States, most professional sport teams are owned by individuals and set up as partnerships.

A semiprofessional sport team refers to a sport establishment made up of semiprofessional athletes. A semiprofessional athlete is defined as "one who is paid to play and thus is not an amateur, but for whom sport is not a full-time occupation, generally because the level of pay is too low to make a reasonable living based solely upon that service . . ." (Wikipedia, 2006). Setting up either as a profit-oriented firm or a nonprofit 501C3 organization, a semiprofessional sport team in the United States is commonly established for the sake of bringing a sport entertainment product to a particular local community. They provide the athletes with a professional opportunity while they complete degrees and/or begin their work careers, and with a path toward the "big professional sport league." The 750 senior amateur teams affiliated with the American Football Association (AFA) are good representations of the semiprofessional sport teams in the United States. More detailed discussion can be found in the section pertaining to administrative or regulatory associations in professional sport.

INTERCOLLEGIATE AND INTERSCHOLASTIC ATHLETIC DEPARTMENTS

Intercollegiate sports is one of the unique aspects of both the higher education system and the sport industry in the United States. More than 4,000 colleges and universities play intercollegiate sports and compete under the sanction of three national governing bodies: the National Collegiate Athletic Association (NCAA), the National Association for Intercollegiate Athletics (NAIA), and the National Junior Collegiate Athletic Association (NJCAA). As of 2005, about 1,024 institutions were affiliated with the NCAA (National Collegiate Athletic Association, 2006) and approximately 283 small colleges are associates of the NAIA (NAIA, 2005). The NJCAA has about 550 member institutions.

Each individual institution that holds membership with a national collegiate athletic association usually competes in a geographically-determined conference at a competition level that matches its operating philosophy and financial resources.

Table 1-3. A Summary of the Differences Among Institutions in the Three Divisions of the NCAA

Division I

Division I member institutions have to sponsor at least seven sports for men and seven for women (or six for men and eight for women) with two team sports for each gender. Each playing season has to be represented by each gender as well. There are contest and participant minimums for each sport, as well as scheduling criteria. For sports other than football and basketball, Division I schools must play 100% of the minimum number of contests against Division I opponents—anything over the minimum number of games has to be 50% Division I. men's and women's basketball teams have to play all but two games against Division I teams; for men, they must play 1/3 of all their contests in the home arena. Schools that have football are classified as Division I-A or I-AA. I-A football schools are usually fairly elaborate programs. Division I-A teams have to meet minimum attendance requirements (17,000 people in attendance per home game, OR 20,000 average of all football games in the last four years, OR 30,000 permanent seats in their stadium and average 17,000 per home game, OR 20,000 average of all football games in the last four years, OR be in a member conference in which at least six conference members sponsor football or more than half of football schools meet attendance criterion). Division I-AA teams do not need to meet minimum attendance requirements. Division I schools must meet minimum financial aid awards for their athletics program, and there are maximum financial aid awards for each sport that a Division I school cannot exceed.

Division II

Division II institutions must sponsor at least five sports for men and five for women or four sports for men and six for women, with two team sports for each gender, and each playing season represented by each gender. There are contest and participant minimums for each sport. Division II schools must meet minimum financial aid awards for their athletics program, and there are maximum financial aid awards for each sport that a Division II school cannot exceed. Division II teams usually feature a number of local or in-state student-athletes. Many Division II student-athletes pay for school through a combination of scholarship money, grants, student loans, and employment earnings. Division II athletics programs are financed in the institution's budget like other academic departments on campus. Traditional rivalries with regional institutions dominate schedules of many Division II athletics programs.

Division III

Division III institutions have to sponsor at least five sports for men and five for women, with three team sports for each gender, and each playing season represented by each gender. There are minimum contest requirements for all sports and minimum participant requirements for individual sports. Division III athletics feature student-athletes who receive no financial aid related to their athletic ability, and athletic departments are staffed and funded like any other department in the university. Division III athletics departments place special importance on the impact of athletics on the participants rather than on the spectators. The student-athlete's experience is of paramount concern. Division III athletics encourages participation by maximizing the number and variety of athletic opportunities available to students, placing primary emphasis on regional in-season and conference competition.

For example, the member institutions of the NCAA are divided into three divisions (i.e., Division I, Division II, and Division III) based on several criteria, which include, but are not limited to, number of sports sponsored and number of financial aid awards for their athletics program. The institutions having a football program in Division I are further grouped into two competition levels (i.e., Division I-A and Division I-AA). Stadium capacity and records of attendance are determinants used in making such distinctions and groupings. Although the mission and scope of operations of athletic programs in U.S. universities and colleges vary considerably, there is one thing in common: They all provide an athletic entertainment product (i.e., sport games) to their students, faculty, staff, and other constituents, such as their alumni and local communities. Table 1-3 summarizes the differences among institutions in the three divisions of the NCAA.

The intercollegiate athletic departments in those 2,000-some institutions that support athletic programs are a major sport event producer in the sport industry. Based on the level of participation with the national governing body it is affiliated with, an intercollegiate athletic department supports a certain number of sports. For instance, Ohio University has 18 intercollegiate athletic programs, competing mainly in the Mid-American Conference (MAC). The athletic departments in large colleges and universities, in a certain way, are set up and operated as a business enterprise within educational institutions. As such, some of them are incorporated, such as the one at the University of Florida (University Athletic Association, Inc. at the University of Florida).

Almost all the high schools in the United States have an interscholastic athletic department, which is set up to develop and implement athletic programs in the school based on the rules and regulations established by its state interscholastic athletic association. More than 800 schools that are affiliated with the Ohio High School Athletic Association, for example, compete in girls basketball in four divisions. In football, only 716 schools sponsor the sport at 6 different divisions or levels. The size of school and its financial capabilities determine the number of sports it sponsors.

MUNICIPAL AND/OR COUNTY PARKS AND RECREATION DEPARTMENTS

A municipal and/or county parks and recreation department is a unit of local government that is funded by local tax appropriation. Its mission is to provide opportunities for local residents to participate in various leisure and sports activities regardless of their age, skill, and ability. To fulfill such a mission in the sense of provision of sport activities, they organize and sponsor a variety of adult and youth athletic leagues and programs all year long. As a whole, the municipal and/or county parks and recreation departments are the largest producer of sport-related activities, particularly sport games and competitions in the United States. In addition to the provision of sport programming, the local parks and recreation departments also operate a variety of sport facilities, such as golf courses, tennis courts, swimming facilities, baseball/softball fields, etc.

RECREATIONAL SPORTS ESTABLISHMENTS

Recreational sports establishments are firms and organizations primarily engaged in operating facilities featuring lifetime activities (e.g., golf) and various active physical fitness conditioning or recreational sports activities, such as swimming, handball, and racquet sports (U.S. Census Bureau, 2002). More than 35,500 business establishments were classified by the U.S. Census Bureau in 2002 as recreational sports establishments (U.S. Census Bureau, 2002). As a main source of income, most of these types of business establishments rely primarily on membership dues or fees paid by users. They also generate income from operations such as food and beverage sales, equipment rental, and instruction. The distinction between a recreational sport establishment that is included in the sport producing sector and a sport facility that is listed under the sport-supporting sector is that the former is operated to provide sport programming and services (e.g., sport leagues and lessons), in most cases, to their members, while the latter is used as a facility by clients who are not affiliated with it. Sports and fitness activities are the main line of operations for this type of business establishment. On the contrary, sports facilities, especially stadiums and arenas, are often used to hold many nonsport events. Detailed discussion on the sport facilities and buildings is provided later in this chapter.

INDEPENDENT PROFESSIONAL ATHLETES AND OTHER INDEPENDENT ACTIVITY PRODUCERS

Independent professional athletes are those individuals who primarily engaged in participating in live sporting events for the sake of their own financial well-being (U.S. Census Bureau, 2002). They make decisions independently on various matters, such as competition schedules and endorsements. Independent professional athletes are commonly seen in tennis, golf, track and field, bowling, and automobile racing. Other independent activity producers include the owners of race participants, such as race cars, horses and dogs. They enter the race participants into events and competitions for prizes and endorsements. Sport trainers and instructors are the third group of people who are independently engaged in providing specialized services to athletes and the general public. Sport medicine clinics and tennis schools are examples of this type of independent sport activity producer. According to the 2002 U.S. Economic Census (U.S. Census Bureau, 2002), there were 2,752 independent professional athletes and other sport activity producers in the United States.

The Sport-Supporting Sector

All the firms and organizations other than those included in the sport activity producing sector make up the sport-supporting sector of the sport industry due to their special role in supporting the production of sport activities. Based upon their distinct purpose and functions, these firms and organizations are placed into six sport-supporting subsectors.

THE SUPPORTING SUBSECTOR I: ADMINISTRATIVE AND/OR REGULATORY SPORT ORGANIZATIONS

The administrative and/or regulatory sport organizations refer to those organizations in the sport industry that are formed specifically to perform administrative and/or regulatory duties for and promote the interest of their members. Examples of administrative sport organizations include the American Association for Professional Athletics (AAPA) and the National Football League Players' Association (NFLPA). On the other hand, those organizations, such as the National Basketball Association (NBA) and the United States of America (USA) Volleyball, that are created mainly to make and interpret rules of competition for their members, and reinforce the policies set by the organization among members, are considered regulatory sport organizations. Four types of administrative and/or regulatory sport organizations are discussed in the following section.

Administrative and/or Regulatory Organizations in Professional Sport

A professional sport league is created by individual team owners to perform various administrative functions as a regulatory body. It is through this body that the owners want to ensure the quality of the presentation of professional sport competitions as a business and entertainment product to its consumers. So, it is the primary responsibility for a professional sports league to create and maintain a constructive environment for its players to compete. Their activities include, but are not limited to, setting up competition schedules, negotiating collective bargaining agreements with players unions, making various rules (e.g., determining order of amateur draft) and regulatory policies to enforce its management rights, and negotiating national TV agreements.

A professional sport league is categorized as either a major or minor league. In seeking to define a major league, no definition has been universally accepted (Wikipedia, 2006). According to Wikipedia (2006), there are only four major professional sports leagues in the United States, which have "the largest fan bases and television audiences (and therefore, the largest revenues and player salaries)." Specifically, they are Major League Baseball (MLB), the National Basketball Association (NBA), the National Football League (NFL), and the National Hockey League (NHL).

Li, Hofacre, and Mahony (2001) believe that a major league is one that has a scope of operations nationwide, competes for media coverage from national television networks, attracts consumer dollars across the nation, and fills its affiliated franchises with the best available players. Using this definition, five men's professional sports leagues and one women's league in the United States are identified as major leagues. In addition to the four professional sports leagues as mentioned above, Major League Soccer (MLS) and the Women's National Basketball Association (WNBA) should also be labeled as major professional sports leagues.

The Arena Football League (AFL), to a certain extent, meets some of the criteria as mentioned above; however, it is still perceived by the public as an entity with a semi-major league status due to the fact that it is secondary to NFL in many aspects. The Canadian Football League is the only major league exclusively in Canada.

A professional sport league would be labeled as a minor league under two basic conditions. If a professional sport league voluntarily takes a secondary stance not to compete economically against the existing major league in the same sport even though its operations are national in scope, the league is a minor league. A league of this type does not try to compete with its major league counterpart for the same type of players, or for the same financial resources, such as national television revenues and consumer dollars. The Continental Basketball League (CBA) is an example of this type of minor league. The second condition for a professional sport league to be considered as a minor league exists if it operates in a designated geographical region and it becomes inherently noncompetitive in both the sporting and economic senses to the league playing at the major level. There is usually more than one minor league in the same sport across the nation because of such geographical separation. Regardless, minor leagues and their affiliated teams often have agreements with teams in major leagues that make them operate and function as a farm system for teams in those major leagues. All major sports leagues in North America, except the WNBA, have their minor league systems. The NFL has its minor systems in both North America and Europe (i.e., the Arena Football League and the NFL Europe).

In general, the minor league teams in North America compete against teams at their own level. For example, both minor league baseball and minor league soccer have a pyramid-like delivery system to supply talented players to their respective major leagues. Based on the size of the market and level of competition, a league playing minor league baseball is classified as either a Pony league/Rookie league, or an A, AA, AAA league. The higher the classification, the higher its level of competition. The number of leagues and teams decreases as the level of competition goes up. Most of the minor league baseball teams are affiliated with a major league franchise. The latter usually assumes some operating costs of the affiliated club (e.g., player salaries, travel expenses, etc.).

The minor league system serves two critical economic roles for major league teams:

> It is a reserve system for major league franchises. A replacement player is called up from AAA when a major league player is hurt.

> It is a training ground for player development. For example, in baseball, players drafted by a major league franchise from colleges and high schools are usually sent to its affiliated minor league teams for development and future use.

Another good example to illustrate the relationship between a major league and its minor leagues and how the former uses the latter as a farm system in North America is the United Soccer League. The mission of the organization is to provide systematic training and opportunities for soccer players to work through the pipeline toward Major League Soccer, the top level of the pyramid. An agreement was reached by MLS and USL in 1996 to allow the USL to act as a farm system for MLS. There are also four levels beneath it. The immediate level is the A-League. It had 28 teams in 1998, including three in Canada. Under an agreement with MLS, one of the teams in the league is stocked entirely with players identified and supported by MLS and other teams are affiliated with individual MLS teams. The next tier in the pyramid is called Division III Professional League. Forty teams played in the 1998 season. Again, all of the teams are associated with teams in MLS. The Division III Professional [Soccer] League is the lowest level of professional soccer in the system. The next two levels, the Premier Development Soccer League and National Youth League, are composed of amateur soccer teams. In addition to the four leagues mentioned above, a women's amateur soccer league, W-League, and a men's indoor soccer league, I-League, are also affiliated with the USL (United Soccer League, 2006).

There was not a minor league in professional football until the creation of the American Football Association in 1980. The goal of the organization is to advance and promote professional football at the minor league level. The AFA is an umbrella organization that consists of several semi-professional/minor leagues in professional football. The Association and its member leagues together produce a national playoff series, in which the league champions and wild card teams participate. Two major differences exist between minor league football and other sports that also have minor league operations. First, the American Football Association has no backing or support from its major league counterpart, the NFL and its major league affiliates. In other words, those minor leagues are not recognized as development leagues or the farm system for the NFL. Second, the Association takes care not only of minor league professional football teams, but also of all levels of nonprofessional football leagues.

The National Lacrosse League is the only professional lacrosse league in the world. Due to its limited scope of operations (mainly the northeastern part of the United States and southeastern region of Canada), the NLL is still perceived as a minor league. The league was founded in 1997 as a result of the merger of two indoor lacrosse leagues, the Major Indoor Lacrosse League and the professional Indoor Lacrosse Leagues. Currently, it has 11 franchises.

There are also some administrative or regulatory associations in professional sport that are mainly developed for individual sports, such as the National Association for Stock Car Auto Racing (NASCAR), the Professional Golf Association (PGA), the Ladies Professional Golf Association (LPGA), and the Dupont World Team Tennis (the only professional tennis league in the United States of America).

Regulatory Sport Organizations in College

As mentioned previously, there are three national governing bodies in college sport, the NCAA, the NAIA, and the NJCAA. The National Collegiate Athletic Association is the largest one. To a great extent, it represents how collegiate sports are governed in the United States. With this in mind, the discussion on administrative or regulatory sport organizations in college will mainly use the NCAA as an example.

As a national governing body in college sport, the NCAA governs, promotes, and furthers the purposes and goals of intercollegiate athletics by acting as a control agent for all the member institutions. It sets regulatory rules and policies with the hopes that the member institutions will benefit economically as a whole through the implementation and enforcement of these rules and policies.

In 2005, the NCAA sponsored and administered 88 championships in 23 sports for its member institutions in three divisions. More than 24,000 men and women student-athletes annually compete in these events for national titles.

Specifically, there currently are 10 National Collegiate Championships for which all divisions are eligible—three for men, four for women, and three men's and women's events. There are 25 National Collegiate Division I Championships (12 men, 13 women), 25 National Collegiate Division II Championships (12 men, 13 women), and 27 National Collegiate Division III Championships (13 men, 14 women) (National Collegiate Athletic Association, 2006). Several major sports sponsored by the NCAA are described in the following section.

All three divisions of the NCAA sponsor football, but not all member institutions play football. As mentioned before, due to the difference in size and financial resources, two levels of competition are also created among the institutions that play football in Division I, commonly known as Division I-A and Division I-AA. There are 117 institutions playing in eleven Division I-A football conferences. Eight schools that do not hold joint membership with any those aforementioned conferences, such as Notre Dame, are also competing at Division I-A level as so-called "independents." Another 118 schools are affiliated with Division I-AA football playing in fourteen athletic conferences (National Collegiate Athletic Association, 2006).

The NCAA brought in $471 million in the 2003–2004 academic year (National Collegiate Athletic Association, 2006). The money was derived primarily from a contract with CBS Sports for television and marketing rights for a number of NCAA championship events, foremost of which is the Division I Men's Basketball Championship. Total television and marketing rights fees represent 86% of the Association's operating revenue. Additional revenue sources include 10% from championships and special events, 2% from sales, services, and contributions, and the rest (2%) is investment. Of the approved operation budget, a total of $280.13 million (62% of the Association's total expenditure budget) was distributed to the NCAA Division I membership during the 2003–2004 fiscal year. The NCAA allocated approximately $61 million to Championship and special events in all three divisions, which was about 16% of the total budgeted expenses. Over 76 million, or 17% of the budget, was spent on the programs, services, and activities that benefit the membership, such as drug testing, drug education, promotions, legal fees, publications, research, sports sciences, seminars, conventions, student and youth benefits, scholarships and catastrophic injury insurance. Management and general operations of the association account for the remaining $24.6 million, or 5% of the budget.

Besides affiliating with a national governing body, a collegiate athletic department also joins a particular regional athletic conference so that its athletic teams can compete against other institutions in the same conference. A collegiate athletic conference is a group of institutions that conducts competition among its members and determines a conference champion in one or more sports. To a certain extent, a collegiate athletic conference operates just like a league in professional sport. It conducts conference championships for the sports it sponsors. Each championship helps to determine teams and/or individuals that will represent the conference in national post-season competition. It also negotiates various sponsorship deals for the conference championships and television opportunities for all sports with national and regional TV networks and radio stations.

There are about 128 athletic conferences affiliated with the NCAA, competing at three different divisions and football designations. The Atlantic Coast Conference (ACC), the Big 12, the Mid-American Conference, and the Southern Conference are examples of those athletic conferences.

Administrative or Regulatory Sport Organizations in High School

In the United States, high school athletics as a whole is administered at the state level and little or no national high school athletic competition is held. The National Federation of State High School Associations (NFHS), which consists of high school athletic/activity associations in the 50 states plus the District of Columbia, is an umbrella organization of state associations. As stated in its mission statement, the NFHS provides leadership and national coordination for the administration of interscholastic activities, including sports (National Federation of State High School Association, 2005). However, its leadership is provided only through the publication of competition rules in 16 sports for both boys and girls, and it does not organize any national championships in all sports under its purview. The high school athletic associations of individual states are the main sponsors and organizers of athletic competitions among high schools within a state. The competition is usually held at multiple levels, such as AAAA, AAA, AA, and A, based on the type and size of participating schools. In Ohio, for instance, the Ohio High School Athletic Association (OHSAA) is created to regulate, supervise, and administer interscholastic athletic competition among its member schools. It is also created to determine the qualifications of individual contestants, coaches, and officials, to provide information through literature and other materials to facilitate athletic relations among member schools, and to establish standards for sportsmanship and competition.

There are also many associations across the nation that are created for the sake of organizing competition in certain sports at the high school level, such as the Interscholastic Sailing Association (ISSA). It governs secondary school sailing in the United States, in both independent and public high schools.

Administrative or Regulatory Organizations in Other Amateur Sport

In addition to the administrative and regulatory sport organizations mentioned above that operate mainly to provide support to the presentation of sports competition at both the professional, intercollegiate, and interscholastic levels, many other administrative and regulatory sport bodies are also involved in, and contribute considerably to, the economic activities of the sport industry. Examples of this type of administrative and regulatory sport organizations include the United States Olympic Committee (USOC), some 50 individual sports federations, the Amateur Athletic Union (AAU), and the Women's Sports Foundation. There are also many other administrative and regulatory sport governing bodies that are developed for specific demographic markets, such as disabled, gay/lesbian, etc. In addition, many amateur sport organizations are created as administrative and regulatory governing bodies at the state or local level. Georgia State Games Commission, one of some 40 state games organizing agencies around the country, is one of the examples. The following section is a brief description of the USOC. It is hoped that the description will provide hints as to what an administrative and regulatory organization in amateur sport does to contribute to the advancement of sport in the United States.

The United States Olympic Committee (USOC) is one of the biggest nonprofit sports organizations in the United States of America in terms of its budget and scope of operations. The mission of this organization is to assist and facilitate the participation of every American in sport and provide "leadership and guidance for the Olympic Movement" in the United States (USOC, 1998). Specifically, the USOC is responsible for

1. Supporting Olympic and/or Pan American sports in the United States,

2. Sponsoring US teams and underwriting their expenses in the Olympic and Pan American Games, and

3. Endorsing the bid of an American city for the hosting right of the Winter and Summer Olympic Games as well as the Pan American Games.

Public Law 95-606, or the Amateur Sports Act (ASA) of 1978, empowered the USOC to be the coordinating body of all Olympic-related athletic activities in the United States. In other words, the law gave the USOC the right (1) to control the Olympics-related phraseologies and logos, and (2) to control over more than 72 national governing bodies (NGB) and amateur sports in the United States. These NGB are responsible for organizing and sanctioning various national competitions in their jurisdiction. If the sport is worldwide, the NGB of it in the United States is recognized by the international federation of the sport as the official representative in the country. The revenues and funds that the USOC receives mainly come from several major sources:

1. A cut of the revenues generated from the sales of American television rights for the Summer and Winter Olympic Games;

2. The sponsorship and advertising revenues from corporations using the Olympic rings in the United States;

3. Royalty fees from the sales of Olympic-related merchandise or goods that bear an Olympic symbols; and

4. Private donations.

In 2003, the USOC raised approximately $83.67 million to support its various operations.

THE SUPPORTING SUBSECTOR II: SPORTING GOODS MANUFACTURERS, WHOLESALERS, AND RETAILERS

The sporting goods manufacturers, wholesalers, and retailers include the companies that either manufacture sporting goods or companies that distribute and sell those products in the sports and recreation market. Sporting goods is an umbrella term including equipment and gear for various sporting and recreational purposes. The U.S. Census Bureau (1997) divides sporting goods into four basic categories: (1) athletic and sport clothing, (2) athletic and sport footwear, (3) athletic and sport equipment (e.g., exercise equipment, golf equipment, team sports equipment, and related accessories), and (4) recreational transport (e.g., bicycles and snowmobiles). As of 1999, close to 900 companies in the United States are categorized in this sector (Patino, 1999). According to the Sporting Goods Manufacturers Association, there are about 2,500 manufacturers and national brand distributors of sporting goods in North America.

There are many sporting goods manufacturers in the United States producing athletic and sport clothing, athletic and sport footwear, and athletic and sport equipment for a variety of sport and physical fitness activities. The leading ones include Nike, Rawlings, Reebok, Spalding, and Wilson.

In general, there are two types of sporting goods stores. The fist type represents those retail stores that are affiliated with major chains that carry a variety of sporting goods for a multitude of sports, such as the Sports Authority and Dick's Sporting Goods. Both are popular chains that offer a variety of sports equipment and sports apparel. The other type of store remains devoted to one or two sports and has a more targeted approach, such as Golf Galaxy or SoccerPost.

The sales of sporting goods are made through a comprehensive distribution and sales system. Sporting goods manufacturers traditionally rely on various sporting goods wholesalers and retailers to distribute and sell their products. While continuously using the external distribution channels, many companies today have formed their own wholesale and retail networks. For example, Nike has extensively utilized three of its own retail structures to sell its products directly, including Niketowns, the Nike stores, and the Nike factory outlets. As a new marketing strategy, the in-house retail system can help the sporting goods companies achieve greater consumer loyalty and strengthen their competitiveness, ultimately leading to greater market shares.

THE SUPPORTING SUBSECTOR III: SPORTS FACILITIES AND BUILDINGS

The sports facilities and buildings refer to those public assembly facilities that are primarily used to host sport-related events. In general, sports facilities and buildings include stadiums, arenas, sports complexes, sports halls of fame, racetracks, and facilities used only by a single sport, such as bowling alleys, skiing facilities, and ice/roller skating rinks. Many public assembly facilities (e.g., convention centers) that usually have large and spacious exhibit halls can be utilized for various sports programming. Nevertheless, since sport is not the main line of operations of those facilities, they are not considered sport facilities. For example, the Savannah Civic Center is not viewed as a sport facility due to the fact that it was built as a multipurpose facility and sports are not the main tenant of the facility.

The mission of sports facilities and buildings varies depending on size. For large stadiums and arenas, they are used for two basic objectives: (1) to provide a competition venue for a local professional sports team or teams or for the owners of race participants, and (2) to support local economic development through contracting international, national, and regional sporting events to the facility. For example, the mission of the Indiana Convention Center and RCA Dome in Indi-

anapolis is to provide a state-of-the-art home venue for the Indiana Colts and to bring in events that can generate economic benefits to the state of Indiana and the city of Indianapolis. For many small sport facilities, such as ice/roller skating rinks and bowling alleys, maximization of their use is a main goal pursued persistently by owners of these facilities.

The scope of operations of the facilities varies also depending on the type of the facility ownership. There are two types of sports facilities in terms of ownership: (1) publicly owned facilities and (2) privately owned facilities. A large number of sport facilities today are owned by government. The Indiana Convention Center and RCA Dome is managed by the Capital Improvement Board of Managers (CIB), which was created in 1965 by the Indiana General Assembly and empowered to finance and manage capital improvements. The Indiana Convention Center and RCA Dome hosts some of the largest events in the country each year. It is a facility that exudes all of the charm, hospitality, and versatility of the heartland city in which it is nestled.

THE SUPPORTING SUBSECTOR IV: SPORT MEDIA

The term "sports media" encompasses a large segment of the sport industry that entertains consumers with special forms of sport-related products. These products range from electronic news and reports about sports events on television, cable, and radio networks to players' stories and team statistics in print sources like magazines and newspapers. The existence of the sports media signifies a unique relationship with the media and what the media intends to distribute and sell, that is, the sporting activities (e.g., games and events).

In general, the sports media consists of three major segments: the sport broadcast media, the sport print media, and the Internet sport media. The sport broadcast media refers to the media segment that delivers sports-related messages to the public through various electronic channels, such as television and radio broadcasting and cable networks. The sport print media communicates with the readership through various printing materials, which include magazines and newspapers. The Internet sport media is a newly expanded media segment which delivers sport-related information to the viewer or reader via the Internet.

Sport Broadcast Media

The sports broadcast system and the presentation of the broadcast media in the United States are configured in a relatively complicated, three-tier structure. At the national level, several media conglomerates, such as the American Broadcasting Company (ABC), the National Broadcasting Company (NBC), the Columbia Broadcasting System (CBS), and the FOX Broadcasting Company along with their sports programming divisions together present extensive coverage of sports events, ranging from professional sports games to amateur college athletic competitions, and from the Super Bowl to the Indy 500. Nevertheless, since the sports events covered by these media giants account for just a relatively small portion of their total programming, they are not considered part of the sport industry. In addition to the sport programming delivered by these national television networks, the sports-only cable channels at the national level, such as the Entertainment and Sports Programming Network (ESPN), the Golf Channel, and Fox Sports Net, a subsidiary of the FOX Broadcasting Company, also produce various sports programming to the national audience. Since these media companies are primarily engaged in producing sports-related media programs, they are regarded as one of the important components of the sport-supporting sector.

It must be pointed out that there are some entertainment cable networks, such as the Home Box Office (HBO), a Division of the Time Warner Entertainment Company, which also provide sports programming on a pay-per-view basis. Professional boxing is the most common sport included on these channels. Again, because the focus of these channels is not normally sport-oriented, these cable networks do not fall under the umbrella of the sport industry.

The second tier of sports presentations through the broadcast media is contributed by the so-called "superstations" and other regional networks. WGN-TV based in Chicago and the Turner Broadcast System (TBS) in Atlanta are examples of the superstations which make their signals available to a national audience, but do not have the same status as other national networks. The same argument used above in the discussion of whether or not HBO is a sport company holds true here. WGN-TV and TBS are not sport entities. However, there are some real sport-oriented regional networks, such as the nine regional cable sports channels owned by FOX Sports (e.g., the Fox Sports Midwest, the Fox Sports South, the Fox Sports Southeast, the Fox Sports Rocky Mountain, the Fox Sports Northwest, Fox Sports West, and the Sunshine Network) which come much closer to achieving that designation.[1]

Local television and radio stations constitute the third tier of sports programming. Despite being locally owned and run, these stations have an affiliation with national networks. In addition to carrying the signals of those sports events that are broadcasted nationally by the networks they are affiliated with, they often provide news and live coverage of games played by local teams at both professional and collegiate levels, and sports activities held in the community. Programming at these local stations is predominately concerned with news and can in no way be called a "sport station."

Sport Print Media

The sport print media refers to the publications that are devoted primarily to sport, ranging from sports almanacs to sport magazines. Sport print media are a traditional source of information sought by consumers. There are mainly two types of sport print media: one for the general population and one for profession-

---

[1] Fox owns 54 percent of the Sunshine Network's ownership.

als. *Sports Illustrated* and *ESPN The Magazine* are examples of sport publications for the general population that satisfy a consumer need for information in sport. Stories about players and teams, and special commentaries on issues, are their common themes and ingredients. On the other hand, the readership for professional sport publications, such as the *Athletic Business*, the *Sports Business Journal*, and the *Sport Marketing Quarterly*, is primarily professionals in the field of sport. The contents of those publications are therefore technically oriented.

Sport Internet Media

As a result of the drastic development in communication technologies, the sport Internet media has gradually become a pervasive form of influence over many people's daily lives. Together with the two traditional forms of sport media (i.e., the sport broadcast media and the sport print media), the sport Internet media looks to have a promising future. According to the Turkey Sports Poll (King, 2005), even though the Internet is ranked the third most popular choice for sport fans to receive sports information behind television (39% and newspaper (31.9%) in 2005, it will surpass both television and newspaper, the two traditional media forms, to become the major source of sports information for sport fans in 2010. The most highly surfed sport Internet media sites today include ESPN.com, SI.com, and USA Today Sports.

THE SUPPORTING SUBSECTOR V: SPORT MANAGEMENT FIRMS

The sport management firms refer to those companies and corporations that provide services to sport firms and organizations, and to individual athletes. There are approximately 2,735 firms in the United States involved in event marketing and management, consumer promotion, public relations, and corporate sponsorships in sport and entertainment (U.S. Census Bureau, 2004). The services rendered by sport management firms include, but are not limited to, (1) organizing, promoting, and/or managing sports events, (2) representing and managing professional athletes, (3) providing marketing services (e.g., sponsorship evaluation, negotiation and market research, naming rights sales, public relations, and other sports marketing services), and (4) providing legal and financial consultation to sport firms and organizations, and to individual athletes.

Not all sport management firms offer the same services to their clients. Some of them may specialize in only one or more of the above-mentioned areas. For example, Baker and Hostetler is a law firm that mainly handles legal issues like intellectual property, licensing, and labor matters for clients in the sport industry, while Hawk Sports Management provides consultative services in the area of endorsements, product licensing, sport celebrity appearances, marketing concepts, and sponsorship programs to a diverse client base including NASCAR drivers, teams, race tracks, various racing entities, professional golfers and tournaments, and licensing and marketing companies. Some of them may only provide services to a particular sport, such as the Cohen Marketing Group, which specializes in marketing the sport of hockey. The International Management Group (IMG) and Octagon Worldwide are two of the largest sport management firms in the United

States. The following is an example to illustrate the services provided by the Octagon Worldwide.

Octagon Worldwide has over 1,000 employees in 60 offices across 24 countries. It owns and manages more events around the world than any other sport management firm. Through its four divisions, Octagon Worldwide provides services and expertise to sport organizations throughout the world. The four divisions are sport marketing (consulting, events, promotions, public relations, and property representation), television and news media (negotiating, distributing and producing high-quality sports and entertainment programming), athletes and personalities (representing world-class clients across all disciplines of sports and entertainment), and music and entertainment (developing fully-integrated music and entertainment-based content).

THE SUPPORTING SUBSECTOR VI: STATE, MUNICIPAL, AND COUNTY SPORT COMMISSIONS AND AUTHORITIES

In North America, sport has been widely recognized by community leaders as an essential instrument in the economic development of their communities. Thus, many states, municipalities, and counties have formed quasi-governmental sport organizations to facilitate and coordinate sport development. Sport commissions and sport authorities are two basic types of those structures. They usually have distinct operating functions. However, in some cases, a sport entity is created to take on all the responsibilities that are assumed by both structures.

Sport Commissions

There are two levels of sport commissions, state and municipal. A sport commission at the state level is commonly set up as a private entity primarily for the sake of (1) promoting and developing the sport industry in a certain state, (2) serving the needs and interests of residents in the state for sports, and (3) using sports to boost economic development in that state. For example, the Florida Sports Foundation, Inc. is the official sports promotion and development organization for the State of Florida (Florida Sports Foundation, 2004). It coordinates the efforts of the 17 regional sports commissions within the state and promotes the state as the world's premier sports destination.

Sport commissions at the municipal level sometimes are also called sport councils (e.g., the Greater Savannah Sports Council). A municipal sport commission is a sport development agency that is specifically created to market a particular municipality as an attractive destination for amateur and professional sporting events. They are either associated with the local convention and visitors' bureau/chamber of commerce or formed as independent nonprofit organizations. Whatever the case, the primary goals of a municipal sport commission is to solicit and secure amateur and professional sports events that will stimulate the local economy, to promote and enhance the image of a particular community, and to provide entertainment and participatory opportunities to local residents to improve their quality of life. For example, the mission of the San Francisco Sports

Council (SFSC) is "to enhance the economic growth, image and quality of life in San Francisco by actively attracting, hosting and supporting significant amateur and professional athletic events, conventions, exhibitions and related activities" (Cabrera, 2005).

A sports commission may also perform other functions, which include

1. Advertise and promote these sports events;

2. Help sports event sponsors and other groups to find athletic facilities, accommodations, and businesses;

3. Develop a bank of volunteers from which sports event sponsors can draw;

4. Produce sports events, educational exhibits, and clinics in-house;

5. Measure and report economic impact of sports events to its members, city officials, and the community at large;

6. Develop charitable and/or non-charitable sports and fitness programs for people of all ages but primarily for underprivileged youth in the area;

7. Offer training programs to amateur athletes competing in local, regional, national, and/or international competition; and

8. Support the development and maintenance of amateur and professional athletic facilities (Cabrera, 2005).

The USA/Russia Olympic Boxing Exhibition, the Women's Sports Foundation Summit, and the USA Volleyball Junior Olympic Championships are just few examples of the events attracted to the Central Florida area by the Orlando Area Sports Commission.

Sport Authorities

Sport authorities are another type of quasi-governmental organization that are primarily responsible for (1) securing funds and investment to construct sports facilities, (2) managing the sports facilities that are funded and owned by local government, and (3) obtaining a sports franchise or franchises. The responsibility in fund security includes borrowing money, issuing debt, and collecting fees and charges for events held in the facility. For example, the main purpose of the Harris County-Houston Sports Authority is responsible for securing $367 million in financing to construct the Reliant Stadium in Houston, Texas (Harris County-Houston Sports Authority, 2006). The facility management function of a sport authority is exemplified by the responsibilities of the Tampa Sports Authority. The Tampa Sports Authority is responsible for planning, developing, and maintaining sports and recreational facilities for residents of Tampa and Hillsborough County. The Authority currently owns and operates three sports facilities, the new Raymond James Stadium, the Legends Field, and the Ice Palace Arena, and manages three public golf courses.

In many cases, a sports authority is empowered either by a specific state legislation or by a local ordinance dealing with matters related to sports facility financing. For instance, specific state legislation in Florida was enacted that provided each county with absolute discretion to create its own form of sports, entertainment, or cultural authority. In case of the Tampa Sports Authority, it was created by the Florida Legislature in 1965.

Summary

An overview of the sport industry is given in this chapter. The overview and discussion is based on a model that groups all the sport-producing industrial units into two major sectors: (1) the sport-producing sector and (2) the sport-supporting sector. The sport-producing sector consists of companies and organizations that produce sport activities (e.g., games and events) and services. The sport-supporting sector, on the other hand, includes companies and organizations that help the firms, organizations, and individuals in the sport-producing sector produce quality sport activities. There are six subsectors: administrative and/or regulatory sport organizations, sporting goods manufacturers, wholesalers and retailers, sports facilities and buildings, sport media, sport management firms, and state, municipal, and county sport commissions and authorities.

Chapter Questions

1. Explain how the North American Industry Classification System defines an industry.
2. Compare and contrast the three models constructed to depict the sport industry in the United States of America: the two three-sector models proposed by Meek and by Pitts, Fielding, and Miller, and the two-sector model by Li, Hofacre, and Mahony.
3. Describe the two-sector model in terms of its components and explain the rationale for the model.
4. Provide a brief overall description of the types of companies and organizations included in the sport-producing sector.
5. Briefly describe the sport organizations included in the "administrative and/or regulatory sport organizations" supporting sector.
6. Briefly describe the sport organizations included in the "sporting goods manufacturers, wholesalers, and retailers" supporting sector.
7. Briefly describe the sport organizations included in the "sport facilities and buildings" supporting sector.
8. Briefly describe the sport organizations included in the "sport media" supporting sector.
9. Briefly describe the sport organizations included in the "sport management firms" supporting sector.
10. Briefly describe the sport organizations included in the "state, municipal, and county sport commissions and authorities" supporting sector.

Learning Activities

1. Organize a class presentation where students are randomly asked to assume the role as the general manager of XYZ International and then describe the sport industry in the U.S. to the class.
2. Identify a sport business or organization that has been discussed explicitly in the chapter in terms of its sector association in the model and argue where it should go.
3. Review the North American Industry Classification System (NAICS).

Chapter Two

BASICS OF ECONOMIC ANALYSIS

What is Economics?

To understand what economics can bring to the analysis of sport, it is useful to define economics. While many definitions of economics exist, the unifying theme among most of them is the problem of scarce resources and unlimited human wants. There are not enough resources available to produce goods and services to satisfy the unlimited wants of people. Because of this situation, we are forced to make choices. If you cannot have everything you want, you must decide among alternatives. Economics brings to sport an approach to understanding decision making.

As economists try to explain decisions, a basic assumption is often made about decision makers, namely that they are rational. Rational decision makers compare the expected benefits of a choice with the expected costs. Given this assumption about decision making, economists believe incentives matter. If you alter the expected benefits and costs associated with a decision, an individual's behavior is likely to change in a predictable manner.

One example of analysis based on this assumption is a study of the impact of adding a third on-court official in college basketball (McComick & Tollison, 1990, pp. 59–72). Adding a third official to help police the court increased the expected cost to a player of engaging in behavior that could be interpreted as a foul. Given the increase in expected cost, we would expect players to change their behavior. While controlling for other factors (for example, differences in the abilities of the teams) that would influence the number of fouls, adding a third official was found to reduce the amount of fouls by 34%.

> ### Economic Resources
>
> *Economists divide resources into four categories:*
>
> *Capital—human-made devices that help people produce goods and services, for example, machinery, tools, and buildings.*
>
> *Labor—human effort, mental and physical, that helps people produce goods and services.*
>
> *Land—all natural resources that help people produce goods and services.*
>
> *Entrepreneurial Ability—the talent to bring resources together that helps people produce goods and services.*

As economists try to explain decisions through examination of expected benefits and costs, they are not trying to explain the behavior of all of the people all of the time but rather most people most of the time. While the third official may not have caused each player to change behavior, some players did change their behavior, such that the overall effect was a reduction in fouls as the expected cost of committing a foul increased. We can increase our understanding of the sport industry by examining decisions within the framework of expected costs and benefits. Decision makers in sport include individuals, firms (for profit and not for profit), and governments.

Economic Systems

The expected costs and benefits decision makers in sport face are influenced by the type of economic system used to make decisions in society. Every society faces the basic problem of scarce resources and unlimited human wants. Societies use different combinations of approaches to answer basic questions (What to produce? How to produce? For whom to produce?) which arise from scarcity. Three basic approaches to answer the questions that arise due to scarcity are command, market, and tradition.

In a command system, decisions are made by an authority (for example, government). The authority decides how resources will be used. In a traditional system, decisions are made according to past practices and cultural beliefs. In a market system, decisions are made through the interactions of potential buyers and sellers. In sport, as in societies, a combination of systems is used to allocate resources and production.

In sport, some choices are made through markets, while others are made through command and tradition. The decision to support a particular professional sports team is often rooted in tradition. People's allegiances are influenced by family, friends, and past behavior. The NCAA makes decisions as the central authority over intercollegiate sports. Its decisions affect the allocation of resources and production among its member schools. The interaction of potential buyers and sellers in markets also makes decisions in sport. In Major League Baseball, the salaries of free-agent players is largely decided by the market for those players.

Command, tradition, and market are not isolated from one another in sport or society. They interact with each other to make decisions. Team allegiance is influenced by decisions made through markets and command. The actions of the NCAA are effected by choices made through markets and tradition. The salaries of free agent baseball players are affected by command and tradition.

While all three systems exist in sport and society, most of the focus of this text is on the operation of markets. Over the last twenty years the use of markets as a way to allocate resources and production in the world has grown.

Economic Models

As economists try to explain decision making in markets (and elsewhere), they often use economic models. Economic models are simplifications of reality. They do not duplicate all of the features of the world but rather strip away some of the complexities of life. Since they are simplifications, economic models will not be realistic in every way.

Models are used in both microeconomics and macroeconomics. Microeconomics examines the choices of individual decision makers, primarily households and firms. Macroeconomics is the study of the economy as a whole. Among the topics covered in macroeconomics are the nature and causes of inflation and unemployment. While macroeconomic issues affect the sport industry, the focus of this book is microeconomics because of our interest in behavior of decision makers in the sport industry.

A basic model used in microeconomic analysis is supply and demand. The model of supply and demand is a tool economists use to describe the operation of competitive markets. As a model it is a simplification of reality. While models like supply and demand are simplifications, some students find their use difficult. To use a model to explain, it is important to know the assumptions and methods of the model.

The assumptions and methods of a model can cause students to question the usefulness of models. Assumptions by their nature make a model less realistic. The methods of models in economics, such as graphs and equations, can be intimidating to students. While both of these statements are true, they do not mean models are useless to students interested in the sport industry.

A highway map of a state is a model. It is a simplification of the road system designed to help us make better choices as we travel. A highway map is unrealistic in many ways. A state is not a flat piece of paper that can be folded and placed in a glove box. To use a highway map a person must know what lines represent geographic boundaries, rivers, and roads.

When using the model of demand and supply a person must know the difference between a change in demand and a change in quantity demanded. While the terms demand and quantity demanded sound similar, they refer to different concepts just as a blue line may be a river while a red line a road on a map. In Chapter 4, you will learn the assumptions and methods of demand and supply just as you once learned the assumptions and methods of maps.

Firms and the Nature of Profit

While demand and supply describes the operation of a competitive market, other economic models explain the decision making of firms. Broadly defined, a firm is an organization that acquires resources to produce goods and services. We will use the term firms to refer to for-profit organizations. Examples of firms in the sport industry include Nike, Callaway Golf Company, Foot Locker, Gold's Gym, and the Pittsburgh Pirates.

Firms may be organized as sole proprietorships, partnerships, and corporations. Each type of organization offers benefits and costs to the owners of the firm. The primary advantage of the sole proprietorship and partnership forms of business organization is simplicity. Both are easy to legally establish. The primary disadvantage to both is unlimited liability. The assets of owners of sole proprietorships and partnerships are at risk if the firm fails. Creditors of the firm may seek the assets of the owners to satisfy debts of the firm.

The primary advantage of the corporate form of business organization is limited liability. Owners of corporations face less risk because if the firm fails only the amount of their investment in the firm is at stake. Creditors of the firm cannot sue the owners of the corporation to recover debts of the corporation. A significant disadvantage of the corporate form of business organization is the expense of meeting tax and regulatory requirements.

Economists have developed theories to explain the actions of firms. A useful starting point in some theories of how firms behave is an assumption of profit maximization. Before the strengths and weaknesses of the model of profit maximization can be assessed, it is important to understand the nature of profits in economics. The profit accountants measure is different than the profit economist use in their analysis of firms. Economic profit and accounting profit have the same definition:

$$Profit = Total\ Revenue - Total\ Cost.$$

The concepts differ primarily because of differences in the definitions of total cost. Economists define total cost to include all of the opportunity costs of production, while accountants include only explicit costs. Opportunity cost is the value of the best alternative given up when a decision is made. Opportunity costs include explicit cost, which involves expenditures of money, and implicit costs, which refer to non-monetary expenditures. Implicit costs are likely to vary from decision maker to decision maker.

Consider the decision to drive from New York to San Francisco. There would be implicit and explicit costs of making the trip. By keeping track of spending on the trip, you could record the explicit costs of the trip. A large part of the implicit cost of the trip would depend on the value you place on your time. If you are driving, you are not doing other things. The best alternative use of your time is an implicit cost of driving from New York to San Francisco. Since the best alternative use of time is likely to vary from person to person, the implicit costs of driving will differ among people.

Economics is about decision making. In making decisions, both implicit and explicit costs are relevant. Accounting is a way of keeping track of information and communicating. Since implicit costs may vary among people, it is difficult for accounting systems to keep track of them. Accounting largely ignores implicit costs not because they are unimportant but rather because of the difficulty they create in tracking and communicating information about a firm.

Economic and accounting profits also differ in their definitions of total revenue. Just as there can be implicit costs, there can also be implicit revenue. Accountants do not consider implicit revenue; economists often do not consider it. Just as implicit costs are non-monetary, implicit revenues are also non-monetary returns. The satisfaction of being one's own boss may be part of the return for an owner of a small business. In the case of the sport industry, it is important to realize the role implicit revenue may play in decision making.

A willingness to trade off explicit revenue for implicit revenue influences decision makers in the sport industry. In an interview, the CEO of the triple A affiliate of the Boston Red Sox stated, "I would rather trade out some of the financial side to work here—people are in really good moods and it's energizing to see the kids' eyes light up when they come to the ballpark" (Tim Reason, 2002, para. 25). To the extent implicit revenue influences decision makers, it should be included in analysis of choices made in the sport industry.

Profit Maximization

When economists talk about profit maximization, they include both implicit and explicit revenues and costs. In economics, early models explaining the behavior of firms concentrated on the maximization of short run profits (Salvatore, 2001, p. 11). This approach ignores the willingness of firms to sacrifice profits in the short run to earn additional profits in the long run. Profit maximization is viewed today as maximizing the present value of a firm's current and future profits.

Both current and future profits matter to decision makers in firms. Future profits must be adjusted to take into account changes in the purchasing power of the dollar. For example, $100,000 earned today is worth more than $100,000 earned 10 years from now. Increases in the average level of prices decrease the amount of goods and services that can be purchased with $100,000 over time. The present value of $100,000 in profits in 10 years is the worth of those profits today.

If current and future profits are independent, then there are no trade-offs among profits across different time periods and the two views of profit maximization are equivalent. In this case, maximizing current short-run profit is consistent with maximizing the present value of the firm. If decisions about current profits affect future profits, the two approaches are not equivalent.

The original and revised profit maximization models can be understood using a sport industry example. Converse may decide between producing Sneaker A and Sneaker B. Sneaker A will produce $200,000 in profits this year and the present value of future profits is $500,000, Sneaker B will produce only $100,000 in profits this year, but the present value of future profits is $800,000. In this example, current profits are not independent of future profits. There is a trade-off between current profit and future profit. Although the original profit maximization model suggests Converse would have chosen to produce Sneaker A in order to maximize short-term profits, the revised model suggests Converse will produce Sneaker B because that will add the most to the long-term value of the firm.

As shown in the example, the two approaches to profit maximization may lead to different behavior. However, analysis based on the two types of profit maximization generally yields similar conclusions (Thomas & Maurice, 2005, p. 15). Much of the analysis in this book is based on maximizing current profit.

Constraints on Firms

As firms attempt to maximize profits, they face limitations that constrain their actions. Cost and revenue conditions act as constraints. The demand for a product limits the ability of a firm to generate revenue. The availability of resources influences costs. A health club deciding whether or not to buy additional weight equipment must compare the additional revenue the weights will generate to the additional costs of the equipment. The potential revenue from the equipment will be influenced by the demand to use the equipment, the costs by availability.

Other factors also constrain the actions of firms. Government laws and regulations limit what firms can do to increase profits. In many states, horse-racing tracks would like to add slot machines and other forms of gaming to the mix of products they offer. The managers of these tracks believe the increase in revenue from the additional forms of gaming would be greater than the increase in cost. However, laws in some states do not allow tracks to offer other forms of gaming, which constrains the ability of firms to earn additional profit.

Firms are legally obligated to obey government laws and regulations. Public opinion, while not legally binding, may also limit the actions of firms. Sporting good manufacturers such as Nike are subject to public pressure regarding their production facilities in less developed countries. Websites exist urging consumers to boycott Nike products because of employment practices at some of their facilities. Nike has adopted a "Code of Conduct" of conditions for workers and factories. Following the "Code of Conduct" may increase Nike's cost of production but Nike has decided it is in the best interest of the firm to be responsive to public opinion regarding working conditions in less developed countries.

Contractual relationships between a firm and other decision makers constrain the actions of a firm. A major league baseball team is limited in its actions by contractual relationships with individual players, stadium authorities, Major League Baseball, and many others. Releasing a non-performing player without additional pay may increase the profits of a team, but if the player has a guaranteed contract, this is not an option. Moving to a new city may increase a team's profit, but if the team is bound by a lease agreement to its current location or if the team cannot obtain approval from its league, moving is not an option.

Alternatives to the Model of Profit Maximization

The model of profit maximization has been criticized for being "too narrow and unrealistic" (Salvatore, 2001, p. 13). Decision makers in firms are likely to be concerned with results other than profit. Sales, growth, and their own satisfaction are likely to be of interest to managers. Expecting decision makers to engage in maximization and to make optimal decisions is unrealistic given the information available to managers in firms and the ability of managers to process information.

Given these criticisms of the model of profit maximization, alternative models have been developed. The alternatives can be classified into two broad categories: maximizing and satisficing. The maximizing models assume managers attempt to make optimal decisions but have goals other than profit maximization. The satisficing models assume managers make choices to meet minimal standards rather than trying to make the best possible decision.

MAXIMIZING MANAGERIAL UTILITY MODEL

The separation of ownership and control in large corporations is the driving force behind this model. While stockholders own the firm, it is management who makes decisions daily about the operation of the firm. In this model, managers are assumed to maximize their own satisfaction (utility) rather than profit. While owners would prefer profit, managers are willing to sacrifice profit to make themselves better off. Managers will spend so as to increase their satisfaction even if the expenditures increase costs more than revenues.

For example, an executive at Churchill Downs horse-racing track, with no significant stake in ownership, has an incentive to use company resources to acquire perquisites (e.g., company car, executive fitness center, plush office furniture) that reduce profit but add to her satisfaction. The executive may also hire more staff (to reduce her work load or for the joy of power) than is consistent with maximizing profit.

To reduce the incentive of managers to trade off profits for other types of returns, various mechanisms to tie managerial compensation with profit have been developed. One method is the use of stock options. Management is given the right to buy stock at a set price. If management is successful at increasing the value of the firm, stock prices rise and the stock options become valuable. Stock options may also be used to give non-management workers an incentive to increase the value of the firm. The American Basketball League, a women's professional basketball league in the late 1990s, offered players stock options in the League to increase their incentive to see the League prosper (Crawford, 1997).

The use of stock options gives managers and others an incentive to increase the price of a firm's stock. This incentive may have perverse effects if managers act in a way to increase the value of the firm in the short run that reduces the long-run value of the firm or if managers are tempted to bend or break accepted accounting practices to increase the short-run price of stock.

A second force giving managers an incentive to follow the wishes of stockholders is the threat of hostile takeover. If managers increase their satisfaction at the expense of profits, there is the possibility of an outside group offering to purchase the firm. The outside group will offer to purchase the firm because of a belief that they can increase the value of the firm. A change in ownership is likely to result in a change in management.

The managerial utility yields some insights into the behavior of firms. If managerial compensation is not tied to profitability, managers may act to increase their own satisfaction at the expense of profit. Stock options are used to try to tie the interests of management with those of shareholders. The threat of hostile takeover disciplines managers to consider the interests of shareholders rather than maximize their own satisfaction.

SALES MAXIMIZATION MODEL

In this model, managers are assumed to maximize sales subject to earning enough profit to satisfy the owners of the firm. This model is related to the managerial utility model. Managerial salaries rise with sales (Lambert, Larcker, & Weigelt, 1991, p. 395). By maximizing sales, managers are able to increase their salaries and their satisfaction. One explanation for owners allowing managers to focus on sales is that maximizing sales may be consistent with long-run profit maximization. The evidence on this relationship is mixed with some studies indicating the goals are inconsistent (e.g., Armstrong & Collopy, 1996), while others (e.g., Zabojnik, 1998) suggest sales and long-term profitability maximization are consistent.

If sales and profit maximization are inconsistent, the use of sports metaphors in talking about competitors may lead to lower profits (Armstrong & Collopy, 1996, p. 197). Sports metaphors may lead managers to focus on selling more than their rivals rather than maximizing profit. Managers in the sport industry need to be aware that using the language of sport may influence decision makers to make choices that reduce profit.

GROWTH MAXIMIZATION MODEL

This model may be viewed within the context of managers or owners. Managers may be interested in maximizing growth because of the link between firm size and managerial compensation. There is evidence that growth maximization is consistent with maximizing the value of a firm (Greer, 1992, p. 77). To the extent that this is true, owners interested in profit may allow managers to pursue growth maximization. In some situations, growth and profit maximization are likely to be inconsistent (Thomas & Maurice, 2005, p. 16).

Some owners in the sport industry may be willing to sacrifice profit for growth to maximize their utility. An owner's satisfaction may be influenced by factors other than profit, such as a desire for power or public attention. Growth in the sport industry can help an owner achieve these other goals.

SATISFICING BEHAVIOR MODEL

Rather than attempt to do the best that can be done, this model presented by Simon (1959) suggests managers make decisions to meet goals for profit, sales, growth, etc. The goals are not at their maximum levels (which are unknown) but rather at levels acceptable to the decision makers. Managers face too many constraints and too much uncertainty and have to make too many decisions quickly to ever be able to actually determine all the decisions that will lead to profit maximization. Managers look at the expectations of owners and attempt to meet the expectations at a satisfactory level, which will ensure their continued employment and financial well-being.

Owners and their representatives do not know the maximum level of profit that can be achieved, so, instead, set measurable goals on which to judge the performance of managers. For example, the CEO of Reebok may be presented with a set of goals by the company's board of directors. The goals may include targeted levels of sales, profit, and growth. Rather than worry about making the best decisions, the CEO's primary focus will be on meeting these goals.

Satisficing is not necessarily inconsistent with profit maximization (Salvatore, 2001, p. 14). Satisficing can be seen as a rational response to incomplete information. There are costs to obtaining more information. Given the expected costs and benefits of obtaining additional information, decision makers may opt for measurable goals rather than the uncertainty of maximizing profit.

Despite the alternative models, profit maximization is used as the primary basis of the analysis of decision making for a number of reasons. Market competition forces managers to try to do better then their competitors. To do better then their

Reasons to Continue to Use the Profit Maximization Model

competitors, managers may find themselves maximizing the value of the firm. Managers who pursue their own interests at the expense of stockholders may find their firm the subject of a hostile takeover threat and their jobs in jeopardy. While managerial compensation is linked to growth and sales, there is also recent evidence of a strong correlation between profit and compensation (Hirschey, 2003, p. 8). Given this link, managers have an incentive to pursue profits. Competitive capital markets provide an incentive for managers to do the best they can to obtain financing at lower rates. While the model of profit maximization does not predict the actions of all decision makers all of the time, no other model predicts behavior as accurately (Petersen & Lewis, 1999, p.10).

Throughout the remainder of this book profit maximization will be used as the starting point in understanding managerial decisions. The alternative models may be seen as complementing our understanding of decisions derived from an assumption of profit maximization. Managers and owners do sometimes pursue goals other than profit. Even if managers and owners solely focus on profit maximization, they can make decisions that fail to maximize profit. Managers and owners make decisions into the future based on expected revenues and costs. These expectations may prove incorrect over time.

Nonprofit Sport Organizations

There are many public- and private-sector nonprofit organizations in the sport industry. The major difference between the two is public-sector nonprofit organizations, such as high school athletic departments and local recreation departments, often receive much of their funding from government sources, while private-sector nonprofit organizations, such as the Special Olympics, YMCAs, and country clubs, rely more on donations and membership fees.

The actions of nonprofit organizations may in some cases be explained using the model of profit maximization. There is evidence some nonprofit organizations in sport, such as YMCAs (Miller & Fielding, 1995) and university athletic departments (e.g., Sack, 1988), operate in a manner that is hard to distinguish from profit-oriented firms. When nonprofits face increased competition from for-profit firms, there is increased pressure on nonprofit firms to behave as for-profit firms.

While profit-maximizing behavior is not unknown among nonprofit firms, a primary focus on maximizing profits would be a violation of their nonprofit status. Alternative models explaining the actions of nonprofit firms are appropriate. There is not a single best model explaining the behavior of nonprofit firms. Among the models used to explain the behavior of nonprofit firms are Efficiency and Satisfying Contributors. In addition, some of the alternative models to profit maximization have also been applied to nonprofit firms: Management Utility Maximization, Satisficing Behavior, and Growth Maximization Models.

EFFICENCY MODEL

One model suggests that managers of nonprofit organizations attempt to maximize output for a given budget (Thomas & Maurice, 2005, p. 352). For example, a local recreation director may be given a set budget; the director will then try to offer as many participation opportunities as possible for the local community for this set level of costs. Alternatively she may decide before receiving the budget which activities she wants to offer and will then try to minimize the costs of providing all of these opportunities.

The efficiency objective has proven useful in examining decision making in a variety of nonprofit organizations. A difficulty with using the model to explain the actions of managers is deciding on the appropriate measure of output. For example, the Special Olympics and many high school and small college athletic departments may focus on maximizing the number of participants and providing a positive experience for the participants, given the budget. Because the number of participants is easier to quantify than positive experiences, increasing participation is the goal that has a greater impact on decision making.

SATISFYING CONTRIBUTORS MODEL

The satisfying contributors model suggests managers of nonprofit organizations attempt to maximize the satisfaction of the current and potential contributors. Therefore, managers in Division I athletic departments will be motivated by a desire to please their athletic department donor groups, as well as their other ticket holders. Because winning is often important to athletic department donors (e.g., Coughlin & Erekson, 1985; J. S. Hall & Mahony, 1997; Sigelman & Brookheimer, 1983), the pursuit of winning at Division I schools may be an attempt to please the donor groups. The desire of the Special Olympics to maximize participants can also be explained within the context of this model. Donors to the Special Olympics want to be shown their gifts were effective. Demonstrating the positive experience of participants is more difficult than quantifying the number of participants. The desire of nonprofits to satisfy donors has also led them to act more like for-profit firms as donors require evidence of market success to demonstrate effectiveness (Brooks, 2003, p. 503).

GROWTH MAXIMIZATION MODEL

Growth maximization may be a goal underlying managerial decision making in nonprofit organizations because profitability cannot be used as a measure of organizational success. Like managers of a for-profit firm, the managers of nonprofits may seek to maximize growth as a measure of success. As the organization grows, managers gain more prestige, gain more power, become more important, control the distribution of more resources, and are often better compensated (McGuigan & Moyer, 1986).

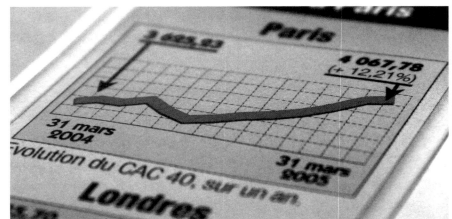

For example, one could argue that the NCAA's growth from a small, basically insignificant organization prior to the 1950s to the dominant organization in college athletics was motivated by the desire of its executives for greater prestige, power, importance, control, and personal compensation. Although

Photo by Gaston Thauvin, courtesy of stock.xchng iv

NCAA executives would certainly argue their decisions were motivated by other goals, all of these factors (e.g., power, personal compensation) have clearly increased during the NCAA's growth, and, therefore, growth cannot be ignored as a motive underlying decision making.

MANAGEMENT UTILITY MAXIMIZATION MODEL

Another model used when examining nonprofit decision making is the management utility maximization model. As was discussed with firms, managers want to maximize their own benefits. Division I administrators realize that it is in their best interest to keep the donors happy because that will generally maximize administrators' personal long-term benefits. Winning, therefore, becomes the goal for nonprofit administrators because they believe that the success of their athletic teams will maximize their own personal benefits.

SATISFICING BEHAVIOR MODEL

Because objectives are often difficult to measure in many public and private nonprofit organizations, managers may engage in satisficing behavior. For example, managers with government agencies that are guaranteed resources may adopt behavior consistent with Simon's (1959) satisficing behavior model. Because it will be difficult for their superiors to determine if they are maximizing or simply satisficing in the pursuit of goals that are difficult to measure, managers in nonprofit organizations may be able to try to achieve a set of goals rather than to make optimal decisions.

As competition in the nonprofit sector increases, there is increased pressure for nonprofits to be as efficient as for-profit firms. The efficiency model of nonprofits may be the best at describing and predicting the actions of nonprofit organizations in the sport industry. However, given the difficulties in measuring the output of nonprofit firms, the other models are also useful at predicting and explaining managerial decisions in nonprofit organizations in certain situations.

An Alternative Model for Sports: The Winning Maximization Model

The models explained in this chapter were developed to explain the actions of for-profit and nonprofit firms across many industries. One theory of managerial motivation is unique to a segment of the sport industry: winning maximization. According to this model, the goal of a sport organization that fields a team to compete with other teams is to maximize wins. This model does not assume profit and other goals are unimportant. Profit and other factors act as constraints limiting the ability of the organization to win on the field.

This model may also be viewed as complementing other models presented in this chapter. Rather than the manager of a firm sacrificing profit to maximize utility, an owner of a professional sport franchise may be willing to sacrifice profit so as to achieve the satisfaction that comes from winning and thereby increase utility. Winning maximization may be a goal for organizations such as the USOC, national governing bodies, NCAA Division I athletic departments, and even some high school athletic departments. Satisfying donors is one reason for a possible emphasis on winning. A second reason for nonprofit organizations to adopt winning as a goal is the difficulty of measuring other outcomes, such as positive experiences for participants.

Summary

The main goal of this chapter was to introduce the reader to economic analysis in the sport industry. Individuals, organizations, and societies are forced to make choices because of scarce resources. Economists explain decision making in terms of expected benefits and costs. To explain decisions, economists use models. Models are simplifications of reality designed to help us understand and explain. To explain the behavior of firms, economists often use the model of profit maximization. Other models (e.g., growth maximization, sales maximization, and satisficing) have been developed to explain the behavior of firms. Economists have applied some of these models to explain the behavior of nonprofit organizations. Economists have also developed models specifically to explain the behavior of nonprofit organizations.

Chapter Questions

1. Explain why adding another official in football to monitor for holding by the offensive line might reduce the number of penalties for holding.
2. Give three examples of the role of tradition in decision making in the sport industry.
3. Why are accounting profits often larger than economic profits?
4. Evaluate the following statement:
    Implicit revenues are more important in decision making in the sport industry than in other industries.
5. How does competition increase the likelihood that firms will try to maximize profit?
6. Can mangers at nonprofit organizations ignore revenues and costs?

Chapter Three

DEMAND, SUPPLY, AND PRICING IN THE SPORT INDUSTRY

Introduction

Variable ticket pricing has become a common practice and ticketing strategy among Major League Baseball franchises. For example, in the 2002 season, the San Francisco Giants added $2 to weekend tickets, the St. Louis Cardinals gave a $1 discount on tickets for April, May, and September games, and the Rockies demanded $7–$8 a ticket for June inter-league series against Cleveland and the New York Yankees, as well as for the two fireworks nights (Antonen, 2002). Those MLB franchises modeled the variable pricing strategy after the airline industry, which charges passengers according to demand when passengers want to fly at busy times.

As the above scenario demonstrates, sport management professionals need a background in demand and supply theory in order to make proper management decisions. In this chapter, we will review several important concepts, including demand, supply, elasticity of demand, and elasticity of supply. We also will discuss the relationship between demand and supply, and the factors affecting consumer demand and supply.

Demand, Supply, and Pricing in the Sport Industry

You were recently hired as a ticket manager for the South Ohio Copperheads, a baseball team affiliated with the Great Lakes League, a NCAA-sanctioned and -sponsored summer college wooden bat league that has been in existence for 3 years. The attendance of the team over the past three years was low. Thus, the general manager has asked you to examine variable pricing and other pricing strategies currently utilized in professional baseball and adopt a better pricing structure conducive to increasing attendance. What would be your recommendation, particularly pertaining to the variable pricing strategy?

Demand

Consumers in any society have needs and wants for a wide range of goods and services. Needs are necessities, such as food, shelter, and health care. On the other hand, wants are things that are desirable but not required for existence. Examples of consumer wants include athletic clothing and entertainment. In general, consumers are buyers who purchase goods and services to satisfy their needs and wants. To satisfy consumer needs and wants, businesses develop goods and services, but there are many ways to satisfy any particular need or want. If people are hungry, they can go to the store and purchase food to prepare at home, or they can choose from a variety of restaurants, from fast food to fine dining, from Chinese to Mexican. If people want to be entertained, they can attend a movie, a concert, or an athletic event, or they can go to a sports bar. If they want to get in shape, they might join an athletic club, purchase home exercise equipment, or hire a personal trainer. Each of these options results in demand for a specific good or service. The choices people make about what to consume and how to consume depend upon many factors. Price is one of such factor.

In simple terms, the willingness and ability of consumers to purchase the goods and services is referred to as "*demand.*" If a consumer has a demand for a pair of athletic shoes, it implies that he or she is willing to exchange money for the good in order to satisfy his or her wants (say, to participate in physical activity). Consumers will not demand what they do not need or want.

There is a basic relationship between demand and the market price of a good and the quantity demanded. The relationship implies the quantity the buyers want to buy at a particular price. Such a relationship between price and quantity sought can be graphically represented with a downwardly sloped curve, that is, the *demand curve*. The demand curve is shown in Figure 3-1. As Figure 3-1 illustrates, if the price for tennis racquets were suddenly cut (say from $60 to $40), more people would want to buy them. If the price were increased (from $60 to $75), fewer people would want to buy them. This important property is called the *law of demand*. The law of demand states that if all things are equal, the lower the price of a commodity, the higher the quantity demanded; and the higher the price, the lower the quantity demanded.

Demand includes all values along the entire range of the demand curve. It is the relationship between all the prices and all the quantities demanded for a good or service. In Figure 3-1, as the price of tennis racquets rises, the number of racquets sold declines. *Quantity demanded* is the amount of specific goods or services that individuals (singly or as a group) will purchase at some specific period of time and at some specific set price. Point A in Figure 3-1 demonstrates that at $80, 2,000

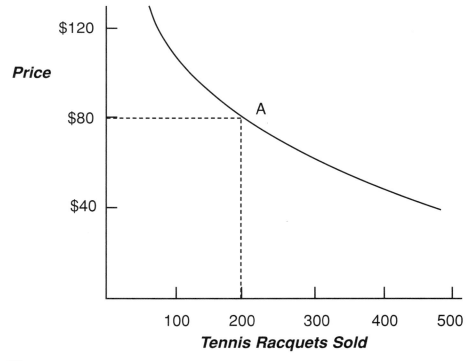

Figure 3-1. Demand Curve

Table 3-1. Trends of Participation in Water-Based Recreational Sport in the United States (in thousands), 1990–2003

	1990	1993	1998	1999	2000	2001	2002	2003
Boardsailing/Windsurfing	1,025	835	1,075	624	655	537	496	779
Sailing	5,981	3,918	5,902	5,327	10,835	10,593	9,806	10,648
Scuba Diving	2,615	2,306	3,448	3,095	2,901	2,744	3,328	3,215
Snorkeling	n/a	n/a	10,575	10,694	10,526	9,788	9,865	10,179
Surfing	1,224	n/a	1,395	1,736	2,180	1,601	1,879	2,087
Wakeboarding	n/a	n/a	2,253	2,707	3,581	3,097	3,142	3,356
Water Skiing	19,314	16,626	10,161	9,961	10,335	8,301	8,204	8,425

Source: American Sports Data, Inc. (2003). *The Superstudy of Sports Participation* (Volume III): *Outdoors Activities*. Hartsdale, NY.

people will be willing to purchase a tennis racquet. A *change in quantity demanded* refers to the effect of a change in price on the quantity demanded. If the price of tennis racquets decreases to $60, there will be a change in quantity demanded from 2,000 to 3,000.

The demand curve represents the willingness of people to pay for additional units of goods or services. The downward slope of the curve implies that people are less willing to pay for additional units of some good or service. This is the concept of *marginal benefit*. A player in a softball league is willing to pay $50 for one pair of turf shoes but would probably not be willing to pay $50 per pair for 5 more pairs of shoes. The (marginal) benefit received from the 10th pair is much less than that received from the first pair.

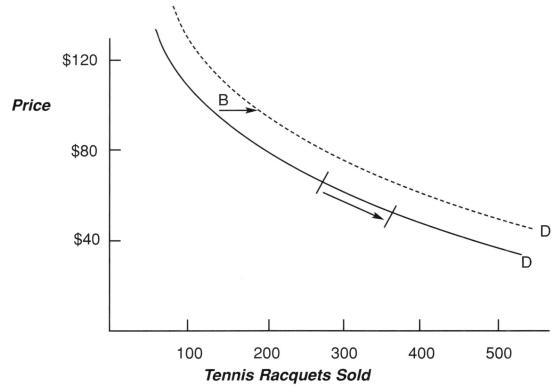

Figure 3-2. Quantity Demanded and Demand Curve

A *shift in demand* refers to non-price factors that cause a shift of the entire demand curve. A shift in demand means that at each price, more (or fewer) units will be demanded. For example, the level of water-based recreational sport participation overall seems to show an upward trend since 1990. As Table 3-1 shows, overall, sailing, scuba diving, surfing, and wakeboarding are water-based recreational sport activities in which participation soared over the 13-year period from 1990 to 2003. Particularly, there was roughly a 78% increase in the number of people who sailed and little less than a 23% hike in the number of enthusiasts who scuba dived. The average real income seems to play a great role behind the increase in participation in water sports. In Figure 3-2, Arrow A represents a change in quantity demanded, and Arrow B represents a shift in demand.

Caution needs to be taken while discussing price as it relates to demand and supply, as it is often difficult to identify outcomes that result from changes in prices. As such, economists use a phrase "all things being equal" to place a limit on conclusions that can be drawn based solely on price changes. For example, an increase in ticket prices should result in a decrease in the number of ticket purchased. Nevertheless, the demand for NFL game tickets remains strong even if ticket prices have gone up about 65% over the last ten years from $35.75 in 1996 to $58.95 in 2005 (Team Marketing Report, 2006). In this case, "all things were not equal" because other considerations entered into the equation, such as the popularity of that particular sport. For the sake of the discussion, the assumption or phrase "all things being equal" will be used continuously in the remaining sections of this chapter.

DETERMINANTS OF DEMAND

Why does quantity demanded for a good tend to fall as price rises? There are two main reasons. First is the *substitution effect,* and the second factor is *income effect.* Demand is affected by the price of other related goods. When the price of a good rises, consumers tend to substitute other similar goods for it. The income effect comes into play when the price of a commodity goes up; consumers may suddenly find themselves poorer than they were before. For example, when gasoline prices double, American consumers have in effect less income and may be forced to curtail their consumption of gasoline.

What determines the market demand for a particular good or service? Evidently, the price of the good or service itself plays a big role. Nevertheless, many other factors also influence consumers' willingness to purchase or their demand for the good or service: average levels of income, the size of the market, the prices and availability of related goods, individual tastes, and special influences.

Certainly, those who have more income are more able and likely to satisfy wants through purchases. In general, as household income rises in a society, consumption rises and the demand curve shifts to the right (at each price, more goods will be demanded). However, other income issues also influence demand. When economic conditions change (either positively or negatively), not all segments of the population are affected equally. If an economy is booming, some people may see their income rise considerably whereas others may notice little impact. Changes in government policies create different economic impacts for different income groups. For example, in 1994, the U.S. government passed a law eliminating the deductibility of country club membership fees as a business expense. Not all clubs were affected in the same way by the change. Many older, high-cost clubs that cater to a high-income personnel have experienced a decline in membership (Walker, 1999) whereas many clubs that appeal to a more medium-income audience are thriving. More of the high-cost clubs had members affected by the deductibility provision. A second issue in examining how income affects demand is that, as income rises, demand may either rise or fall. For some items, demand rises as income rises. These items, called *normal goods*, would include steaks, yachts, cellular phones, stadium luxury boxes, or resort vacations. For other items, demand declines as income rises. These items are called *inferior goods*. Commonly used examples are Spam and bologna. As people gain more income, they reduce their purchase of less desirable items in favor of more desirable ones. It is open to debate as to whether sport activities are normal or inferior goods. Even though most sport activities are considered normal goods, some economists suggest baseball (Noll, 1974) or hiking and backpacking (Walsh, 1986) are inferior goods. Other economists (Siegfried & Eisenberg, 1980) do not support these assertions, stating that the evidence is not clear-cut.

The size of the market or the total market demand (i.e., the number of buyers in the market) is the second factor affecting consumers' overall demand for a certain good or service. Clearly, New York City demands more sport-related entertainment products than Columbus, Ohio, as the former has more than 8 million people in 2000, which is over 10 times as many people as in the latter. No wonder New York has nine professional teams playing at the major level and Columbus, Ohio, only hosts one NHL team and one Major League Soccer team.

As previously discussed, the price and availability of related goods influence the demand for a commodity as consumers will substitute other similar goods for a commodity when its prices rises. *Substitutes* are goods or services that also satisfy consumers' wants and needs. When the price of playing golf rises, people may turn to other leisure activities that can satisfy their desire for recreation. So, instead of playing a round of golf, they may choose to play tennis, provided that the cost of playing tennis is acceptable in relation to playing golf. Thus, the existence of alternatives or substitutes and the price of those alternatives are important. *Complements* are products that are used jointly. Both tennis and golf require the use of a ball. If the price of tennis or golf balls suddenly rises, it can affect many golfers and tennis enthusiasts' choice of activity. If the price of a slate of golf balls suddenly costs $9 more, it may mean a golfer will lose equivalently $3 every time he or she loses one ball. Such increases in the cost of playing golf may deter the player from further participation and subsequently the player may choose to play tennis instead. Mullin, Hardy, and Sutton (2000) state that the ancillary costs of a sport activity often equal or exceed the price of the sport activity itself. It implies that the increases or decreases in other related items will change the total cost of consumption of an activity even if the price of the core activity is constant. Team Marketing Report created the fan cost index (FCI) to track the cost for a family of four to attend a professional sports game. The FCI included four average-price tickets, four small soft drinks, two small beers, four hot dogs, two game programs, and two adult-size caps (Team Marketing Report, 2006). According to Team Marketing Report (2006), it cost $329.82 for a family of four to attend a NFL game in 2005. A family with children involved in ice skating will spend dollars on equipment, lessons, ice time, transportation, and food. A change in the prices of these other items creates shifts in the demand curve. When the price of playing a round of golf rises, people may start to substitute it.

Consumer tastes or preferences, as a subjective element, also influence consumers' demand for a certain commodity. Tastes reflect consumers' social and historical backgrounds, traditions, religion, and values. For example, badminton is a sport that is profoundly appreciated by people in many countries in Asia. As such, the demand for badminton racquets and shuttlecocks is higher in California where there is a large Asian and Asian American population than in Kansas. Changes in taste over time also affect demand. Injuries caused by aerobics have led athletic clubs to offer low-impact aerobics, such as step aerobics, slide aerobics, water aerobics, and tap aerobics. Racquetball, a booming activity in the 1970s, drastically declined in appeal in the 1980s, leaving athletic club managers with empty courts. As the number of people participating in downhill skiing decreases, resorts are adding whitewater rafting, mountain biking, and snowboarding. The increase in popularity of a variety of extreme sports has led to the strong demand for skateboards and skating facilities. The more people desire an activity, the higher the demand for it. As the appeal of an activity declines, demand decreases. However, changes in taste are more difficult to quantify than are other impacts on demand.

Finally, some special influences are also behind the demand for goods and services. Expectations about future activity can influence current consumption and produce shifts in the demand curve. Many professional sports teams building new stadiums sell current season tickets by linking their purchase to seats at the future stadium. The argument is that fans should buy now because demand will be high when the new stadium opens. New athletic clubs attempt to increase sales by offering locked-in membership prices or suggesting that people should join now because demand will be high for a limited number of memberships. The demand for sport boats are influenced by the expectation of future price increases in sport boats, the availability of docking and marine facilities, new government regulations related to water sports, etc.

The factors behind the demand for sport boats are sketched in Table 3-2. A brief recount of the factors is provided here. As the most important variable, price tends to balance demand and supply. But in addition to the importance of price, many non-price factors also influence the strength of demand for a certain commodity. We cannot lose sight of their importance.

OTHER ELEMENTS OF DEMAND FOR SPORT ACTIVITIES

In addition to the factors listed above, which apply to many firms that supply goods and services, numerous studies have examined demand specifically for sport and recreation activities. These studies suggest several additional factors that are relevant for the sport industry. Table 3-3 shows several factors related to outdoor recreation demand (Walsh, 1986). Age, education, income, and gender are

Table 3-2. (Price and Non-price) Factors Affecting Demand of Sport Boats

Factors Affecting Demand	Example for Sport Boats
The Good's Own Price	Higher own price reduces quantity demand
Average Levels of Income	As incomes rise, more people may purchase sport boats
Size of the Population	Larger population increases sports boat purchases
Prices and Availability of Related Goods	Low gasoline and fishing-related equipment raise the demand for sport boats
Individual Tastes	Americans who live closer to coastal areas buy more sport boats than who reside in inland states with other things being equal
Special Influences	Special influences include availability of docking and marine facilities, expectation of future price increases in sport boats, new government regulations, etc.

significant in discussing demand for activities. In addition, travel time to activities, quality of the attraction, and congestion are relevant.

A number of demand studies have centered on professional sports, especially on American baseball. The studies have focused particularly on price, uncertainty of outcome, and quality of the team. These studies measure demand by attendance at the game. Most of the North American professional sports leagues (and even U.S. colleges) rely heavily on attendance to generate revenue. This is truer for the National Hockey League, Canadian Football League, and Major League Soccer than for the National Football League or National Basketball Association. The latter two leagues, with their reliance on lucrative television packages, are less dependent on attendance.

Table 3-3. Socioeconomic Determinants of Adult Participation in Outdoor Recreation, United States

Socioeconomic Variables	Strength of the Relationship	
	All Adults	Working Adults
Age	-.51***	-.43***
Education	.09***	.09***
Income	.08***	.06*
Race	.07*	.10*
Sex	.08***	.09***
Size of city	-.06***	-.07*
Type of dwelling	-.04	-.02
Hours worked	.02	.01
Vacation time	NC	.08***
Have yard	.07***	.06**
Have park nearby	.09***	.08***
Coefficient of determination, R	.63	.51
Sample size	2,970	1,709

Significance:*=.05; **=.01; ***=.001

Source: Walsh (1986) p. 159, taken from *Heritage, Conservation, and Recreation Service.*

NC = Not calculated because vacation time data were not available for those not employed in a paid job.

Siegfried and Eisenberg (1980) found price, quality of excitement of play (not necessarily winning), and promotional efforts are determinants of attendance in minor league baseball; however, price was not as important as other studies have suggested. The authors proposed that minor league teams tended to be located in smaller cities, with fewer available substitutes. In addition, they suggested that profit maximization was not the only objective of the clubs and that the clubs engaged in creating a general atmosphere that attracted fans. Although Cairns, Jennett, and Sloane (1986) had limited success in estimating professional sports attendance using price and income variables, Gruen (1976) found betting at the horse tracks to be influenced by both price and income. This may be because there are many substitutes for betting, particularly at the horse tracks.

Several studies have explored the impact of the uncertainty of outcomes on attendance. This issue is of particular interest in the sport field, especially because one of the characteristics often used to define sport is that the outcome of an event is uncertain (Leonard, 1998). Many individuals make (and lose) large amounts of money by betting on that uncertainty of outcome. Knowles, Sherony, and Haupert (1992) suggest that uncertainty is a significant determinant of Major League Baseball attendance, especially when the home team is slightly favored. Attendance (demand) is higher when the game is likely to be a close one. The authors argue that a league is best served, in terms of profit maximization for the league, when competitive balance exists across the league. Competitive balance enhances the uncertainty of outcome.

Supply

Meek (1997) estimated that the sport industry produced $152 billion worth of goods and services in 1996. The Street & Smith's SportsBusiness Journal believes the size of the sport industry should be $194.64, calculating with 2001 data. Who determines what and how much to produce? Why have some firms been successful whereas others have failed? Why do firms produce athletic shoes rather than dress shoes? Why do they produce more basketball shoes and fewer aerobics shoes? These are questions related to supply. Sports organizations have an inventory (supply) of events, apparel, and information that they are willing to trade for cash from someone who wants to attend an event, wear apparel, or read a sports magazine (demand). Figure 3-3 is a supply curve that illustrates the relationship between price and supply for tennis racquets.

Supply is the quantity of a good that firms willingly produce and sell. Holding equal other things, such as costs of production, the prices of related goods, and the organization of the market, the quantity of a good supplied is related specifically to its market price. The relationship between the amount of a commodity that firms are willing to produce and sell with other things being equal, and its market price is depicted by the so-called *supply curve*.

Figure 3-3 shows a hypothetical supply curve for tennis racquets, which is plotted with data from Table 3-4. The data indicates that, at a price of $20, no racquets will be produced because the firms may devote their production capabilities to other products due to a small or no profit margin on making tennis racquets. As the price per racquet rises (assuming other things stay equal), more firms will turn their attention to tennis racquets. As the price continues to rise (a greater profit margin), more tennis racquets will be produced and supplied. *Quantity supplied* is the number of specific goods or services supplied at some specific

Table 3-4. Supply Data of Tennis Racquets Related to Quantity Supplied to Price

Price (Dollar/Per Pair)	Quantity Supplied (thousands)
20	0
30	150
40	200
60	280
80	350
100	410
120	440

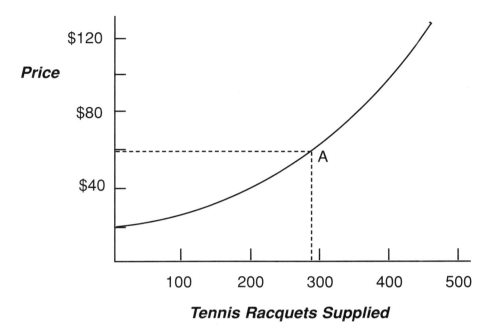

Figure 3-3. Supply Curve

period of time and at some specific price. At Point A in Figure 3-3, if a tennis racquet sells for $60, 280,000 of them will be produced. A *change in quantity supplied* refers to the effect of a change in price on the quantity supplied. If the price of the athletic shoes decreases to $30, only 130,000 tennis racquets will be supplied.

A shift in supply refers to non-price factors that cause a shift of the entire supply curve. If the entire supply curve shifts, more units are produced at each price. In Figure 3-4, Arrow A represents a change in quantity supplied, and Arrow B represents a shift in supply.

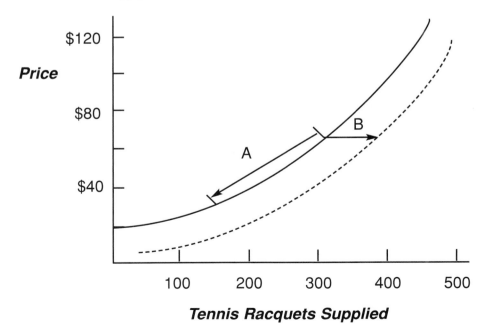

Figure 3-4. Supply Curve

The supply curve represents the effect of prices on quantity produced. It slopes upward, from left to right, because the relationship is generally a positive one. The corollary to the law of demand is the law of supply. With all other things being equal, the higher the price of a good offered, the more will be supplied. On the other hand, the lower the price of a good, the less of it will be supplied. As the price of a product increases, producers can make more profit and will want to maximize that by producing more. They may also shift from making a lower-priced item to a higher-priced one (as long as production costs are similar). In addition, because there are profits to be made, additional producers will enter the market.

The cost of production is a key factor that underlies supply decisions. When production costs for a good are low relative to the market price, it is profitable for producers to supply a great deal. When production costs are high relative to price, firms that produce little may decide to produce something else instead. In addition, other factors that affect supply decision include technology, prices of inputs needed to make the product, prices of related goods, number of suppliers, and special influences.

Technological improvements affect costs in a number of ways. They act to lower costs and also increase profits, which shifts the supply curve to the right. Over the years, improvements in production processes and in materials have made many goods more plentiful at lower prices. Today, avid sports fans are purchasing foot-wide satellite dishes to put on their roofs and, in some cases, paying nothing for the dishes as long as they purchase programming. Compare that to a few years ago when a six-foot-wide dish might cost several thousand dollars. The growth of cable television, including pay-for-view, and direct broadcast services have increased the number of sporting events available to the viewer (Hugh-Jones, 1992).

All the elements a firm uses to make products, including materials, labor, and machines, are called inputs. Generally, the higher the cost of inputs, the lower the profit realized, and the fewer the number of items that will be supplied at each price (shift in supply curve to the left) assuming technology did not change. If the cost of inputs declines, profit increases and the greater the number of items that will be supplied (shift in supply curve to the right). For example, when sport industry manufacturers use foreign labor, the result is much lower-cost labor inputs than would be possible in the United States. Shoe manufacturers make more profit and produce more shoes. What would happen if shoe manufacturers were suddenly forced to increase the wages they pay in other countries?

Another major factor influencing supply is the prices of related goods, particularly goods that can be readily substituted for one another in the production process.

The number and expectations of suppliers influence supply. As firms make more profits, new firms enter the market hoping to also profit. Over time, more products are offered at every price along the supply curve. The sport industry has seen tremendous increases in supply in recent years. Existing sports leagues have expanded their schedules, and new professional sport leagues (e.g., WNBA, MLS, Arena Football) have provided more events. Additional sports (e.g., Extreme Games) are now available for consumers to watch, either in person or on television. The supply of skate parks has doubled, responding to the growth in the

Table 3-5. (Price and Non-price) Factors Affecting Supply of Sport Boats

Factors Affecting Demand	Example for Sport Boats
The Good's Own Price	Higher own price increases profitable production level and raises quantity supplied
Technology	Improved technology in manufacturing lowers production costs and increases supply
Input Prices	Cutting the wages of workers lowers production cost and increases supply of sports boats
Prices of Related Goods	Number of suppliers
Special Influences	If government lowers standards on water pollution-control equipment, supply of sport boats may increase.

number of people roller blading. The increase in supply will eventually result in a decrease in prices, but in the short term, supply will increase at a given price. The growth in supply provides for increased competition. On the other side, as firms leave a market, perhaps because of too much competition and less opportunity for profit, supply decreases.

Some special influences affect supply. For example, weather conditions have a strong bearing on the ski industry. Government regulations and policies on taxes and subsidies also affect profits and supply. Many cities have imposed an amusement tax on sporting events as a way of generating revenue. Sport organizers claim that the tax decreases profits, and they would prefer to take their inventory of events to a place where there is no tax. In contrast, subsidies lead to an increase in supply. Municipalities routinely subsidize recreational programs and facilities and, increasingly, subsidize corporate sport in the guise of stadiums and arenas. Table 3-5 offers a brief summary of all the factors influencing the supply of sport boats.

Demand and Supply and Price

As mentioned previously, consumers demand different amounts of a good as a function of its price. Similarly, producers willingly supply different amounts of the good depending on its market price. What happens when the quantity supplied and quantity demand meet? The answer is that the forces of supply and demand operate through the market to produce an equilibrium price and quantity, which is called a market equilibrium. In such an equilibrium state, the amount that consumers demand and the amount that producers supply is in balance, and prices remain constant; price and quantity tend to stay the same as long as other things remain equal. For example, the number of bottles of sport drink available for sale is equal to the number of bottles desired by buyers if a state of equilibrium exists. Figure 3-5 shows a graphical presentation of a market equilibrium that combines the demand curve from Figure 3-1 with the supply curve from Figure 3-3.

The market equilibrium is located at point C where the two curves intersect. When the price per tennis racquet is $95, suppliers want to sell more than demanders want to buy. The result is a surplus or excess of quantity supplied over quantity demanded, shown in Figure 3-5 by the black line labeled "Surplus." The arrows along the curves show the direction that price tends to move when the market of tennis racquets is in surplus. At a low price of $40 per racquet, the market shows a shortage, or excess of quantity demanded over quantity supplied, shown in Figure 3-5 by the black line labeled "Shortage." If a state of shortage or excess demand occurs, the competition among buyers for limited tennis racquets will cause the price to rise. As prices rise, producers create more products until demand is satisfied and prices stabilize, or a market equilibrium is achieved. At point C, where price per tennis racquet is $60 and the quantity is 290,000, the quantities demanded and supplied are equal; there are no shortages or surpluses. No market forces cause the price of tennis racquets to either rise or fall.

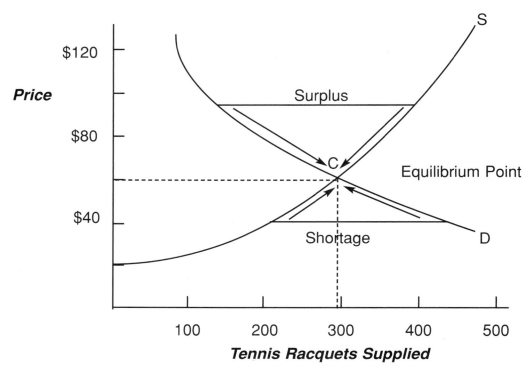

Figure 3-5. Market Equilibrium

In the late 1980s through the 1990s, ice hockey was experiencing growth not just at the professional level but also at the recreational level. The number of participants and teams wanting to play was increasing. However, there were not enough ice rinks to accommodate the demand. Because of the excess demand, ice time became very costly, and recreational teams often practiced or played as late as midnight or 2:00 a.m. New ice rinks were created, and the cost of ice time stopped increasing.

Demand and supply and price are related in other conditions. For example, each year the NCAA conducts a lottery for available Final Four basketball tickets. The lottery is necessary because there are many more people who want tickets than there are tickets available (in 2001, 112,732 people applied for 9,300 tickets available to the general public; NCAA News, 2000). The price of an NCAA Final Four package has risen from $50 in 1988 to $130 in 2005 in spite of an increase in supply (the size of the arenas in which the event is played has increased; National Collegiate Athletic Association, 2004). The NCAA could raise the package price even more because of excess demand. We should note that one of the reasons there is such an excess demand is that the NCAA has intentionally kept prices lower than it could charge. If it allowed prices to freely adjust on the open market, as the package price increased, demand would decrease until equilibrium was reached.

If there is more supply of a product than there is demand, a state of excess supply exists. Some producers will not be able to sell all the goods or services they have. In such a state, producers reduce prices, hoping to capture a larger market share. However, all producers will likely do the same, a strategy that leads to reduced profits for everyone. Ultimately, as prices come down, consumers will be more willing to purchase, and equilibrium is reached. In 1999, a hot golf equipment market cooled, as consumer demand for $400 clubs was filled. The result was lower sales and excess inventories and, ultimately, lower prices (Spanberg, 1999).

The sport industry has its own term for the demand and supply relationship in relation to price. Scalping is buying tickets at a low price and reselling them to consumers who have not been able to satisfy their demand for tickets through a ticket office. Many high-level sporting events experience ticket scalping. A few years ago, Florida State and Notre Dame were scheduled to play in football. Ticket prices were $27 in preseason and sold out. Halfway through the season, both teams were unbeaten, and tickets could be obtained from scalpers for $200. One week before the game, both teams were still unbeaten, and tickets could be obtained from scalpers for $600. Two days before the game, the scalpers' price fell to $400 (Colander, 1998). What happened at each step?

The above situations are covered by the laws of supply and demand:

1. If the quantity demanded is greater than the quantity supplied, prices tend to rise. When quantity supplied is greater than quantity demanded, prices tend to fall. With ice rinks, demand for time resulted in hourly rates increasing from approximately $80 to as much as $200. The opposite was true with golf clubs. The demand for a $400 club turned into a demand for $100 substitutes.

2. The larger the difference between quantity demanded and quantity supplied, the greater is the pressure for prices to rise (if there is excess demand) or fall (if there is excess supply). If the waiting list for Final Four tickets is 10,000 people, prices can rise more than if the waiting list is 100 people.

3. When quantity demanded equals quantity supplied, prices will tend to remain the same.

ELASTICITY OF DEMAND AND SUPPLY

In the above sections, the basic concepts of demand and supply are discussed. The understanding of them as well as the meaning of the equilibrium of demand and supply sets the stage for introducing another economic concept, called elasticity, and the further discussion of the demand and supply relationship. Elasticity, devoting to responsiveness, is a measure of what happens to a variable when another variable is changed. For example, if an organization changes its pricing structure, what happens to sales and revenues? If a team or event raises ticket prices, what happens to ticket sales and/or revenue? If the price of joining a community golf league increases, what impact does it have on participation? Price elasticity of demand and price elasticity of supply are two concepts that will be examined in the following sections.

Note that elasticity measures percentage, not absolute, changes. We compare percentage changes in price to percentage changes in demand and supply. Using percentages allows us to compare change without having to remember the exact unit being used. It also makes it possible to compare elasticities of different goods (e.g., tickets, athletic shoes, memberships).

Price Elasticity of Demand

The law of demand indicates that quantity demand tends to be inversely related to price. Nevertheless, this law does not provide sufficient information for us to know how much quantity demanded will be in response to a change in price. Price elasticity of demand, sometimes also referred to price elasticity, is a measure then used to quantify the amount of change in demand that occurs as a result of change in price, with other things that are held equal. The precise definition of price elasticity of demand is the percentage change in quantity demanded divided by the percentage change in price. The relationship can be expressed with the following formula:

$$\text{Price Elasticity of Demand } (E_D) = \frac{\text{Percentage Change in Quantity Demanded}}{\text{Percentage Change in Price}}$$

To illustrate the calculation of elasticity, a simple case is presented here.

Table 3-6. Example of Price Elasticity of Demand: A Pair of New-Branded Shoes

Sales	January	February
Quantity	2000	1850
Price	$68.99	$72.99

As Table 3-6 shows, in January, the price for the newly-branded athletic shoes is $68.99 per pair and quantity demanded is 200,000 pairs. The price rises to $72.99 in February. As a result of the price increase, consumers reduce their purchase to 185,000 pairs.

$$E_D = \frac{\text{Percentage change in quantity demanded}}{\text{Percentage change in price}} = \frac{-7.5\%}{6.8\%} = [-1.1] = 1.1$$

Where
   Percentage change in quantity demanded
   $= [(1850-2000)/2000] \times 100\% = -7.5\%$
   Percentage change in price
   $= [(72.99-68.99)/68.99] \times 100\% = 6.8\%$

The price increase is 6.8 percent with the resulting quantity decrease being 7.5%. The price elasticity of demand is evidently E_D = 7.5/6.8 = 1.1. The price elasticity is greater than 1 and these newly-branded athletic shoes therefore displayed price-elastic demand within the price range discussed.

Price elasticity of demand is usually a negative number. However, for convenience, economists always drop the negative sign and treat all percentage changes as positive so that elasticity is always a positive number. Its value can vary from zero to infinity; a zero value represents price inelasticity, or little relationship between demand and price. For example, an elasticity of 0.4 means that a 1% increase in the price of a good or service results in a 0.4% decrease in number of units consumed. A good is "elastic" when its quantity demanded responds greatly to price change. Specifically, when a one percent change in price calls for more than a one percent change in quantity demanded, this is price-elastic demand (E_D > 1). On the other hand, a good is "inelastic" when its quantity demanded responds little to price change. Specifically, when a one percent change in price calls for less than a one percent change in quantity demanded, this is price-inelastic demand (E_D > 1). Unit-elastic demand occurs when percentage change in quantity is exactly the same as the percentage change in price (E_D = 1).

Let us compare a baseball and a football team to illustrate how elasticity works. In 1998, approximately 1.4 million fans paid an average ticket price of $7.50 to attend a professional baseball team's games. For the upcoming year, the team management is discussing whether to raise ticket prices. Prices of concessions, parking, and merchandise will remain the same. The team management has to make some judgments about what the change will do to attendance. Table 3-7 presents options.

Table 3-7. Sample Price Elasticity of Demand for a Baseball Team

Price	% P	Quantity	% Q	Elasticity
$7.50		1.40 million		
$7.75	.033	1.35	.036	1.09
$8.00	.067	1.29	.079	1.18
$8.25	.100	1.23	.121	1.21

Table 3-8. Sample Price Elasticity of Demand for a Football Team

Price	% P	Quantity	% Q	Elasticity
$30		58,000		
$31	.033	58,000	.00	.00
$32	.067	58.000	.00	.00
$33	.100	57,900	.002	.02

For the baseball team, would the demand be elastic or inelastic?

$$\text{Elasticity of baseball} = \frac{121}{0.10} = 1.21$$

The answer is elastic ($E_D > 1$): A 10% or $0.75 increase in the price of the average ticket has a corresponding decrease of 12.1% in sales (remember the negative relationship).

As another example, consider a football team in the same town, subject to the same economic environment. Last year they sold out each of their games, for an average attendance of 58,000, at an average ticket price of $30. What would happen if they raise their ticket prices by the same amount as the baseball team? Again, all other prices remain the same (see Table 3-7).

How would you describe the demand for football tickets?

$$\text{Elasticity of baseball} = \frac{0.002}{.100} = 0.02$$

Here the demand is inelastic ($E_D < 1$): The change in price has virtually no impact on the change in attendance.

By now you may be thinking: Wait. What about team performance and other such trivial factors? Keep in mind, economists look at relationships with "all things being equal." In these cases, we assume that the team's performance on the field and other factors are consistent from year to year.

Factors that make demand for goods and services more elastic include

1. More substitutes for that good or service. If a team or athletic club or shoe manufacturer raises its prices, what are the alternatives to spend money? The more alternatives, the more elastic the good or service is.

2. The longer the time interval considered. More substitutes are available in the long run. The growth of ice and dek hockey rinks during the 1990s is an example. In addition, over time, consumers adjust their purchasing habits and develop substitutes. This is the reason economists develop short-run versus long-run demand curves.

3. The less a good is a necessity. Necessities (e.g., prescription drugs, utilities) have fewer substitutes. As previously mentioned, recreation and sport are not considered necessities.

4. The more specifically a good is defined. Sports or recreation taken as a whole has more elastic demand than do individual sports or recreation activities. There are many substitutes for sports as entertainment; there are fewer substitutes for a round of golf or a baseball game.

5. The larger the expenditure for a good relative to one's total income. To buy tennis balls at $3 a can does not result in much impact on one's total income. To be asked to pay a $10,000 initiation fee to join a golf club will result in many people looking at other alternatives.

Table 3-9. Estimated Elasticity of Demand of Selected Recreation Activities, United States

Activity	Demand
Golf (general)	0.12
Golf (club members)	0.70
Tennis	0.20
Outdoor pool	0.23
Attending sports event	0.33
Skiing	0.40
Visiting fairs, amusement parks	0.20
Camping	0.15

Source: Walsh (1986), p. 259.

Siegfried and Eisenberg (1980) found price elasticity of demand in minor league baseball is 0.25. A one percent increase in the price resulted in a 0.25% decline in attendance. They concluded that changes in price did not result in major changes in attendance or that minor league baseball as a product is generally inelastic.

Table 3-9 represents estimated elasticities of demand for several recreational activities. Although these elasticities are generally low, for some activities, such as belonging to a golf club (0.70), demand is more affected by changes in price than is true for other activities, such as golf in general (0.12).

Price Elasticity of Supply

What happens to supply if price is changed? Economists use price elasticity of supply to measure percentage change in quantity supplied that occurs relative to change in price. It depicts the responsiveness of the quantity supplied of a good to its market price. The following is the mathematical expression or formula for price elasticity of supply:

$$\text{Price Elasticity of Supply } (E_S) = \frac{\text{Percentage Change in Quantity Supplied}}{\text{Percentage Change in Price}}$$

Again, a simple case is presented here to illustrate the calculation of the price elasticity of supply.

As Table 3-10 shows, the price for a pack of 12 golf balls is $14.5 and quantity supplied is 1000 packs in January. The price falls to $12.99 in February. As a result of the price decrease, producers reduce their supply to 850 packs in that month.

Table 3-10. Example of Price Elasticity of Supply: Supply of Golf Balls

Sales	January	February
Quantity	1000	850
Price	$14.50	$12.99

$$E_S = \frac{\text{Percentage Change in Quantity Supplied}}{\text{Percentage Change in Price}} = \frac{-15\%}{-10.4\%} = 1.44$$

Where
Percentage Change in Quantity Supplied
= [(850-1000)/1000] × 100% = -15%
Percentage Change in Price
= [(12.99-14.50)14.50] × 100% = -10.4%

The price decrease by 10.4% leads to the decrease in quantity supplied 15%. The price elasticity of supply is then 1.44 (E_S = -15/-10.4). The price elasticity of supply is greater than 1 and the golf balls therefore displayed price-elastic supply within the price range discussed.

If the price of a golf club declines from $400 to $300 (a 25% decrease), producers start to reduce their production of the clubs, perhaps by 10%. The supply elasticity would be 0.40. If the price of tennis balls declines by 10% and 10% fewer tennis balls are produced, the supply elasticity would be 1.0. When we compare the two figures, it is clear that the supply of tennis balls would be more responsive to changes in price than would be the supply of golf clubs.

Sport managers need to be aware of this relationship because they are often changing prices. Ticket prices are an example, not just for team sports, but for ski resorts, golf courses, and major events. Athletic clubs and country clubs adjust membership prices. Sellers of sponsorship, advertising, and signage should consider the impact of pricing changes on their sales.

Price elasticity of supply is also affected by available substitutes, but the influence is felt most when considering time factors:

1. The longer the time period being considered, the more elastic is supply. Over a longer time period, producers have more opportunities to adjust production and supply.

2. Ease and cost of adding supply. How easy is it to add new supply? To add more rounds of golf may require building a new course whereas increasing the number of available spots in a 10K race requires little in costs. The former is more difficult and costly time- and money-wise.

What does this mean to an administrator with a sport organization? If you are making decisions for the previously described baseball team, you have less flexibil-

Photo courtesy of iStockphoto

ity in your options, at least in ticket prices. Your sales are responsive to changes in ticket prices. If you are making decisions for the football team, you have more flexibility. You can change prices without having to worry as much about the impact on demand. For almost any sport organization like an athletic club, event, or resort, a sport administrator must attempt to determine what the impact of price changes will be in order to make smart pricing decisions.

DEMAND, SUPPLY, AND REVENUE

An understanding of the relationship among demand and supply and price, and price elasticity of demand and supply helps clarify the impact of price changes upon total revenue for an organization. Total revenue is by definition equal to the price charged per unit of some item times the number of units sold (TR = P × Q). For example, a golfer buys three slates of balls at $6 each; the total revenue is $18. What happens to total revenue if price changes (keep in mind that if price changes, demand is likely to change). Three types of relationship exist between total revenue and price changes:

1. If demand is elastic, the relationship is inverse; that is, an increase in prices results in a reduction in total revenue.

2. If demand is inelastic, the relationship is positive. It means an increase in prices results in an increase in total revenue.

3. If demand is unit elastic, a rise in prices has no impact on total revenue.

Tables 3-11 and 3-12 illustrate what happens to total revenue for various price changes with the baseball and football teams. For the baseball team, the jump from $7.50 to $8.25 (an increase of 10%) results in a decline in demand and a loss

Table 3-11. Total Revenues for Sample Baseball Team

Price	% P	Quantity	% Q	Elasticity	Total Revenue (P x Q)
$7.50		1.40 million			$10.50 million
$7.75	.033	1.36	.029	.88	$10.54
$8.00	.067	1.29	.079	1.18	$10.32
$8.25	.100	1.23	.121	1.21	$10.15

Table 3-12. Total Revenues for Sample Football Team

Price	% P	Quantity	% Q	Elasticity	Total Revenue (P x Q)
$30	58,000	$1.74 million			
$31	.033	58,000	.00	.00	$1.80
$32	.067	58.000	.00	.00	$1.86
$33	.100	57,900	.002	.02	$1.91

in total revenue of $350,000. However, for a smaller price increase—from $7.50 to $7.75—although demand declines by 40,000 people, revenue actually increases by $40,000. It may be beneficial from a ticket revenue standpoint for the baseball team to accept some decline in attendance to maximize revenues. Of course, this is with all things being equal. In practice, the sport manager needs to consider impacts on ancillary revenue such as concessions and parking.

Table 3-11 shows that for the football team, the impact of the rise in prices is clear: Revenue increases. A 10% rise in ticket prices, from $30 to $33, results in a 9.7% rise in revenue, or an addition $1.71 million. In this case, maximizing revenue does not necessarily involve a decline in attendance.

Price Discrimination

Price discrimination is another element entering our discussion of supply and demand. In using the baseball team as an example, we used a single ticket price. However, rarely when we go to a baseball game is there just one price for tickets. Rather, there is a range, giving consumers an option of how much they will spend. This is true for many sports venues. Ski resorts vary prices by weekend/weekday or half-day use; athletic clubs have family, single, and social memberships; and weekend 10K events have different prices for early and late registration and/or for walkers. This concept, called price discrimination, recognizes that different segments of consumers have different price elasticities.

Table 3-13 illustrates the concept of price discrimination for users of a ski resort. The elasticity for day skiers, who are likely to live close to the resort, is 0.30, whereas for skiers on vacation trips, the elasticity is almost 0.09. For the latter, demand is more inelastic. People going to ski on vacation are not as concerned about changes in price as are those who ski on a day pass, perhaps because the lift ticket price itself is a smaller portion of the overall cost of the vacation or because they have a higher income level.

Table 3-13. Price Elasticity of Demand for Ski Lift Tickets

Day tickets	0.35
Weekend use	0.22
Vacation trips	0.087

Source: Walsh (1986), p. 279.

Using the concept of price discrimination, sport managers may have more flexibility in changing prices for certain consumer segments and less flexibility for others. As another example, prime behind-the-plate seats in baseball are more likely to be inelastic whereas bleacher seats are more likely to be elastic. Businesses and high-income attendees are more likely to purchase prime seats. For them, the cost of tickets is likely to be a small percentage of their total income, or they may write off the tickets as a business expense. Either way, they are less concerned about price.

Forecasting Demand and Supply

Sport managers can use their knowledge of demand and supply to forecast events or conditions. Forecasts are basically predictions. For example, a sports apparel company may want to project demand for its clothing over the next 3 to 5 years to determine whether or not it should open a new production line or new stores. Before developing new slopes, a ski resort manager might want to estimate the future demand for ski days. One of the goals of forecasting is to reduce uncertainty on the part of the sport manager in making decisions. With good estimates of what would happen, given changes in price, demand, and supply, better decisions are possible. However, forecasting does not eliminate uncertainty. It only provides a tool to the manager to assist in making decisions.

Forecasting, or demand estimation, is a complicated topic and is the focus of entire academic courses. However, sport managers should be aware of some basic considerations. People looking at doing forecasts need to consider several relevant factors. An important beginning point is to determine what a forecast is intended to accomplish. Who will use the predictions? How will they be used? What format is most useful? What is the relevant time period? After answering these questions, the forecaster considers general factors:

1. General economic conditions, such as GDP or population distributions

2. Industry conditions, in either the sport industry or specific segments of it (e.g., clubs, sporting goods)

3. Income levels of the population

4. Consumer habits and tastes

5. Market potential for various groups

6. Government regulations and laws, including enacted laws, agency regulations, and court decisions. For example, many ski resorts use Forest Service land for slopes. Are changes in regulations governing the use of that land imminent?

Although important to do, forecasting is not an easy task. It requires thorough analysis of what has happened as well as assumptions about what will happen. Economists have developed elaborate models in many industries; however, these models have not been frequently applied to sports. The following description is a brief summary of techniques used in developing economic forecasts that have been used in the sport industry. It is not designed to be a comprehensive explanation.

OPINION POLLS, MARKET RESEARCH, AND SPENDING PLAN SURVEYS

They are three common techniques used to identify changes in people's activities. These techniques can help determine who consumers are, why and how they make the purchases they do, and what future plans consumers have for spending. Such surveys are done by individual businesses, industry groups (for example, the National Sporting Goods Association provides extensive information on sporting goods consumers), and research centers (the Survey Research center at the University of Michigan is one example). Doing market research and polls has many advantages and disadvantages. A course in research methods provides a useful background.

EXPERT OPINIONS

These experts may be corporate executives in an industry or salespeople for a business. *Street & Smith's SportsBusiness Journal* provided an example of the former when it brought together six of what it deemed the "masters of their various disciplines" to describe what they see happening in the sport industry in the 21st century (Schoenfeld, 1999). Business can also look within the organization. A resource often overlooked is a business's own sales staff. Who else is in continual contact with consumers, talking with them, asking them what they are going to want? Although this technique may be useful, it also has disadvantages, not the least of which is that using a selected group of people does not necessarily give a representative view.

ANALYSIS OF PAST DEMAND DATA

Another way to make projections is to look at past demand and use it to determine how supply might be adjusted. This can be a useful technique, especially if the manager is trying to predict what is going to happen in the very near term. However, using such a method does present difficulties, one of which is that conditions under which a company operates change, especially over a longer period. For example, the sport apparel business is one that is subject to fads. What has been a hot item over the past 3 years may very well be out-of-date in the next year. As a result, using past information can provide a very misleading picture of the future. A variety of statistical techniques have been developed, including time series analysis and constant compound growth rates, to improve the use of past data. Knowledge of statistics and econometrics is helpful.

Even though each of these techniques has disadvantages, those disadvantages should not dissuade the sport manager from using them. A bad scenario occurs when the manager does not attempt to determine what the future holds and how to position the organization to meet future demands.

Summary

Supply and demand are basic economic concepts. In fact, they can be used to answer many of the questions we have about why industries and individuals make the decisions they do. The general law of demand states that, all things being equal, the lower (higher) the price of some item, the higher (lower) the quantity demanded. The general law of supply states that, all things being equal, the higher (lower) the price of a good offered, the more (less) of a product will be supplied. Many factors influence supply and demand; the major one is price. In making decisions, sport managers need to consider elasticity of demand and supply, or the responsiveness of demand and supply to changes in prices. Sport managers can use their knowledge of supply and demand in making forecasts and decisions for their organizations.

Chapter Questions

1. What would be your recommendation for the Great Lake Baseball League, particularly pertaining to the variable pricing strategy?
2. What is the difference between demand and quantity demanded? What is the difference between change in quantity demanded and a shift in the demand curve?
3. What is the difference between supply and quantity supplied? What is the difference between change in quantity supplied and a shift in the supply curve?

4. You are a ski resort operator. In the next 5 years, what factors might affect your business in terms of supply and demand?
5. The U.S. women's soccer team won the World Cup in 1999. If you're in the soccer business, how might that influence your decision making?
6. What is elasticity? Elasticity of demand? Elasticity of supply? Distinguish between elastic and inelastic demand and supply.
7. What makes demand for some goods and services more elastic? What makes supply of some goods and services more elastic?
8. If you're the CEO for the baseball and football teams that are considering raising their prices, what would your decision be? How much would you raise the prices? Why?
9. Many professional athletes make millions of dollars each year whereas the salaries of elementary school teachers are a fraction of that. We pay huge amounts to some people to "play," whereas others, responsible for shaping the abilities and attitudes of children, make so much less. How would you argue this makes economic sense, using the concepts of supply and demand?
10. Why do organizations use price discrimination?
11. What methods are available for managers to forecast demand and supply?

Learning Activities

Complete an application project of economic principles. This project is designed for you to see the relevance and application of economics to the sport industry. Use the following guidelines to complete the project:

1. Complete a bibliography and a portfolio of research material related to such concepts as demand, supply, price elasticity of demand, price elasticity of supply, and price discrimination topics. Material can come from a variety of sources, such as professional journals, magazines, Internet, etc. You need to find at least two articles pertaining to each of the concepts.
2. Discuss history of pricing of the goods and services in the sport industry field and how the price as well as nonprice factors have influenced the decisions of sport executives in production.

Chapter Four

MARKETS AND THE SPORT INDUSTRY

Introduction

The purpose of this chapter is to explain and predict managerial decision making by understanding the nature of the markets in which a firm operates. The decisions managers face depend on the conditions in the market where the firm sells its products. Since some firms in the sport industry operate in more than one market, managers at those firms will face a different set of decisions across the markets of the firm.

Markets may be characterized by their features: the types and degrees of rivalry present, the existence of barriers to entry, and the amount of control over price held by a single firm in the market.

Types of Rivalries in Markets

Rivalries in markets include: consumer-consumer, producer-producer, and consumer-producer rivalries (Baye, 2003, pp. 10–11). All three types of rivalries can be found in the sport industry. Auctions for sport memorabilia are examples of markets where consumer-consumer rivalry plays a significant role. The more consumer-consumer rivalry, the higher the price the auction winner pays. In the market for record home run baseballs, the degree of consumer-consumer rivalry has varied significantly. Mark McGwire's seventieth home run ball sold for $3 million while Barry Bond's seventy-third home run baseball sold for $517,500. The purchaser of both balls explained, "If it weren't for me and another guy, the McGwire ball would have sold for $1.3 million" (Rovell, 2003, para. 8). Because of the intensity of consumer-consumer rivalry, the price was increased by $1.3 million. Consumers would like to pay lower prices but consumer-consumer rivalry increases the price they pay.

As health clubs try to win members in a community, they are engaging in producer-producer rivalry. The existence of other health clubs forces a health club to offer more services and to charge a lower price. While each health club would like to charge higher prices, the extent of producer-producer rivalry limits the prices they can charge.

Producer-consumer rivalry is present in naming rights negotiations between a stadium authority and a company. The stadium would prefer a higher price for the naming rights, the company a lower price. The negotiations are likely to be complex as both parties attempt to get more of what they want in the agreement. The stadium authority can increase the price of the rights by bundling different products (for example, the use of a suite) with the naming rights. The company can reduce the dollar price by offering non-monetary returns (for example, a computer firm could offer hardware or software) to the stadium authority.

Producer-consumer rivalry is a battle over consumer and producer surplus. Consumer surplus refers to value received by consumers in excess of the price they paid. If you were willing to pay $150 for a new pair of running shoes and had to pay $115, you would have received $35 of consumer surplus. Producer surplus is revenue received in excess of the minimum price the producer would have accepted for the product. If the shoe seller would have accepted a price of $100, the producer received $15 of producer surplus. In the negotiation process between a stadium authority and a company, the stadium authority attempts to increase producer surplus, the company the amount of consumer surplus.

DEFINITION AND EXAMPLES OF BARRIERS TO ENTRY

Barriers to entry are factors that make it difficult for a new firm to enter a market (Hirschey, 2003, p. 365). According to this definition, barriers include advertising, product differentiation, patents, product bundling, economies of scale, and legal barriers. Nike makes it difficult for a new firm to enter the athletic shoe industry by advertising and product differentiation. Through advertising Nike has built brand loyalty, which a new firm must overcome to enter the industry. By producing many different types of athletic shoes, Nike makes it difficult for a new firm to find an unserved niche in the athletic shoe industry.

When government grants a firm a patent for an invention, it gives the firm the exclusive right to sell a product for twenty years (McConnell & Brue, 2005, p. 218). Nautilus International uses patents to try to keep other firms from entering markets for its exercise products (Herzog, 2004, p. 1).

By bundling services (for example, weight training and aerobics classes) together into a single membership package, a health club can make it more difficult for a new firm to enter the market for any one of the services. The firm can tell potential customers they do not have to settle for just one service but rather can have a menu of services by buying membership in their club. A firm that wants to enter the market for aerobics classes may feel it must also enter the other markets to be competitive. Entering all the markets makes it more difficult for a new firm to enter any of the individual markets.

Economies of scale are a long-run cost concept. When economies of scale exist, producing more output lowers the average cost of production. In the retail sporting goods industry there are economies of scale. Retailers with large volume have access to quantity discounts from suppliers, which lowers their average cost of production relative to smaller firms. If a firm wants to enter the general sporting goods market at a small size, it will be at a cost disadvantage relative to larger firms.

As a result of this barrier, entrants into the sporting goods retail market tend to be small specialty firms. While a small specialty firm will be at a cost disadvantage, it can compete in the market by offering better service than larger retail firms. The cost of providing service at a general sporting goods store would be higher than at a specialty store given the diversity of products sold at a general sporting goods store.

Legal barriers may make entering a market difficult. In Illinois a person who wants to be an athletic trainer must obtain a license from the state (Illinois Department of Professional Regulation, 2006). To obtain the license a person must complete an approved program in athletic training at an accredited college or university and pass a written exam. These legal requirements make it difficult to enter the market for athletic trainers.

BARRIERS TO ENTRY AND LONG-RUN ECONOMIC PROFITS

For a firm to earn economic profit in the long run there must be barriers to entry. When a firm is making economic profit, its total revenue exceeds total cost. Included in total cost are the costs of the owner's time and any other resources supplied by the owner. At an economic profit of zero, a firm would continue to operate because all costs are covered. If economic profits are positive, the firm is more than covering all its costs. An industry where firms are making more than enough to continue to operate is an attractive industry to enter. If there are no barriers to entry and firms in an industry are making economic profit, new firms will enter the market. As new firms enter an industry the ability of existing firms to earn economic profit is reduced. Over time, given a lack of barriers to entry, firms will eventually earn zero economic profit.

Health clubs provide an example of the relationship between economic profit and barriers of entry. For example, the first health club in an area to offer classes in a trendy new type of exercise (past examples include spinning [on exercise bikes] and Pilates), is likely to experience a spike in membership. Increased membership increases the profitability of the club.

As managers at other health clubs observe increased activity at a rival club, they will begin to offer similar programs. As other clubs offer similar programs, the spike in membership and profitability the original club had will diminish. Had barriers to entry existed in the market for classes in the trendy exercise, economic profits could have continued until there was a change in consumer taste away from that form of exercise, decreasing demand for the classes.

Given the importance of barriers to entry to long-run profitability, firms often attempt to maintain them. As other firms have begun to market products similar to Nautilus International's Bow-flex training machine, Nautilus has spent millions of dollars defending its patents in court (Herzog, 2004, p. 1) In 2004, Nautilus International planned to spend double on research and development because of the expiration of patents.

THE NATURE OF BARRIERS TO ENTRY AND THE ENFORCEMENT OF ANTITRUST LAWS

Barriers to entry play a significant role in the enforcement of antitrust laws in the United States. Broadly speaking, the purpose of the antitrust laws is to promote competition. Barriers to entry make it difficult for new competitors to enter a market. There is controversy in economics over what barriers to entry are harmful to competition. According to Robert Bork, some barriers, advertising, product differentiation, product bundling, and economies of scale are types of efficiency and should not be condemned as anticompetitive (Bork, 1978, pp. 310–311).

Within the context of Bork's view of barriers to entry, Nike's advertising and product differentiation are consistent with the firm attempting to serve customers. Efficiency is not just cutting costs but also offering what consumers want (Bork, 1978, p. 319). Nike's advertising evidently gives consumers what they want given their response to it. Nike's product differentiation is profitable only if consumers like it. According to Bork's approach, Nike is serving its customers through advertising and product differentiation and is not building anticompetitive barriers to entry.

Proponents of the view that advertising is a barrier to entry that reduces competition cite the association between intense advertising, product differentiation, and high profitability (Mann, 1974, p. 155). According to this view Nike's advertising and product differentiation are attempts to build barriers to entry. By building barriers to entry Nike is able to earn economic profit in the long run by keeping potential competitors out of the market.

Antitrust laws and the sport industry are covered in Chapter 11. The alternative views of barriers to entry will be used to explain why different economists want different enforcement and interpretation of the antitrust laws. The enforcement and interpretation of the antitrust laws has significance for the sport industry.

CONTROL OVER PRICE AND MARKET STRUCTURE

The types of decisions managers have to make are influenced by the level of competition in the markets in which their firm competes. One way of assessing the level of competition in a market is by examining the degree of control a firm has over the price of its output. The more control a firm has over price, the less competitive the market. A firm's control over price is linked to the structure of the market in which it competes.

Economists use models to describe four basic market structures: pure competition, monopolistic competition, oligopoly, and monopoly. These models can be characterized in terms of the number of producers in the market, the homogeneity of the product, the amount of power over price of a firm, the level of barriers to entry, and the extent of non-price competition. For three of the four models, pure competition, monopolistic competition, and monopoly, there is relatively little controversy. About oligopoly, economics offers no single vision of how firms behave but rather speaks in a "babble of voices" (Sullivan, 1977, p. 7). Pure competition, monopolistic competition, and monopoly are covered in this chapter, oligopoly in Chapter 5.

Table 4-1 contains a description of the characteristics of the four basic models. As we examine the behavior of firms within each of these markets, we will assume the goal of a firm is to maximize profit. To understand profit maximization, the nature of costs and revenue must be explored.

Table 4–1. Market Structure

Market Structure	No. of Producers	Type of Product	Power Over Price	Barriers to Entry	Non-Price Competition
Perfect Competition	Many	Standardized	None	Low	None
Monopoly	One	Unique	Much	High	Advertising and Product Differentiation
Oligopoly	Few	Standardized or Differentiated	?	?	Advertising and Product Differentiation
Monopolistic Competition	Many	Differentiated	Some	Low	Advertising and Product Differentiation

COSTS, REVENUES, AND PROFIT MAXIMIZATION

In the short run the total cost of production may be split into two categories, fixed and variable costs. Fixed costs are costs that do not change with the amount of output produced. As additional units of output are produced, variable costs increase. For example, STS builds race cars. The company has a year-long lease on a production facility that requires a rent payment of $2,000 per month. The rent payment is a fixed cost because STS must pay $2,000 per month whether zero or ten cars are produced. STS purchases engine components from a supplier. The more cars STS produces, the more engine components they purchase. The cost of the engine components is a variable cost; the more cars produced, the greater the spending by the firm on components.

The long run is a length of time such that there are no fixed costs. All costs are variable in the long run. In the long run, STS's lease will expire and it will no longer face the fixed cost of $2,000 per month in rent.

Marginal cost can be thought of in two ways. It is the increase in cost from producing one more unit of output or the rate at which costs change as production changes. Average fixed cost is fixed cost divided by the quantity of output produced. Average variable cost is variable cost divided by the quantity of output produced. Average total cost is total cost divided by the quantity of output produced. Average total cost equals average fixed cost plus average variable cost. Table 4-2 contains hypothetical cost information for a golf club manufacturer. The marginal cost figures in Table 4-2 are the rates at which total costs change as output is increased.

The total revenue of a firm equals the price of its product multiplied by the quantity of output. Average revenue is total revenue divided by the quantity output. Marginal revenue is the change in revenue from producing one more unit of output.

Marginal revenue and marginal costs are the keys to determining the profit maximizing level of output. As long as marginal revenue exceeds marginal costs, profits are ris-

Table 4-2. Hypothetical Cost Information for a Golf Club Manufacturer

Quantity	Fixed Cost	Variable Cost	Total Fixed Cost	Average Variable Cost	Average Total Cost	Average Cost	Marginal
0	$21600	$0	$21600	Undefined	Undefined	Undefined	Undefined
1	21600	$765	$22365	$21600	$765	$22365	$731
2	21600	1464	23064	10800	732	11532	668
3	21600	2103	23703	7200	701	7901	611
4	21600	2688	24288	5400	672	6072	560
5	21600	3225	24825	4320	645	4965	515
6	21600	3720	25320	3600	620	4220	476
7	21600	4179	25779	3086	597	3683	443
8	21600	4608	26208	2700	576	3276	416
9	21600	5013	26613	2400	557	2957	395
10	21600	5400	27000	2160	540	2700	380
11	21600	5775	27375	1964	525	2489	371
12	21600	6144	27744	1800	512	2312	368
13	21600	6513	28113	1662	501	2163	371
14	21600	6888	28488	1543	492	2035	380
15	21600	7275	28875	1440	485	1925	395
16	21600	7680	29280	1350	480	1830	416
17	21600	8109	29709	1271	477	1748	443
18	21600	8568	30168	1200	476	1676	476
19	21600	9063	30663	1137	477	1614	515
20	21600	9600	31200	1080	480	1560	560
21	21600	10185	31785	1029	485	1514	611
22	21600	10824	32424	982	492	1474	668
23	21600	11523	33123	939	501	1440	731
24	21600	12288	33888	900	512	1412	800
25	21600	13125	34725	864	525	1389	875
26	21600	14040	35640	831	540	1371	956
27	21600	15039	36639	800	557	1357	1043
28	21600	16128	37728	771	576	1347	1136
29	21600	17313	38913	745	597	1342	1235
30	21600	18600	40200	720	620	1340	1340
31	21600	19995	41595	697	645	1342	1451
32	21600	21504	43104	675	672	1347	1568
33	21600	23133	44733	655	701	1356	1691
34	21600	24888	46488	635	732	1367	1820
35	21600	26775	48375	617	765	1382	1955
36	21600	28800	50400	600	800	1400	2096
37	21600	30969	52569	584	837	1421	2243
38	21600	33288	54888	568	876	1444	2396
39	21600	35763	57363	554	917	1471	2555
40	21600	38400	60000	540	960	1500	2720

ing. To maximize profits a firm wants to produce all the units of output where the additional revenue of a unit (marginal revenue) exceeds the additional cost of producing that unit (marginal cost). As long as profits are rising they are not maximized.

If marginal revenue is less than marginal cost, profits are falling. To maximize profit a firm does not want to produce units of output where the additional revenue (marginal revenue) from the unit is less the additional costs (marginal costs) of producing the unit. Table 4-3 contains hypothetical cost and revenue information for a golf club manufacturer. As long as marginal revenue exceeds marginal costs, profits increase.

In a graphic representation of marginal revenue and cost, the profit maximizing output occurs where marginal revenue equals marginal costs. At any other output level profits are either rising or falling. If profits are rising or falling they are not at their maximum.

Table 4-3. Hypothetical Cost and Revenue Information for a Golf Club Manufacturer

Quantity	Price	Total Revenue	Marginal Revenue	Variable Cost	Average Variable Cost	Marginal Cost	Fixed Cost	Total Cost	Average Total Cost	Profit
0	1500	0		0	Undefined		500	500	Undefined	-500
1	1470	1470	1470	765	765	731	500	1265	1265	205
2	1440	2880	1410	1464	732	668	500	1964	982	916
3	1410	4230	1350	2103	701	611	500	2603	868	1627
4	1380	5520	1290	2688	672	560	500	3188	797	2332
5	1350	6750	1230	3225	645	515	500	3725	745	3025
6	1320	7920	1170	3720	620	476	500	4220	703	3700
7	1290	9030	1110	4179	597	443	500	4679	668	4351
8	1260	10080	1050	4608	576	416	500	5108	639	4972
9	1230	11070	990	5013	557	395	500	5513	613	5557
10	1200	12000	930	5400	540	380	500	5900	590	6100
11	1170	12870	870	5775	525	371	500	6275	570	6595
12	1140	13680	810	6144	512	368	500	6644	554	7036
13	1110	14430	750	6513	501	371	500	7013	539	7417
14	1080	15120	690	6888	492	380	500	7388	528	7732
15	1050	15750	630	7275	485	395	500	7775	518	7975
16	1020	16320	570	7680	480	416	500	8180	511	8140
17	990	16830	510	8109	477	443	500	8609	506	8221
18	960	17280	450	8568	476	476	500	9068	504	8212
19	930	17670	390	9063	477	515	500	9563	503	8107
20	900	18000	330	9600	480	560	500	10100	505	7900
21	870	18270	270	10185	485	611	500	10685	509	7585
22	840	18480	210	10824	492	668	500	11324	515	7156
23	810	18630	150	11523	501	731	500	12023	523	6607
24	780	18720	90	12288	512	800	500	12788	533	5932

THE SHORT-RUN SHUT-DOWN RULE

If a firm is making profit in the short run, its best output level is where marginal cost equals marginal revenue. If a firm is making a loss in the short run it has a different decision to make. It must decide whether it is better to produce the output where marginal revenue equals marginal costs or if it should shut down and produce zero units of output. If the firm shuts down in the short run it will earn a loss equal to its fixed cost. For STS, the loss will be $2,000 per month, the amount of its rent payment that it must make no matter how many cars it produces.

The decision to operate or shut down in the short run depends on the relationship between revenue and variable costs. If revenue exceeds variable costs, the firm should produce in the short run. It can use its revenue to pay its variable costs and apply the remaining revenue to pay part of fixed costs. The best output level to produce will be where marginal revenue equals marginal costs. Where marginal revenue equals marginal costs a firm maximizes profit or, in this case, minimizes losses.

The firm should shut down in the short run and make a loss equal to its fixed costs if revenue is less than variable costs. If the firm would operate, its loss would equal fixed costs plus that portion of variable costs the firm's revenue did not cover. Rather than lose an amount larger than fixed cost, the firm should shut down and lose an amount equal to its fixed costs.

The decision rule for shutting down in the short run can be stated in terms of price and average variable cost. If price is greater than average variable costs, the firm should operate. If price is less than average variable cost, the firm should shut down.

PURE COMPETITION

In a purely competitive market managers do not have to make decisions about price because an individual firm has no control over the price of the product it sells. In a purely competitive market there are many buyers and sellers, none large relative to the market. The product in a purely competitive market is homogeneous. Since buyers perceive the product as the same no matter which firm produced the good and there are so many producers, no individual firm can change the price of the product by changing production. The price of a product in a purely competitive market will be determined by the interaction of supply and demand, as described in Chapter 3.

A purely competitive market does not have barriers to entry or exit. It is easy for firms to enter and to leave the market. If firms in the industry are earning positive economic profit, new firms will enter the market. As new firms enter the market, the supply of the product increases. As supply increases, the price of the product falls. As the price of the product falls, the profitability of firms in the market is eliminated. If firms had been earning losses, firms would have exited, supply decreased, price risen, and losses eliminated. Given this process, firms in a purely competitive market in the long run earn zero economic profit because of the lack of barriers to entry and exit.

While managers in a purely competitive market do not have to make pricing decisions, they do have to decide how much output to produce. To maximize profit, mangers need to compare marginal revenue and marginal cost. In a purely competitive market the output of one firm does not change the price of the product. If a firm sells another unit of output its total revenue will increase by the price of the product. In pure competition the marginal revenue of selling one more unit is the price of the product. For pure competition, the profit maximization rule may be restated as price equals marginal cost. If the information in Table 4-2 was for a purely competitive firm and the price of the product was $1,340, the profit maximizing output would be 30. At an output of 30, the firm would earn zero economic profit. At any other output level the firm would make a loss. The best output the firm can produce is where price equals marginal cost.

There are no good examples of markets in the sport industry that fit the description of pure competition. Pure competition can be thought of as a benchmark. The model of pure competition describes the most competitive situation; other models describe markets that are less competitive.

MONOPOLY

Monopoly describes a market in which there is one seller of a product that has no close substitutes. Because of the lack of substitute products the control over price of a monopoly is not limited by the actions of other firms. A monopolist is limited only by consumer demand for the product. Given the negative relationship between price and quantity demanded, all else held constant, if a monopolist expands output, price will fall. If a monopolist decreases output, price will rise.

A monopolist can choose any price and output combination on the market demand curve. To maximize profit a monopolist should produce the output where marginal revenue equals marginal cost. By deciding on a level of output, a monopolist has also chosen a price, the price that will sell that amount of output.

Whether or not there are monopolies in the sport industry depends on how you define the market. The National Football League has a monopoly in the professional major league football entertainment market. They do not have a monopoly in the market for football entertainment. In that market, they compete with college and high school football. An important issue is the extent to which consumers view the products as similar. The more consumers and potential consumers view the products of different firms as similar, the further the market is from monopoly. The more consumers and potential consumers view the product of a firm as unique, the closer the market is to monopoly. If consumers and potential consumers view the product of the National Football League as unique, the NFL is a monopoly.

In Chapter 11 on antitrust issues in the sport industry, the importance of defining the relevant market in cases involving monopoly will be examined. Another issue explored in Chapter 11 is the role of unfair business practices compared to superior business practices in maintaining monopoly. From the view of society, a monopoly maintained through superior business practices is more acceptable than one maintained through unfair business practices.

For profitable monopoly to persist into the long run there must be barriers to entry. If there are no barriers to entry new firms offering the same or similar products would enter the market. Unfair business practices and superior business practices can enable a monopolist to remain the only firm in a market. The NFL has experienced other leagues attempting to enter the market for major league professional football over the last thirty years, the World Football League and the United States Football League.

Price and Output in Monopoly

The relationship between price and marginal revenue is different for a firm with control over price than for a firm in a purely competitive market. For the purely competitive firm, selling one more unit increases total revenue by the price of the product. Marginal revenue equals price. Because for a firm with some control over price selling another unit causes price to fall, marginal revenue is less than price. Total revenue increases by less than the price of the additional unit sold because the price that is charged for all units is now lower.

Table 4-4 contains hypothetical revenue information about the Exo Corporation. The firm has developed and received a patent for a new type of exercise equipment. Exo has a monopoly because consumers and potential consumers view the device as unique with no close substitutes. As Exo expands output, the price it can charge for its product decreases.

If the firm produces 12 units, it can charge a price of $1,140. To sell 13 units the price must be lowered to $1,110. When the thirteenth unit is sold for $1,110, the first twelve units now are also sold at $1,110 rather than at $1,140. To sell the thirteenth unit, revenue decreases on the first 12 units sold by $30 each because of the lower price. Instead of increasing total revenue by $1,110, the thirteenth unit increases revenue by $750, the revenue from selling just the thirteenth unit $1,110 minus $360, the decrease in revenue from the first 12 units.

If the marginal cost of producing each machine is $600 and constant, the profit maximizing output for Exo is 15 units. If Exo produces 15 units, it can sell each of them at a price of $1,050. Exo's profitability depends on the average total cost of producing 15 units. If the average total cost is $1,000 at 15 units of output, Exo's profit per unit is $50. Exo's total profit is $750.

The ability of Exo to continue to earn profit over time depends on the strength of barriers to entry. If other exercise equipment companies can develop similar products without violating Exo's patents, entry will occur and Exo's profits will decrease. Nautilus International's experience suggests that firms will risk law-

Table 4-4. Hypothetical Revenue Data for the Exo Corporation

Quantity	Price	Total Revenue	Marginal Revenue
1	1470	1470	1470
2	1440	2880	1410
3	1410	4230	1350
4	1380	5520	1290
5	1350	6750	1230
6	1320	7920	1170
7	1290	9030	1110
8	1260	10080	1050
9	1230	11070	990
10	1200	12000	930
11	1170	12870	870
12	1140	13680	810
13	1110	14430	750
14	1080	15120	690
15	1050	15750	630
16	1020	16320	570
17	990	16830	510
18	960	17280	450
19	930	17670	390
20	900	18000	330
21	870	18270	270
22	840	18480	210
23	810	18630	150
24	780	18720	90

suits for patent infringement to enter a market they believe is profitable (Herzog, 2004, p. 1). If the average total cost of production of 15 units is $1,300, Exo faces a different decision, to operate or shut down. If it operates, it will lose $250 on each unit produced for a total loss of $3,750. To decide whether or not to operate, Exo should compare the price to the average variable cost of production. If marginal cost is $600 and constant, average variable cost is also $600 and constant. Exo can sell 15 units at $1,050 each. Since the price $1,050 is larger than average variable cost $600, Exo should operate and produce 15 units.

The difference between average total cost $1,300 and average variable cost $600 is average fixed cost $700. If the average fixed cost of producing 15 units is $700, the fixed cost is $10,500 (average fixed cost $700 multiplied by the number of units 15). If Exo shuts down, it will lose $10,500, its fixed cost.

Operating Exo will lose $3,750, which is better than shutting down and losing $10,500. Exo's monopoly does not guarantee them profit. If it has developed a machine that is expensive relative to consumer demand, it will earn a loss. If your firm sold tennis balls made of cement you would have a monopoly, but your firm would not be profitable.

MONOPOLY AND SOCIETY

Monopoly imposes costs on society. Relative to a competitive firm, a monopolist produces less output. A monopolist restricts output to increase the price to maximize profit based on marginal revenue and marginal cost. A firm in a purely competitive market cannot change the market price, so it has no incentive to restrict output.

A competitive firm will continue to produce output as long as consumers are willing to pay a price at least equal to the cost of producing another unit (marginal cost). A monopolist will produce another unit only as long as marginal revenue at least equals marginal cost. In a monopolized market, a consumer can be willing to pay what it costs to produce another unit, but the firm will not serve the customer because increasing output puts downward pressure on price.

In major league professional sports, the restriction of output takes the form of fewer franchises in the leagues (Quirk & Fort, 1992, p. 359). To maximize profits, the leagues restrict the number of franchises below the number that could be supported. By restricting the numbers of franchises, leagues are able to increase the value of existing franchises.

A second criticism of monopoly is their potential inefficiency in production. Monopolies do not face the same pressure to be efficient that competitive firms face. In a competitive market, if you are less efficient than your rivals, your firm may not survive. A monopoly does not have rivals generating pressure to be efficient. A health club in a city large enough to support only one club does not face the same pressure to be efficient in serving customers that a club in a large city with many other clubs faces.

Being inefficient is not costless to a monopolist. Inefficiency raises costs, reduces revenues, and leads to less profit. Owners of a monopoly who want to maximize profit need to be concerned with inefficiency.

While owners are likely to be concerned with inefficiency, managers may not be concerned. In cases where managers are not the owners, inefficiency may be a way for them to increase their utility. In general, becoming efficient is not an enjoyable process. Reducing inefficiency is likely to be a stressful process. Managers may be willing to accept inefficiency if it makes their lives more pleasant by reducing stress, even if it means less profit for the owners.

The manager of a monopoly health club in a small city might be willing to ignore a problem employee who alienates customers rather than deal with the situation. The manager increases his utility (by avoiding an unpleasant task) even though it means lower profits for the owner. In a competitive market, the manager would face additional pressure to correct the problem given the movement over time toward zero economic profit.

While monopoly imposes costs on society, it may also benefit society. Firms in a competitive market have incentives to innovate and invent, but may not have the ability to finance spending on research and development. Monopolists are under less pressure to invent and innovate because barriers to entry shield them from competition. Monopolists have some incentive to invent and innovate because it can lead to increased profit.

Monopolists are more likely to have access to financing for research and development than competitive firms because of the possibility of monopolists earning profit in the long run. Monopoly may lead to more invention and innovation than competitive markets. A golf club manufacturer with a patented profitable golf club may use some of its profit on research to develop new clubs. A golf club

Photo by Aaron Murphy, courtesy of stock.xchng iv

manufacturer without a patent-protected product may be less able to finance research on new clubs.

MONOPOLISTIC COMPETITION

Monopolistic competition describes a very competitive market. Like pure competition, it describes situations where there are a large number of firms, each small relative to the market and no barriers to entry or exit. Monopolistic competition may be thought of as pure competition with just a tiny touch of monopoly. The touch of monopoly in monopolistic competition comes from product differentiation. In purely competitive markets, there is no product differentiation; managers do not make decisions about product differentiation. In monopolistically competitive markets, managers must make decisions about the degree and nature of product differentiation.

In monopolistically competitive markets, product differentiation gives firms some degree of control over price. The extent of control is very limited because like pure competition there are many firms selling a similar but not identical product. The model of monopolistic competition approximates the market for health clubs in a large city. Health clubs differ in their location, hours, equipment, classes, etc. Because they differ, health clubs may charge different prices. If all health clubs were exactly the same in every way (a homogeneous product), they could not charge different prices. It is product differentiation that gives managers at health clubs some control over price. The degree of control over price is limited, given the similarities of health clubs.

The market for athletic shoes at the retail level fits the model of monopolistic competition. If retail athletic shoe stores are earning economic profit, more firms will enter the market. As new firms enter the market, existing firms face a reduced demand. The decreased demand for existing firms reduces their profitability. As long as firms are earning economic profit there is an incentive for new firms to enter the market. If the typical retail shoe store had been earning a loss over time, firms would exit the market. As firms exit the market the demand facing those firms which remain increases. The increased demand at the remaining stores reduces the losses earned by those stores. As long as firms are making losses there is an incentive for firms to exit the market. In the long run, firms in a monopolistically competitive market will earn zero economic profit.

PRODUCT DIFFERENTIATION

Managers at monopolistically competitive firms must decide on the degree and nature of product differentiation for their products. As long as the additional revenue (marginal revenue) from additional product differentiation exceeds the additional cost (marginal cost), the firm should continue to differentiate its product. If marginal cost exceeds marginal revenue, additional product differentiation would decrease profits.

There are different types of product differentiation in the sport industry. Differences in the condition of sale are a type of product differentiation. Health clubs may make membership a condition of the sale of classes. Some clubs require membership for people to take classes; others allow people to take classes without being members. As part of the condition of the sale, some exercise equipment manufactures offer money-back guarantees. The availability of alcoholic beverages at spectator sport facilities differentiates venues.

Differences in the product are another type of product differentiation. One model of running shoes is physically different than another model. Golf courses differ in their design; some are easier than others, some more attractive than others. Bowling centers may differentiate themselves by the amount of wax they use on lanes, since a bowling center may increase the scores of customers through how they wax the lanes. Given different waxing practices, a game at one bowling center is different from a game at another center.

Differences in the image of products are also a type of product differentiation. If consumers perceive products are different, there is product differentiation even if the products and conditions of the sale are identical. Endorsement of a product by a sports figure can make consumers believe a product is different from otherwise identical versions of the product.

Advertising can be used as a tool in product differentiation. Through advertising, firms can make potential consumers aware of differences in products and the condition of the sale. Advertising can create the perception of differences among products even if the products are essentially the same. The optimal amount of advertising depends on the marginal revenue (additional revenue from another unit of advertising) and marginal cost (additional cost of another unit of advertising).

Through advertising and product differentiation, managers may increase the control over price of the firm. Advertising and product differentiation provide an aspect of monopoly to firms in a monopolistically competitive market. The availability of similar products from other firms reduces the control over price of a firm in a monopolistically competitive market.

PRICE DISCRIMINATION AND TWO-PART PRICING

Price discrimination is charging different consumers different prices not based on cost differences. A minor league baseball team that charges senior citizens a lower price than other customers is practicing price discrimination. There is no difference in the cost of producing a seat for a senior citizen compared to another customer, yet the senior citizen pays a lower price for admission.

Firms with some degree of power over price practice price discrimination to increase revenue and profit. To practice price discrimination, a firm with some control over price must be able to segment the market based on the elasticity of demand of consumers and potential consumers and keep customers from reselling the product. When price discriminating, a firm wishes to charge consumers who are more sensitive to price (more elastic demand) a lower price while charging those who are less sensitive to price (less elastic demand) a higher price.

Senior citizens are believed to have a more elastic demand for minor league baseball entertainment, so the team charges them a lower price. Families are also perceived to have a more elastic demand for tickets, so teams will often charge lower prices for children, reducing the average price paid by a family attending a game. The team will not let an adult use a child's ticket or a non-senior citizen a senior citizen's ticket because it would make it difficult to maintain the price for adult tickets.

By offering a lower price to children and seniors but not adults, a team increases revenue. The lower price to those with more elastic demand increases revenue from those consumers. The increase in revenue from the increase in the number of children and seniors who attend games more than offsets the reduction in revenue from the lower prices charged to those children and seniors who would have attended anyway. Adults are not offered lower ticket prices because the increase in revenue from an increase in the number attending games would be less than the reduction in revenue from the lower prices charged to those who would have attended the game anyway.

If a firm can charge different prices to consumers based on their sensitivity to price, it can earn additional revenue compared to charging all consumers the same price. A ski resort may do this by offering lower prices during the week than on the weekend. People who are more price sensitive (more elastic demand) are more likely to make the effort to go skiing during the week than those who are less sensitive to price. By offering the lower price during the week, the ski resort is allowing customers to sort themselves by their sensitivity to price.

This strategy will increase revenue if the increase in revenue from more people skiing during the week offsets the decrease in revenue from fewer people skiing during the weekend and the lower price charged to those who would have skied during the week anyway.

A seller who negotiates directly with each buyer over price will practice price discrimination. The seller will try to charge each buyer the highest price the buyer is willing to pay, even if the cost of production does not vary across buyers. An agent representing an athlete in negotiations to endorse products will attempt to get the highest price for the athlete that each firm is willing to pay.

A firm may increase revenue and profit by charging an initiation fee plus a price for the use of a product (Baye, 2003, pp. 404–406). In an optimal two-part pricing system, the firm should charge the marginal cost for each unit consumed. Profit in an optimal two-part pricing system comes from the initiation fee. Each consumer should be charged the highest initiation fee the consumer is willing to pay.

Two-part pricing is used in some segments of the sport industry. A golf course that charges an initiation fee and a monthly membership fee is practicing two-part pricing. Different membership levels can be used as a way of getting some consumers to reveal the highest price they are willing to pay as an initiation fee. By offering different types of membership, a golf course can charge different consumers different initiation fees based on their willingness to pay.

Summary

This chapter links the decisions faced by firms and the conditions in the market in which firms compete. Markets can be categorized by different characteristics, the types and degrees of rivalry present, the extent of barriers to entry, and the control over price by a firm. The characteristics of markets will influence the choices firms make and the outcomes of those choices.

Markets in which barriers to entry are low are likely to be competitive. New firms will enter profitable markets, increasing competition and reducing the profits of existing firms. The greater the degree of competition, the less control a firm has over the price of the product it sells. In all markets, a firm should compare the additional cost of producing another unit (marginal cost) with the additional revenue from producing that unit (marginal revenue) to maximize profit. Firms with some control over price may increase revenue and profit through price discrimination.

Chapter Questions

1. Give examples of consumer-consumer rivalry, producer-producer rivalry, and producer-consumer rivalry in the sport industry.
2. Define barriers to entry.
3. Why might aerobics instructors lobby government to require licenses for aerobics instructors?
4. Why should a firm compare marginal revenue to marginal cost to maximize profit?
5. Evaluate the following statement:

    If a health club is earning a loss in the short run, it should shut down.
6. How does consumer demand limit a monopolist?
7. Why is inefficiency more likely to persist at a monopoly than at a competitive firm?

Chapter Five

OLIGOPOLY AND THE SPORT INDUSTRY

Introduction

The purpose of this chapter is to explain and predict managerial decisions in the sport industry by understanding the nature of oligopolistic markets. In oligopolistic markets, there are a few firms and the firms recognize their interdependence. The behavior of firms in oligopoly depends on their perceptions of the likely reactions of rivals to any action they take. Because of the variability of perceptions of the reaction of rivals, there is no dominant explanation of oligopolistic markets.

Oligopoly in the Sport Industry

There are examples of oligopoly in the sport-producing sector and the different subsectors of the sport industry. In the sport-producing sector, NASCAR is dominated by a few owners who recognize their interdependence (Blake, 2004). As car owners sell sponsorship rights, they recognize their rivals are likely to react to decisions they make. In the administrative and regulatory athletic association subsector, major sports leagues are in an oligopolistic market in the sale of broadcast rights to network and cable television outlets. There are relatively few sellers of major league sports to television and the sellers recognize their interdependence. In the sports media subsector, network and cable television outlets recognize their interdependence as they sell commercial time during sporting events. Local markets for sports facilities are likely to be oligopolistic in nature. Each venue will recognize its interdependence with other venues in the sports facilities and buildings subsector.

The sports equipment manufacturing subsector is characterized by oligopolistic industries. The top four golf equipment manufactures have 62% of the markets for woods, irons, putters, and balls (Buyers, 2004, p. 7). In the market for athletic footwear, the top four firms have almost 75% of the market (Business Wire, 2000). Tennis ball manufacturing is dominated by four firms: Wilson, Penn, Dunlop, and Spalding (Mankiw, 2001, p. 349).

A market that is not oligopolistic at the national level may be oligopolistic at the local level. At the local level health clubs may compete in an oligopolistic market. There may be only a few clubs in the market, each recognizing its interdependence with the other clubs. The retail market for athletic footwear may be oligopolistic at the national level, where the top four firms have over 70% of the market but not in each local market (United States Census Bureau, 2006). In some local markets, sales may be spread across more firms. At the national level, retail athletic footwear chains are interdependent and realize it.

Oligopoly exists in the sport industry. When decision makers at firms in the sport industry consider the likely reactions of their rivals as they make choices, models of oligopoly can help explain their choices. Alternative models of oligopoly are needed given variations in how firms expect their rivals to react to decisions.

MODELS OF OLIGOPOLY

Six models of oligopoly are presented in this section: cost-plus pricing, kinked demand curve, price leadership, collusion, cartel, and game theory. Cost-plus pricing can be used to explain the level of price set by a firm with control over price. The kinked demand curve, price leadership, collusion, cartel, and game theory models emphasize the role of interdependence in oligopolistic markets.

Cost-Plus Pricing

If a firm has power over price it must decide on the price to charge. To use the profit maximizing rule of producing the output where marginal cost equals marginal revenue requires detailed information on demand and costs. Firms may not have that information. Cost-plus pricing is a method of pricing that requires less information.

Cost-plus pricing begins with an estimate of costs, either average total, average variable, or marginal costs. Under cost-plus pricing, the measure of cost is multiplied by a mark-up factor to determine price. While simpler than the marginal revenue equals marginal cost rule, cost-plus pricing can yield a price consistent with profit maximization.

At the output where marginal revenue equals marginal cost, price equals K times marginal cost, where K is a function of the elasticity of demand for the product (Baye, 2003, p. 395). The more elastic the demand, the more sensitive consumers are to price changes, the lower the profit maximizing mark-up factor. The more inelastic the demand, the less sensitive consumers are to price changes, the higher the profit maximizing mark-up.

If firms in the sport industry that use cost-plus pricing consider the availability of substitutes as they determine the mark-up factor, the prices they charge can approximate profit maximizing prices. A baseball glove manufacturer should use different mark-up factors for different models of gloves if the number of substitutes varies across models. If for low-end gloves there are more substitutes, demand will be more elastic and the profit maximizing mark-up less than for high-end gloves for which there are fewer substitutes and a less elastic demand.

Kinked Demand Curve

While cost-plus pricing can be used to explain how firms determine price, the kinked demand curve model explains why in an oligopolistic industry prices may be rigid. The kinked demand curve model is built on assumptions about a firm's beliefs about its rival. According to the model, firms believe if they raise price their rivals will not follow their lead and if they lower price their rivals will follow.

If the assumptions are correct, small variations in the cost of production will leave price unchanged. If costs increase by a small amount, a firm will not raise price if it believes its rivals will not follow. A firm does not want to be the only one to raise price. If costs decrease a little, a firm does not want to lower price if it believes it could start a price war. The kinked demand curve does not explain how prices change; the only thing it explains is why prices do not change in oligopolistic markets.

The kinked demand curve model is likely to explain the behavior of some oligopolistic firms in the sport industry some of the time. If managers at firms believe their rivals want to harm them, the assumptions of the kinked demand curve model are plausible. Imagine a small city with three health clubs, two of which were started by unhappy former employees of the first health club. If the original health club experiences a small increase in variable cost because of an increase in the prices charged by its laundry service, it may be hesitant to raise rates at the club given the likely reactions of rivals. The kinked demand curve model is likely to explain behavior when managers at different firms do not trust each other and there is little feeling of industry solidarity.

Barometric Price Leadership

The model of barometric price leadership complements the kinked demand curve model. This model explains how prices may increase in an oligopolistic market. In barometric price leadership, one firm in the market raises price in the hope the other firms in the market follow. There is no guarantee the other firms will follow the lead of the firm that raised price. If they do follow, the price in the market increases. If its rivals do not follow the price increase, the barometric price leader reduces price back to the original level. Unsuccessful attempts at barometric price leadership may result in the price rigidity described by the kinked demand curve model as firms come to believe their rivals will not follow a price increase.

The more mangers across firms trust each other and see common interests, the more likely barometric price leadership will occur. If in our example of the three health clubs in a small city there was no feeling of animosity among the owners and all three experienced the same increase in variable cost due to increased laundry prices, one club may decide to raise rates in the hope the other clubs will follow. If rates at all three clubs are increased following the increase in cost across the clubs, a pattern of behavior may be established because firms will assume the others will follow a price increase given an increase in the cost of production.

Successful barometric price leadership results in all firms in the industry raising price. Barometric price leadership is sometimes cited as an example of tacit collusion. In tacit collusion firms act as though they have met but do not actually meet and discuss price.

Collusion

While tacit collusion is legal, collusion itself is not. Collusion is when firms jointly decide price. (Collusion among buyers to reduce the price they pay is covered in Chapter 9.) Firms may legally act as though they have met and all raise price, if they make the decisions independently. It is illegal for firms to coordinate a price increase. If representatives of the three health clubs from the earlier examples were to coordinate raising rates, it would be illegal.

In order for a collusive agreement to increase price, firms must decrease industry output. An agreement to raise price without restricting output will not work because industry price is an inverse function of industry output. Holding demand constant if all three health clubs raise rates, they will sell less output than if they charged lower prices.

The necessity of restricting industry output makes it difficult for firms to successfully fix prices. There is an incentive for firms to cheat on the agreement and to charge lower prices and sell more output. With our health club example, each club has an incentive to cheat and charge a rate lower than the agreed-upon rate. If a club cheats, it is able to gain members by undercutting the rates of its competitors who are following the agreement. Each club has an incentive to cheat; as they cheat, they sell more output. As output increases, price decreases. If each club cheats, rates do not increase despite the agreement to charge higher rates.

Unlike in most of sport, cheaters in price fixing agreements serve society interests. Because of cheating, price-fixing agreements are more likely to fail. Cheaters in price-fixing agreements help keep markets competitive. Nobel Prize winner George Stigler (1964) described the likelihood of successful collusion as a function of the ability of the colluding firms to (1) detect cheating on the agreement and (2) punish firms that cheat. An inability to detect and punish cheaters makes it difficult for a collusive agreement to succeed because of the temptation for individual firms to cheat.

Among the factors that affect the ability of the colluding firms to detect cheating are (1) the number of firms in the agreement, (2) the homogeneity of the product, and (3) the flow of information among the firms. The more health clubs fixing prices, the less likely the agreement will succeed. There are more potential cheaters, so the difficulty of detecting cheating increases. To the extent health clubs offer different services and products, price fixing is more difficult. The sale of different services and products makes it more difficult to detect if a firm is cheating. Differences in prices may reflect differences in products and services rather than cheating on the agreement. The less information that flows among the health clubs, the more difficult to maintain a collusive agreement. To detect cheating by their collusive partners, firms need information on their rivals' actions.

Cartels

A cartel differs from collusion in the existence of a formal agreement to act together to fix prices. One feature of the formal agreement is likely to be mechanisms to detect and punish cheaters. In general, cartels, like collusion, are illegal in the United States.

Prior to 1981 the National Collegiate Athletic Association

Photo by Bob Townsend, courtesy of stock.xchng iv

(NCAA) sold the broadcast rights to college football games for all its members to the national television networks (Horowitz, 1999, p. 202). Acting as a cartel, the NCAA limited output to increase price. In 1981, a group of major football powers within the NCAA sold network television broadcast rights to their games because they believed increasing their output would increase their revenue. The NCAA responded by threatening the "cheaters" with various sanctions. In 1982, two of the football powers, the Universities of Georgia and Oklahoma, responded to the NCAA's sanction by suing the NCAA, accusing the organization of acting as a cartel in the sale of broadcast rights to college football games. In 1984, the Supreme Court ruled in favor of the Universities of Georgia and Oklahoma, ending the NCAA's cartel in the sale of network broadcast rights to college football.

With the end of the cartel sale of network broadcast rights to college football games, the number of college football games on network television has increased (Horowitz, 1999, pp. 215–217). Some schools earn more revenue in the post-cartel environment, others earn less. The overall revenue of NCAA schools from the sale of broadcast rights to college football games is likely to have decreased given the increase in output.

In sport there are examples of legal cartels. While the NCAA is not allowed to act as a cartel in the sale of broadcast rights, the Sports Broadcasting Act of 1961 permits professional "leagues to act as cartels in the negotiation and sale of their broadcast rights, and to be free of any antitrust sanction" (Scully, 1995, p. 27). The National Football League (NFL) is allowed to sell packages of games to television networks and to restrict the sale of television broadcast rights by the individual franchises in the NFL. If an individual franchise were to attempt to sell television broadcast rights beyond league restrictions, the league would punish the franchise.

The NFL's willingness to try to punish a franchise for violating league rules on marketing was demonstrated in 1995 when NFL Properties sued Jerry Jones and the Dallas Cowboys for selling sponsorship rights to companies in violation of the league's common approach to the sale of sponsorship rights (Kass, 1996). Jones responded by suing NFL Properties for being a cartel. While the NFL is allowed to act as a cartel in some markets, it does not have a general immunization from the laws against cartels. Rather than risk losing in court, the NFL settled out of court with Jones, allowing him to keep the sponsorship contracts he had negotiated. Without the ability to punish a "cheater," the league's ability to restrict output to increase revenue and profit was reduced.

For cartels and collusive agreements among firms to raise prices, industry output must decrease. There is an incentive for firms to violate the agreement and to produce more output while their competitors are restricting their output. The success of cartels and collusive agreements depends on the ability to prevent cheating by firms. If firms cheat, the effectiveness of the agreement to increase price is reduced.

Game Theory

Game theory is a method of analyzing decisions when there is interdependence among decision makers. Given the mutual interdependence of firms in oligopolistic markets, game theory may be used to understand the behavior of firms in oligopolies. In game theory, decision makers in firms are compared to players in a game where the payoff to one player depends on her actions and the actions of other players.

Games may be classified as (1) zero or variable sum, (2) sequential or simultaneous move, and (3) one time or repeated games. In a two player zero sum game, if one player wins, the other loses and the amount won by one player equals the amount lost by the other player. In a variable sum game, every player can win, lose, or there may be a combination of losers and winners. Checkers is an example of a sequential move game; one player decides then the other makes his decision. Rock, paper, scissors is a simultaneous move game, each player deciding at the same time what shape to form with her hand. In a NFL season, the Super Bowl is a one-time game. Games in the National Hockey League playoffs are part of a repeated game (at least until the seventh game of a playoff series).

When using game theory to make, explain, or predict decisions, it is important to be careful in the choice of the type of game used. Using an inappropriate game form can lead to poor decisions and analysis. If Major League Baseball (MLB) and the Major League Baseball Player's Association (MLBPA) view contract negotiations as a zero sum game, it will increase the likelihood of a work stoppage as each side wants to win while the other loses. If the parties view negotiations as a variable sum game, they are more likely to try to reach a settlement, particularly if both sides view the payoff to a work stoppage as a loss. For MLB and the MLBPA, viewing negotiations as a variable sum game is made more difficult by the knowledge that any agreement will be analyzed by individuals who view the process as a zero sum game and will be looking for a winner and a loser.

Table 5-1 shows the payoff matrix for two firms in the exercise equipment industry. The payoff matrix is for a variable sum, simultaneous move, one shot game. The companies are deciding whether to invest in research and development and invent a new piece of exercise equipment or to wait until their competitor invents a new product and copy it. Each firm is confident it can work around any patent protection on a machine developed by the other firm.

The first number in each cell of the matrix is the payoff to Firm 1; the second is the payoff to Firm 2. If both firms commit to invent a new product, they each earn $25 in profit this year. If one firm decides to invent and the other firm copies, the inventing firm earns $30 and the copying firm earns $35. Being the sole inventor is more profitable than inventing at the same time as your rival

Table 5-1. Payoff Matrix for Firms in Exercise Equipment Industry

		Firm 2	
		Invent	Copy
Firm 1	Invent	$25, $25	$30, $35
	Copy	$35, $30	$10, $10

because of the length of time it takes the other firm to copy the invention. While the other firm is copying, the inventing firm has a monopoly. While it takes the copying firm some time to get the product to market, it eventually earns $35 because of lower development costs. If both firms decide to copy, no new product is invented and both firms earn $10 on their existing product lines.

If the firms were allowed to jointly decide whether to invent or copy, the choice would be for one to invent and the other to copy. The only issue would be which firm would invent. To come to an agreement, the copying firm could offer to make a payment to the inventing firm. If the firms are not allowed to jointly decide, game theory can provide insight into the likely behavior of the firms.

The ideal situation for each firm is to copy the invention of the other firm. Both firms would like to convince its rival it will not invent a new piece of equipment. However, if both firms plan on copying, there will be no new invention to copy. If there is no new invention, each firm earns less than if a new product had been invented. For both firms, a statement that it is not going to invent is not credible because if its rival does not invent, it is more profitable for the firm to invest in research and development and invent a new product.

Each firm must decide on the likely action of its rival and make its decision accordingly. One approach to this decision is to adopt a secure strategy. Using a secure strategy, a firm assumes its rival will take the action that is least favorable to the firm (Baye, 2003, p. 351). In this example the secure strategy is to assume your rival will not invent a new type of exercise equipment. If your rival does not invent, it is more profitable for you to invent rather than not invent. If both firms adopt a secure strategy, both will invest in research and development and invent a new type of exercise equipment and each earn a profit of $25.

Table 5-2 shows the payoff matrix for two health clubs. Each firm must decide on whether to charge a high or low price for membership. The first number in each cell is the profit of Firm 1, the second, the profit of Firm 2. The profit of a firm depends on its actions and the actions of its rival. A dominant strategy exists if there is a choice that yields the highest payoff no matter the actions of your rival (Baye, 2003, p. 350). For both firms, the dominant strategy is to charge the low price.

If Firm 2 charges the high price, Firm 1 makes the most profit ($15) by charging the low price. For Firm 1, the high price would yield a profit of $10. If Firm 2 charges the low price, Firm 1 makes the most profit ($6) by charging the low price. The high

Table 5-2. Payoff Matrix for Health Clubs

		Firm 2	
		High Price	Low Price
Firm 1	High Price	$10, $10	$2, $15
	Low Price	$15, $2	$6, $6

price would earn Firm 1 $2 profit. Firm 2 is in the same situation; no matter what Firm 1 does, Firm 2 can earn the most profit by charging the low price.

If each firm commits to its dominant strategy, both earn a profit of $6. Each firm could earn more profit if both charged the high price. The willingness of a firm to charge the high price depends on what the firm believes about its rival.

If a firm believes its rival will charge the low price, it will not charge the high price. If a firm believes its rival will join him at the high price, it makes sense to charge the high price and both earn a profit of $10. If the firms collude and agree to charge the high price, each firm could increase its profit by cheating while the other firm followed the agreement to charge the high price. Game theory can be used to demonstrate why firms may be afraid to change price, how price leadership may work, and the temptation to cheat given collusion.

In each case, the optimal decision of a firm depends on the actions of its rival. In oligopolistic industries, managers must consider the likely reactions of their rivals as they make choices. To understand the behavior of firms in oligopolistic markets in the sport industry, the mutual interdependence of firms must be considered.

Summary

This chapter provided an introduction to the behavior of firms in oligopolistic markets. Oligopolies are industries in which there are a few firms and the firms recognize their interdependence. There are many examples of oligopoly in the different segments of the sport industry.

In oligopolies, anticipation of the reactions of rivals influences decision making. Because firms have diverse beliefs about the likely reaction of their rivals, firms will behave differently. A health club that believes its rivals will follow a price increase will make different choices than a health club that believes its rivals will not follow a price increase. Because firms behave differently depending on their assumptions about their rivals, there is no single explanation of how firms behave in oligopolistic markets. Economists have developed alternative models to explain the actions of firms in oligopolies.

Chapter Questions

1. Give examples of oligopolistic markets in different segments of the sport industry.
2. If the number of substitutes for a type of exercise equipment increases, what happens to the mark-up factor, which will generate the most profit for the firm producing the exercise equipment?
3. Is the kinked demand curve model likely to be a good explanation of the behavior of firms in the health club market if the owners of clubs are friends who believe they face similar problems and issues in the industry?
4. From the view of society, are firms that cheat on a price-fixing agreement heroes or villains?
5. What problems can arise if decision makers in a professional sports league view negotiating with television executives over broadcast rights as a zero sum game when it may be a variable sum game?

Chapter Six

- -
SPORT INDUSTRY DELIVERY

Introduction

From an economic perspective, Western City presents many interest issues. Why are the sports offerings structured the way they are? Why are some sports being supplied by the city? Why are others, of the same nature, being supplied by private entities? To whom do benefits accrue? What is public choice theory and does it help us understand how scarce resources might be allocated?

Sports are provided to consumers through three main suppliers (see Table 6-1). Although there is some overlap, each type of supplier has differences in philosophy, objectives, financing, leadership, and membership. In any city or town, examples of each of these delivery systems can be found.

In fact, these suppliers can be viewed as complements rather than competitors, although there are instances where competition does occur. Taken together, they increase the likelihood that consumers' desire for sport will be satisfied.

Government Delivery of Sport

Many economists believe that private enterprise operating in an open market is the most efficient means of providing goods and services to consumers. Why, then, do we find government and community organizations in the business of providing sports services? What constitutes government's proper economic role in

---

Sport Industry Delivery

Western City is a medium-sized city in the western part of the United States that is experiencing explosive population growth. Several new corporations have relocated to Western; housing prices are skyrocketing; and traffic congestion and crime have increased. There are numerous opportunities for recreation and sports in the city. However, there is not enough supply to accommodate demand. Waiting lists have developed for fields and leagues. Current facilities are a mix of city-owned parks, swimming pools, softball and baseball fields, soccer fields, tennis courts, a golf course, recreation centers, as well as privately owned athletic clubs and golf courses. Professional sports in the city include a Triple A baseball club and an A-League soccer franchise. The city allocates approximately one percent of the general operating budget for the recreation department, but it is feeling financial pressures to deal with the population growth. A member of the city council has floated the idea of a .25% increase in the city sales tax to be used for expanding sport and recreation opportunities. A second council member agrees with the tax increase but wants to use it to obtain an expansion franchise in one of the major league sports. A third member strongly disagrees with any tax increase for sports, arguing that if the need truly exists, private enterprise can and should fill it. He would use the increase to improve the city's infrastructure.

Table 6-1. Suppliers of Sport

	Government	Community	Private
Philosophy	Sport for all	Sport for members	Satisfy public demand and make profit
Goals	Contribute to well-being of citizens and area, nonprofit	More limited in membership, people with similar philosophies, generally nonprofit	Profit maximization
Finance	Primarily taxes, user fees	Membership fees, donations, fundraising	Private investment, admissions/user fees, memberships, media
Leadership	Professional, often civil service, and some volunteer	Professional and volunteer	Professional
Membership	Open to all	Organizational restrictions, often on age, residence	Open to those who can pay
Examples	City parks and recreation	Little League, local soccer associations, YMCAs	Private athletic clubs, professional sports teams, bowling alleys, sporting goods

providing services and goods to its citizens? Certainly, we are accustomed to government, at all levels, providing a variety of services. Moreover, although there is general agreement that government should provide some services, there is not agreement as to what kind of, and how many, services. At one end of the continuum are those who believe government should regulate a variety of economic activities; at the other end are those who would assign only minimal responsibilities to government.

One economic viewpoint is that private business, operating in a free market, will always provide services and goods more effectively than will government. In a free market system, private enterprise will recognize and produce goods to satisfy demand. Parties will trade, and both will be better off. If one or both parties do not benefit, trade will not occur. Thus, both sides have incentive for effective trade. In addition, costs of a product will be assumed by those who benefit from the service or good. Because the benefits of sport accrue to those who use sport, they should also bear the costs. When government intervenes in an economy, even more problems are created. Why, then, has government been a major provider of recreational sport services? Since the late 1800s, government intervention in markets has been viewed as important to correct problems coming from a reliance on the market mechanism. The following statement by Walsh (1986, p. 558) concerning the function of a public recreation program articulates that perspective:

> A public recreation program can increase the welfare of society if the resources given up by the private sector (via taxes, opportunity costs) are used to produce greater benefits than they would produce in the absence of the government programs.

Essentially, government redistributes resources for the benefit of the general public. Government is viewed as an appropriate supplier of services, including sports, for many reasons. First, a primary function of government is to service human needs, among which is sport. Sport contributes to the social, physical, and mental well-being of citizens. Second, government can provide services regardless of citizens' ability to pay. Not all residents can afford private services, which are frequently focused on profit maximization.

Through its power to collect revenues, government can afford to subsidize services for those who would not otherwise have access to them because of financial restrictions. Third, governments are longstanding bodies, as opposed to private businesses, which may come and go. Continuity and reliability of services are viewed as desirable. Fourth, government has the power to regulate land for use. Government has or can acquire land (e.g., for fields, arenas), and it can create zoning regulations (e.g., requiring open or green space in real estate developments). Fifth, government can bring together diverse groups within the community to maximize benefits. Creating a recreational sport program may require input and assistance from parks and recreation departments, school districts, public safety, and private entities. Finally, without government regulation, private enterprise can conspire to restrain trade, which does not benefit the public (see detailed discussion on government regulation in Chapter 10).

Economists explain government provision of sport using the concept of *externalities*. Externalities exist when "actions of one party affect the utility or production possibilities of another party outside an exchange relationship" (Brickley et al., 1997, p. 46). Another perspective is that "some benefits or costs associated with the production or consumption of a particular product accrue to parties other than the buyers or sellers [or users] of the product" (Keat & Young, 1992, p. 583). Externalities are relevant when talking about government provision of roads, education, parks, and recreational sport. For example, if a person has no children, why should this person pay for the provision of education? Why not let the private market provide education to those who need it? If education were provided solely as a private enterprise, this person would probably not purchase it. However, does this person (and society) benefit from having educated children? Most would argue the answer is yes. So, even though the person is not a buyer or seller or user of the education services, this person does benefit from them. If the person accrues benefits, then this person should also accrue costs. In the case of education, government collects tax monies (e.g., property tax) from the person to support schools. As such, education has positive externalities.

Does sport also have positive externalities? If a person never uses the city's soccer fields or never attends a professional football game played in a stadium built with funds subsidized from the local government, why should this person support the building of those facilities? This argument was heard frequently throughout the 1990s as taxpayers were asked to bear the costs of new stadiums and arenas for professional sports teams. A positive externalities argument would suggest that the person does benefit from the public investment as the facilities may enhance the general quality of life and make the area more desirable to live in and grow. Specifically, many governments use the following arguments for their provision of sport services:

1. Sport helps to create an appealing community. Ratings of most desirable places to live routinely evaluate the sport culture and provision of opportunities to watch and participate in sport. Cities increase their visibility and enhance their image when they provide such opportunities. This can pay off in direct financial benefits, by attracting businesses to locate in the city and attracting more convention and tourism business (Howard & Crompton, 1995).

2. Sport enhances the health of the community: "A community of physically active people will ultimately be a community with reduced traffic congestion, air pollution, and health care costs" (Seeley, 1997, p. 72).

3. Sport keeps youth occupied and out of trouble, and lessens costs related to youth crime. Since the late 1800s, one of the perceived roles of sport has been to give youth a constructive way to occupy their time. A recent example is midnight basketball leagues for inner-city youth (Gratton & Taylor, 1992; Sailes, 1999).

Negative externalities also exist. A municipal golf course built with taxpayer dollars may provide positive benefits to the entire community, not just to the golfers who use it. However, the golf course may also displace wildlife habitat, result in contamination from use of chemicals, and divert dollars that could be used for other purposes. These negative impacts exist for all city residents. For the city, it is necessary to look at all costs and all benefits to arrive at a decision. Residents of Colorado rejected a proposal to host the 1976 Winter Olympics on the grounds that the harm to the environment and disruption of lifestyle (negative externalities) were too great to justify using tax dollars.

Economists make a distinction between private and public goods. Private goods provide benefits to those who use (pay for) them, and public goods are available for anyone to enjoy. Athletic shoes are an example of private goods because the benefits of wearing them go only to the people who have purchased them. Championship teams are often cited as examples of public goods. When a university football team ends the season ranked number one in the country, its fans receive many benefits, even though they may not have contributed in any way to the success of the team. This concept is called *nonexcludability*. Anyone can share in the benefits of a winning team. A second feature of a public good is that it is nonrival. Many people can enjoy a product or service at the same time. Many people can call themselves fans of the number one team. The same is not true of a private good. Only one person at a time can benefit from wearing the athletic shoes. The concepts of externalities and of public and private goods go hand in hand. When we talk about externalities, we are generally talking about public goods. Thus, education and many sport activities are public goods.

Consider that producers of public goods with either positive or negative externalities may not take into account the impact on nonpurchasers. Their decision to produce (in a free market situation) does not represent the optimal amount for the market system. Government becomes involved in order to remedy this failure.

GOVERNMENT SPENDING

When we look at spending by government, a strong commitment to recreational expenditures is clear. Just at the state and local levels, governments spent close to $32 billion on parks and recreation programs in 2002 (U.S. Census Bureau, 2005). Local government is the level closest to the consumer and provides the most services. For most people, the governing body oversees the city or town in which they live. Depending upon the size of local government, a variety of services are provided. Table 6-2 gives two examples of what a local area might provide. Local governments will generally allocate from one to 2 percent of an annual operating budget on recreation services, including sport. That does not include special requests, such as a new stadium or arena. County government is the next level up, or for unincorporated areas, it may even be local government. Here, the most common participation involves making facilities available.

Table 6-2. Sample Sport and Recreation Provided by Governments of Two Cities

	City A	City B
Facilities:	Golf course Boat launch Recreation centers Swimming pools Tennis courts Playgrounds Parks	Playground Tennis courts Parks
Athletic Programs:	Baseball contests Basketball camp Youth bowling Fishing lessons 5K and 10K race Ultimate frisbee Junior golf clinic Golf tournaments Roller skating Soccer leagues Swimming lessons Tennis clinics Tennis leagues Special Olympics	Basketball clinics Tennis lessons 5K race
Special Events:	Regatta Vintage grand prix Community festivals	Community festival

A special district provides services that cross city and county lines. Perhaps the most common services provider in this category would be public schools. Although schools provide facilities and programming primarily for the students in the district schools, the general population also benefits. People in the community may attend sports contests, use the track for jogging, or play in a summer basketball league in the gym. In some locations, special parks or recreation districts cross city and/or county lines.

State or provincial government provides services in a variety of settings, including state parks and correctional facilities. States also provide subsidies for local provision of sports. An example of state support includes subsidies to state and local sports commissions, state games, and sporting events.

RECENT ISSUES WITH GOVERNMENT SUPPORT

Issues related to government spending on sport exist in virtually every community. In the last two decades, professional sports teams have been very visible in their demands for publicly built stadiums and arenas, along with the threat that the team will leave town if it does not get a new facility. An indication of the extent to which municipal governments have agreed to those demands is shown in Table 6-3.

In Canada, the national government is being pressured to provide subsidies, in the form of tax breaks, for NHL teams (Aubrey, 1999). The Canadian teams argue that they cannot compete in the same market with subsidized (in the form of new arenas) U.S. teams when the Canadian clubs face heavy tax burdens, bad dollar exchange rates, and no subsidies. However, critics of the proposed breaks argue that it is "unconscionable for the government to continue contemplating tax adjustments for the NHL while rejecting schemes to help out Canada's 1.3 million disadvantaged children to play sports" (Aubrey, 1999, p. 2). The debate about how government should spend its limited resources on elite level and/or general participation sports is an ongoing one.

Table 6-3. Taxpayer Share of New Professional Sports Facilities

City	Team	Cost (millions $)	Taxpayer %
Cincinnati	Bengals (NFL)	404	100.0
Raleigh	Hurricanes (NHL)	158	87.3
Miami	Heat (NBA)	228	78.1
Pittsburgh	Steelers (NFL)	233	67.6
Dallas	Mavericks (NBA)/Stars (NHL)	300	41.7
Detroit	Tigers (MLB)	295	39.0
San Francisco	Giants (MLB)	306	8.5
Los Angeles	Kings (NHL)/ Lakers, Clippers (NBA)	350	3.4
Columbus	Blue Jackets (NHL)	150	0

Source: *Street & Smith's SportsBusiness Journal* (May 10–16, 1999), p. 5.

Professional sports is not the only area where issues of who will pay for sports facilities and programs exist. Many cities experiencing population growth face increasing demands for public services from a population that has come to expect government to supply those services. An example of those issues currently under debate is the availability of playing fields for recreational soccer. Organized soccer participation among youth in the United States has increased from 890,000 in 1980 to 3.57 million in 1998 (El Nasser, 1999). With the addition of adult participants, that number increases to more than 17 million. The boom in participation has resulted in a shortage of fields. Who should provide the fields? In November 1998, local communities across the United States approved 200 bond issues for the development of park spaces. Two-thirds of the funds approved were earmarked for recreation facilities, including soccer fields (El Nasser, 1999). Additional funds are coming from sales tax increases, fees charged to real estate developers, donations, and fees assessed to soccer participants.

Although the national visibility obtained from professional sports teams and facilities is often heard as a justification for spending taxpayer dollars, the same cannot be said of youth soccer leagues. Such leagues do not attract national attention. However, the arguments for public support remain similar. Organizers of the 2000 Midwest Regional soccer tournament to be held in Lawrence, Indiana, claim a $35-million economic impact for the city as a result of the tournament (EI Nasser, 1999). More detailed discussion on economic impact studies is provided in Chapter 8.

PUBLIC CHOICE THEORY AND PRIVATIZATION

The historic perspective of government taking on responsibility for a variety of public services began to change in the 1960s as a result of changing economic times and a new economic theory. In the 1960s, a concept called public choice theory emerged in economics. Public choice theory suggests that if public officials monopolize service delivery, the result is oversupply and inefficiency (Boyne, 1998). If government is the only entity responsible for providing roads, maintenance, transportation, education, and recreational activities including sports, then a monopoly exists, and there is no incentive to operate services in an efficient manner. However, if services are provided in a competitive market, the result will be a more efficient service.

In the 1970s, many local and state governments began to experience two trends. The first was a demand for more services, and the second was budgetary constraints that made it difficult to maintain existing levels of services, much less to provide more. Government officials looking for a way to deal with the difficult economic environment found that public choice theory justified the idea of turning some government services over to private enterprise. As such, privatization for diverse services, such as airports, waste management, education, corrections, and recreation, have been attempted by many American cities. *Privatization* is "an array of techniques designed to promote greater involvement on the part of the private sector in the administration or financing of traditional government services" (Auger, 1999, p. 2). There are two reasons why government is willing to privatize services and take on some of the risks and rewards of the free market system:

1. Reducing costs and increasing revenues are motivators. However, there is much disagreement on the financial impact of privatization.

2. There is a belief that private enterprise can operate more efficiently, via enhanced flexibility to adjust services and increased ability to quickly obtain materials and staff. By specializing, private enterprise has more expertise.

Privatization takes many forms. Frequently, private enterprises are contracted to supply services. Waste collection is often handled this way, and a few cities have tried privatizing educational services. Second, some cities and states have suggested use of vouchers, whereby residents are given vouchers to purchase private services. For example, a great deal of discussion is occurring over the use of vouchers in education. Partnerships with voluntary and quasi-voluntary organizations are a third option. In the most extreme case, cities will sell assets to a private firm, thus eliminating the responsibility for the service.

In the United States, certain sport services are targets for privatization. For many years, governments have contracted with private management companies to operate stadiums and arenas. City and county officials believe that private management companies can bring certain managerial and entrepreneurial skills that government does not necessarily have in managing their facilities. One of the leading companies in facility management in the world is SMG World. Founded in 1977, SMG World specializes in venue management, marketing and development for convention centers, exhibition halls and trade centers, arenas, stadiums, performing arts centers, theaters, and specific-use venues such as equestrian centers. Some of the facilities include the First Mariner Arena in Baltimore, the Reliant Astrodome in Houston, and the Ford Center in Oklahoma City (SMG World, 2005).

The operations of many municipal golf courses are gradually being turned over to private companies (Mahtesian, 1997). One of the largest such companies in the United States is American Golf Corporation, which operates over 170 public and private golf courses in 29 states. Founded in 1968, "[Its] approach involves initial investment, improving the course and related infrastructure, dramatically increasing rounds of play . . . and reducing costs largely through more flexible and cost-effective utilization of personnel" (Howard & Crompton, 1995, p. 121). The corporation collects revenues from greens fees, concessions, and equipment and cart rentals in exchange for the right to operate. Interestingly enough, when American Golf Corporation signed an agreement to operate courses for Detroit, city government excluded two courses from the deal, preferring to maintain some level of competition between course managers. The city recognized the difficulty that might arise from providing American Golf Corporation with exclusivity in city-provided golf.

The struggle over obtaining public support for new sports facilities has resulted in public-private partnerships in some cities. Numerous facilities have been financed jointly between public and private entities, including the Bradley Center Arena in Indianapolis, Coors Stadium in Denver, Jacobs Field in Cleveland (Regan, 1996), and the Citizen Bank Park (Munsey & Suppes, 2005). In Lawrence, Indiana, new soccer fields are being built with city-donated land, a bond issue, and investment from private company, Motorsports, Inc. (El Nasser, 1999). The main concern for public-private partnerships is that the goals and objectives of the participating partners may be difficult to reconcile due to the existence of differences in their operating philosophies.

The move to privatization has had mixed results, both in general services and in recreational activities, including sport. While many golfers have been complimentary about the improvements in golf courses taken over by private firms, there were some golfers who have expressed their dissatisfaction with the result of privatization (Lieberman, 1994; Vitullo-Martin, 1998). At most privatized courses, greens fees increase, especially for those who are not residents of the local government unit. Access to courses for individual golfers is also lessened because of increased use of courses for revenue-maximizing golf tournaments. As mentioned above, it is due to the difference in operating philosophies and goals of service provision between the private enterprise and the government. In the extreme case, the private enterprise does not provide the same stability as government does. In 1998, the company contracted to operate the reservation services for California's state parks declared bankruptcy ("A Tighter Rein on Privatization," 1998). Although the private marketplace may indeed produce more efficient operation and provide more revenues to cities, this outcome is not guaranteed.

The move toward privatization is not a fad. Over 70% of state agency and recreation department heads have predicted expansion in privatization efforts in their area (Auger, 1999). As cities continue to face increased demand for services without a corresponding increase in resources to supply the demand, alternatives to direct government supply of services will grow.

Photo by Julie Elliott, courtesy of stock.xchng iv

Aside from private entities, government has also teamed with community-based organizations to supply facilities and programs. The U.S. Tennis Association spent $10 million to build the Louis Armstrong tennis center in New York (Howard & Crompton, 1995) on ground leased by New York City to the USTA. The facility is available to the city for 305 days per year and to the USTA for no more than 60 days. In another instance, both the Los Angeles Olympic Organizing Committee and the Atlanta Olympic Organizing Committee built facilities and turned them over to their respective cities.

Community Delivery of Sport

North America has a history of sports being provided by community-based organizations, sometimes also called voluntary associations. These include groups, such as the Boy Scouts, YMCAs, Little League Baseball, and Rotary and Lions

Table 6-4. Business Forms

	Advantages	Disadvantages
Sole Proprietorship	Low start-up costs Greatest freedom from regulation Direct control by owner Minimum working capital requirements Tax advantage to small owner All profits to owner Ease of formation Low start-up costs	Unlimited personal liability Lack of continuity More difficult to raise capital Unlimited personal liability Lack of continuity
Partnership	Additional sources of venture capital Broader management Limited outside regulation Limited liability Specialized management Ownership is transferable	Divided authority Difficulty in raising additional capital Hard to find suitable partners Closely regulated Most expensive to organize Charter restrictions
Corporation	Continuous existence Legal entity Easier to raise capital Unity of action account having Centralized authority in board of directors	Extensive record-keeping necessary Double taxation Difficult to liquidate investment

clubs. Table 6-4 shows some of the community-based organizations that are involved in the provision of sport. Although some associations, such as Little League or U.S. Youth Soccer Association, are organized around sport(s), others, such as Boy Scouts and Lions, provide sports as one of a variety of activities. Many of these organizations focus on youth sports; however, there are also those that operate for adult participants. Revenue to operate community organizations comes from a number of different sources: membership dues, donations and sponsorships, sales, and government subsidies.

Weisbrod (1977) provides economic rationales for community rather than government provision of sport. First, government may not have adequate information about what citizens really want. Thus, decisions are made on the basis of what officials think citizens want. A decentralized entity may have more local knowledge and a better grasp of what people want. This can be especially true in larger cities where demand is likely to be diverse. It is also true when examining demands of minority interests. A second rationale is that government officials often act in their own self-interest rather than according to the concept of efficiency.

Government has an incentive to provide subsidies to these organizations. This is because government will not have to provide services if they are already provided by those organizations. Although the organizations often have restrictions on who may participate (generally based upon age or residence), they also often serve segments of the community who could not afford to purchase the services on the private market. Thus, community organizations are remedying failures of both the private and government systems. Government subsidies are generally in the form of a tax-exempt status but may also include use of public facilities or grants.

A distinguishing element of community organizations is their reliance on volunteers. As opposed to the private and government sectors, community sports have a free labor resource. Such labor may be provided by participants themselves (main beneficiaries), former participants (former beneficiaries), parents and families of participants (indirect beneficiaries), or nonparticipant-related volunteers (who receive positive benefits from volunteering; Gratton & Taylor, 1992). The use of volunteers means that community organizations can operate at a lower cost than can government or private enterprise.

Generally, people participate (directly or indirectly) in community organizations for reasons of self-interest. They receive some benefit that exceeds their costs. People make a choice about how they are to incur costs of sport participation. If they purchase services from a private enterprise, there is a cash cost. If they obtain services from a government entity, there may be costs related to restrictions on who may participate or how many or when activities are offered. If they participate in community organizations, the cash outlay is smaller than for private enterprise, but there is an opportunity cost. What else could people do with their time if they were not being a coach, chaperone, booster club member, or event organizer? As evidenced by the large number of community organizations that exist, many people believe that benefits exceed costs in evaluating their decision to use community sport suppliers.

The forms of community organizations can range from local, small scale (Moon Area Soccer Association) to national (U.S. Youth Soccer Association) ones. At the most highly organized level, community organizations act in some ways as quasi-private enterprises, with large paid staff and major revenue flows from television and sponsors. They operate closer to a profit-seeking firm. For example, private athletic clubs have argued that some YMCAs should lose their tax-exempt status because they are acting more as private clubs, with upscale services, higher membership prices, and few community services. The dispute between metropolitan YMCAs and private athletic clubs illustrates the blurred line that sometimes exists between community and private enterprises.

Private Delivery of Sport

By far, the majority of organizations delivering sport in the United States are private enterprises. These enterprises take a variety of forms—local to national, small to large, privately owned to publicly held. The involvement of private enterprise in the delivery of service (e.g., sport) emerges because entrepreneurial-minded individuals see the existence of "an opportunity to sell an item demanded by consumers at a price higher than the average cost of producing it" (Colander, 1998, p. 578) to make a profit. By allowing entrepreneurs to earn profit, market economies encourage people to supply goods and services. Entrepreneurs create supply to meet demand.

There are many forms of private enterprise, most of which are organized in three basic forms: sole proprietorships, partnerships, or corporations. According to Colander (1998), of the 18 million businesses in the United States, approximately

Table 6-5. Selected Community-Based, Nonprofit Sport Organizations

	Year Founded	# Members
YMCA	1851	14,000,000
U.S. Youth Soccer Assn.	1973	2,500,000
Little League Baseball	1939	2,500,000
American Bowling Congress	1895	2,250,000
U.S. Tennis Assn.	1881	500,000
Canadian Soccer Assn.	1912	430,000
Canadian Curling Assn.	1990	352,000
Canadian Lacrosse Assn.	1867	150,000
USA Volleyball	1928	125,000
U.S. Slo-Pitch Softball Assn.	1968	125,000
USA Track & Field	1979	120,000
Swimming/Nation Canada	1970	71,000
Disabled Sport USA	1967	60,000
Athletics Canada	1884	20,000
Canadian Amateur Wrestling	1932	15,000
U.S. Luge Assn.	1978	650

Source: Myers, K. J. (1998). *Sports Market Place* (Ed.). Mesa, Arizona: Custom Publishing Inc.

69% are sole proprietorships, 8% are partnerships, and 23% are corporations. However, in terms of total receipts, corporations conduct the vast majority of business. Specific regulations, especially those taxes-related, affect the operations and decision making of each of these business forms. Table 6-5 summarizes the advantages and disadvantages of the three basic forms of business.

Corporations are legal entities, independent of the ownership of the firm. An important reason for choosing a corporate structure is that it limits the liability of owners. As a sole proprietor or partner, an individual is personally liable for any judgment if someone sues my sporting goods store. If someone sues my firm and it is a corporation, I have no personal liability as an owner. Owners in a corporation purchase shares and vote for a board of directors that sets policies of the corporation. Some corporations have very limited ownership and are not available in an open market (privately held), whereas many sell shares to the general public (publicly held). In the United States, many sport organizations are corporations.

Sport organizations may be corporations themselves, such as Nike, American Skiing, and the Boston Celtics. Table 6-6 lists several sports teams owned as part of a parent corporation. It is important to understand that ownership structure affects the firm's objectives and operations.

CORPORATE OWNERSHIP

Corporate ownership of sport entities is an old concept. In 1869, the Cincinnati Red Stockings were financed through a joint stock association that raised $15,000

Table 6-6. Selected Professional Sports Teams Owned by a Parent Corporation

Team	Parent Company
Atlanta Braves (MLB)	Time Warner Inc.
Atlanta Thrashers (NHL)	Time Warner Inc.
Chicago Cubs (MLB)	Tribune Co.
New York Knicks (NBA)	Cablevision Systems Corp.
Philadelphia Flyers (NHL)	Comcast Corp.
Philadelphia 76ers (NBA)	Comcast Corp.

in capital. That year, the club earned a profit of $1,700, a return-on-equity of 11.3% (Gorman & Calhoun, 1994). In 1876, Spalding began operations with $800 in capital on its way to becoming the first national sporting goods manufacturer (Spalding Sports Worldwide, Inc., 1999). The company remains a privately held corporation.

Professional sports has experienced a mix of individual and corporate ownership. Throughout the late 1800s and into the 1900s, there were publicly held baseball teams, but they soon died away, affected by economic conditions and poor performances. Today, although five Major League Baseball clubs are owned by corporations, just one, the Cleveland Indians, is traded publicly on its own. In 1923, the Green Bay Packers sold $200 shares in the team to people in the community. As recently as 1998, they sold additional shares. The Packers remain the only publicly held football club because the NFL has a rule forbidding corporate or public ownership of teams. The intent of such prohibition is to have owners focused on football and to avoid having corporate ownership change the way NFL owners operate. In the NHL, seven teams are owned by corporations. In 1986, the Boston Celtics raised $48 million by selling 40% of the team to the public, and it remains the only publicly held franchise in the NBA. Five NBA teams are owned by corporations. At league levels below the four major leagues, many teams are held by corporations, but they are not publicly traded. An exception is the Orlando Predators of the Arena Football League, which made a public offering in 1997.

It is not only North America where the concept of public ownership of professional sports exists. In the 1990s, there was much discussion among European football clubs of making public stock offerings in an effort to produce additional revenue. One of such examples is Borussia, which went public in 2000. It is Germany's only publicly listed football club.

Outside team sports, publicly held companies are common. From sports apparel/footwear (Nike, Rawlings) to sport products (Callaway Huffy) to resorts (American Skiing Company, Vail) to motor sports (CART, Speedway Motorsports) to facilities (Family Golf Centers, Hollywood Park), there are many com-

Table 6-7. Market Capitalization for Selected Publicly-Held Sport Corporations

Corporation	Capitalization (000,000)
Nike	$17,174
International Speedway	2,024
Speedway Motorsports	1,695
Callaway	1,052
Reebok	1,001
SportsLine	771
Vail Resorts	645
Hollywood Park	413
Panthers	431
Family Golf Centers	171
Huffy	155
K2	150
Cleveland Indians	115
American Skiing	113
Rawlings	74
Boston Celtics	32
Orlando Predators	22

panies in which the public can purchase shares. Table 6-7 lists several sports corporations and their market capitalization. Capitalization equals price of a share multiplied by the number of shares outstanding.

The desire or need of a corporation to create revenue with which to operate the firm is the major motive of why it makes shares available to the general public. In 1999, Churchill Downs announced plans for a secondary stock offering, which could raise as much as $75.3 million (Mullen, 1999). The 1998 initial stock offering for Championship Auto Racing Teams resulted in $80 million. The Cleveland Indians raised $60 million in its 1998 stock sale. SportsLine USA, Inc. went public in 1997 and collected $28 million. Proceeds from public offerings pay down debt, finance acquisitions, and engage in capital construction.

Although public offerings are common in the general business world, professional sports has been slower to adopt that model, especially the "small-market" teams. It would seem the benefits would outweigh the costs. It could be a way to raise revenue for the team. By so doing, the team could also lessen its reliance on government subsidies or on ticket or media revenue. Selling stock to raise funds, however, has several disadvantages. One is a potential loss of control over the firm. If unhappy shareholders can gather enough votes (shares), they have the power to make change. Even a minority of shareholders can make operations difficult. Ascent Entertainment Group Inc. agreed in 1999 to sell its sports teams (the Colorado Avalanche and Denver Nuggets) and Pepsi Center for $400 million. Angry shareholders filed suit claiming that the sale price was too low (Kaplan & Mullen, 1999) and that an officer of Ascent would excessively benefit. Florida Panthers

Holdings Inc. was sued by several investors upset about the company's diversification into real estate (Kaplan, 1999). Nike has faced criticism from shareholders as well as the general public over its Southeast Asia manufacturing operations.

A second disadvantage for a firm to go public is that public ownership requires financial information be made available to the public and to potential competitors. Many companies are reluctant to allow such information into the public. Competitors can use the information to their own advantage. In the case of professional sports teams, arguments that the team is losing money may not be supported by financial statements. As a privately held corporation, a company is not required to disclose its financial information. A longer period of recovery from investment is another reason.

If there are few financial benefits to be obtained from the purchase of professional team stocks, why does the public still buy them? It does not seem to make financial sense. However, from an economic perspective, a person still obtains benefits from being a shareholder of such stocks, even if the benefits are not financial ones. These benefits might include demonstrating team loyalty and the uniqueness of being an owner (albeit on a small scale). For a relatively small cost, the benefits are high.

Generally, publicly held companies make their stock available without restrictions. Professional sports teams have been more careful in selling their stock. In most of the cases where professional teams have publicly sold shares, the percentage available for sale is limited. The Celtics' sale of 40% ownership is an example. Franchises sell only a limited percentage of shares in the club, thus retaining majority ownership. The Packers placed many restrictions on their community ownership, including no payment of dividends, no trading of the stock on an exchange, no stock appreciation, and limited voting rights. For most publicly held stocks, there is an economic incentive to purchase. The goal is that, either through stock appreciation or dividends, the stockholder will obtain income that exceeds the possible income from any other use of the money invested. This is the concept of opportunity cost.

SINGLE-ENTITY OWNERSHIP

In the major professional sports, individual players sign contracts with individual clubs. However, labor costs for any individual club are not independent of labor costs for another club. What one owner pays a player affects what other owners will have to pay. This environment is a result of free agency and arbitration. When one owner is willing to pay a player far beyond what has been typical, other owners become upset (more in-depth discussion on labor issues will be provided in Chapter 8).

An attempt to overcome this problem is a structure called *single-entity ownership*. Rather than having one owner for one club in a league, a group of owners jointly owns all clubs in the league. Today, this structure appears in Major League Soccer. In 2005, Bain Capital Partners LLC (a powerful Wall Street buyout firm) and Game Plan International (an upstart sports advisory company) have made a dramatic joint proposal to buy all of the NHL's 30 teams for as much as $3.5 billion US. If the deal has gone through, the NHL would evolve into a single ownership structure.

In MLS, investors participate in the league as a whole but receive the right to operate one of the 12 franchises. Players sign contracts with the league, which then allocates them to specified teams. Although a franchise operator can request certain players, there is no assurance that such a request will be honored. The league allocates players for the benefit of the league rather than the benefit of an individual club. In this case, profit maximization of the league as a whole is the goal. The franchise operator makes decisions about marketing and operation of the club but does not have unlimited authority.

Such a structure eliminates the possibility of owners driving up labor prices by competing for players. It has dispensed with a free market for players and has centralized control, essentially moving from an oligopoly to a monopoly. Leagues can plan their labor costs, which contributes to long-term survival. However, single-entity ownership also has disadvantages. One is a legal threat. Major League Soccer players have sued the MLS and argued that their ability to obtain jobs is being unfairly restricted (restraint of trade). However, in a recent ruling, the court was in favor of the Major League Soccer, citing that the Sherman Antitrust Act only prohibits collective activity by plural economic factors which unreasonably retrain competition. The court also declaimed that the player hiring policy was a unilateral activity of a single firm and the Sherman Antitrust Act did not apply to unilateral activity. Finally, the formation of the league was not in violation of the Clayton Act because it does not involve the acquisition or merger of existing business enterprises (*Street & Smith's SportsBusiness Journal*, 2002).

A second problem is free riders. If revenues and expenses are handled through a central office, there is less incentive for any individual club to maximize profit. The advantage of a free market is that owners who make profits keep profits. Under a centralized operation, an individual operator may be able to gain a "free ride" on the success of other operators.

Single-entity ownership also has disadvantages for its investors. For most investors in professional sports, a reward for investing is the ability to operate a team—to make decisions about player acquisition, marketing strategies, and operations. MLS restricts investors' ability to conduct business. In addition, under ordinary circumstances, the MLS might also be a good candidate for a public stock offering. League officials currently want to expand, which will be expensive. A public offering could raise the capital necessary to undertake growth. However, until the MLS resolves issues regarding player allocations, it is unlikely that the league would be willing to make a public offering, which would require opening up the books.

MERGERS, ACQUISITIONS, AND STRATEGIC ALLIANCES

The past two decades have seen a flurry of activity among corporations in terms of acquiring and merging with other companies or forming a strategic alliance. Many well-known companies have been part of such behavior, including Westinghouse and CBS, Daimler-Benz and Chrysler, Amoco and British Petroleum, Norwest and Wells Fargo banks, and U.S. West and Qwest. The sport industry has echoed this general business activity. Examples include Sportsline.com acquiring MVP.com, Comcast controlling 100% of the Outdoor Life Network after purchasing shares from the Fox Entertainment Group, Inc. in 2001, Nike buying Converse in 2003, and the merger of Adidas-Salomon AG and Reebok International in 2005. The decision of engaging in such behavior is generally based on the results of benefit and cost analysis.

Consumer goods and services are generally provided through a series of steps described as the *chain of production*. Figure 6-1 shows two chains of production, one for a consumer good, such as an athletic shoe, the other for a service, such as a round of golf. Each point in the chain represents some activity by a firm to move the product or service toward the end consumer. The chain for a consumer good is more involved than that for a service. This is especially relevant in the sport industry where much of what organizations provide is represented by the shorter chain.

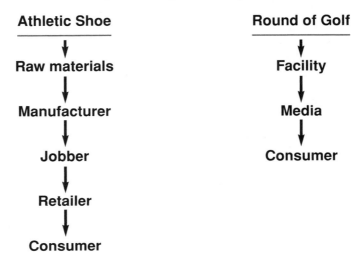

Figure 6-1. Chain of Production

Given their own operating environment and including the competition they face, firms have to continually make decisions about how to move products and services along the chain in a way that will best satisfy consumers. Strategic decisions that firms can make to accomplish this include mergers, acquisitions, and formation of strategic alliances. Mergers and acquisitions result in firms being integrated along the chain of production. *Horizontal integration* is "the combining of two companies [at the same level] in the same industry" (Colander, 1998, p. 760). In 1996, American Skiing, an operator of several ski resorts in the Northeast, acquired SKI Ltd., another operator of Northeast ski resorts. The result was a single company that owned seven resorts (Gilpin, 1996). For American Skiing, benefits came from more integrated marketing and advertising and the ability to offer more options to consumers. In 1990, sporting goods manufacturer Spalding acquired Dudley, the premier manufacturer of softballs (Spalding Sports Worldwide, Inc., 1999). Spalding, which considers itself a premier sporting goods company, was now able to offer one additional product to its business consumers and keep them within the Spalding sphere of influence.

Vertical integration is "a combination of two companies that are involved in different phases of producing a product, one company being a buyer of products the other company supplies" (Colander, 1998, p. 760). A firm will then operate at more than one point on the chain of production. Vertical integration may be either backward, where a firm moves closer to the supply of inputs, or forward, when a firm moves closer to the ultimate consumer. In the sport industry, many media companies have engaged in vertical integration. An example is Cablevision Systems Corp., which acquired the New York Knicks and New York Rangers in 1997, giving them control over the product as well as the delivery system (Burgi, 1997). Media company acquisitions of sports franchises have been common occurrences in North America and Europe. In most cases, media companies have found it cheaper to buy their product (teams) rather than pay escalating rights fees.

Some firms practice both horizontal and vertical integration. During 1998 and 1999, SportsLine, a global Internet sports media company, acquired International Golf Outlet (a retailer of fine golf equipment), Golf Club Trader (an Internet retailer specializing in used pro-line golf equipment), and Infosis Group Limited's Sports Division (a provider of sports information for SportsLine; CBS SportLine, 1999). The first two acquisitions allowed SportsLine to diversify horizontally, providing a wider range of items to offer through its Internet delivery system. The last acquisition is an example of vertical integration in that SportsLine acquired one of its information suppliers. In addition, SportsLine and CBS have combined. CBS gained enhanced access to Internet delivery whereas SportsLine gained the visibility that comes with the CBS name, as well as cash.

A firm might want to merge with or acquire another firm for many reasons (Brickley et al., 1997, p. 356). One is to increase power and influence. Generally, the larger the company, the more power it tends to have. One of the concerns with mergers and acquisitions is that firms can develop too much power and influence. At the extreme, such consolidation would result in monopoly power. That is why the government occasionally reviews, and even disallows, a merger or acquisition. There was discussion about American Skiing's gathering too much power in the Northeast ski resort industry although no antitrust investigation occurred (Gilpin, 1996).

A second reason relates to transaction costs. Going outside the company for inputs and outputs involves costs, including searching out partners. Escalating rights costs for sporting events are a major cost for media companies. Measuring the quality of a supplier's production also involves costs. At every point along the chain of production there are costs. The necessity of coordinating such activities as production, transportation, and pricing decreases the opportunity for profit. Additionally, a company's reputation depends on its suppliers because poor suppliers or retailers can cost reputations.

Third, companies want to ensure the supply and quality of important inputs. Quality reflects on reputation. For example, makers of wooden bats depend on growers of wood to supply a good product. No matter how good the bat maker, if the wood is not good, baseball players will be unhappy. In addition, shortages occur in the marketplace. A sporting goods retailer who also controls the manufacture of items to be sold has much more control over the amount produced and has more assurance of consistency of supply. A cable television company depends on programming. If the cable company owns a baseball or basketball or hockey team, it has consistent supply and does not have to compete on the open market.

Mergers and acquisitions have both costs and benefits. They also raise many issues, not the least of which is government interest in maintaining competition. Several of the firms mentioned above have faced antitrust concerns. Chapter 10 will talk more about antitrust issues.

Strategic alliances have existed in the business community for many years, but it is a fairly new concept among sport organizations. A *strategic alliance* is a form of cooperation between two or more industrial sectors for the sake of cutting costs and maintaining quality simultaneously as well as increasing synergy (Berger, 2001; Park & Richard, 1996; Schifrin, 2001), and accomplishing mutually compatible goals that would be difficult for each to accomplish alone (Spekman & Isabella, 2000). In business terms, a strategic alliance typically involves technology swaps, joint research and development, and the sharing of complimentary assets. Strategic alliances have been used for such purposes as gaining access to new markets, channels, and knowledge; realizing economies of scale; enhancing capabilities; sharing of marketing costs; broadening the product lines; and learning new skills (Lachowetz, 2001). According to Schifrin (2001), strategic alliances take many forms, including outsourcing, information sharing, joint marketing, and partnership. Many people would consider a strategic alliance to be the same as a joint venture. By definition, a joint venture is essentially any collaborative effort short of a merger among firms with respect to production, research and development, distribution or marketing of products or services (Metge, Nathanson, & Levin, 1996). The collaborative effort usually benefits the parties involved.

The rationale for the formation of strategic alliances is severalfold. First, the companies involved in the alliance aim at achieving competitive advantages for the partners. For example, the formation of an alliance between sports organizations and businesses in a community will increase the competitiveness and attractiveness of the community over other regions in bidding for sports events, attracting visitors, and enhancing the community's reputation and visibility. Second, both partners put in resources and access to competencies or share complementary assets. Such arrangement ensures that each partner can have access to competencies it lacks and can share competencies with its partner. For example, a partnership or alliance commonly exists in many cities between their sports commissions and the intercollegiate athletic programs in the cities. The sports commission can assist its collegiate athletic partner in promoting certain events that foster economic development in the community. The sports commission can provide event management functions via the provision of security, issuing permits or helping with ordinances and zoning regulations. On the other hand, the collegiate athletic partner can provide entertainment, cultural programming, and promotion of city-sponsored events at its venues and through its media outlets. In addition, the involved partners can share facilities (e.g., buildings, fields, pools, courts, gymnasiums, meeting space) and programs, as well as co-develop major cultural facilities. Third, strategic alliances are developed to stimulate growth. The skills gained through new partnerships can introduce new techniques, market segments, or new geographic markets, and can help boost revenue opportunities by gaining greater returns from existing customers, channels, and products (Spekman et al, 2000).

A strategic alliance between firms in the same sport industry sectors and a partnership between a sport organization and non-sport organizations are two approaches to which sport organizations apply the strategic alliance theory. Examples of the former approach include the alliance formed to combine marketing efforts of the Phoenix Suns and Coyotes, and the partnership created between the Korean and Japanese soccer for hosting the World Cup. Many intercollegiate athletic programs adopted the latter approach in outsourcing their marketing services to marketing firms, such as Host Communications, International Sports Properties, Learfield Communications, and Viacom.

Summary

Sport is supplied via several delivery structures, each of which has implications for how it ultimately reaches the consumer. Government-supplied sport reallocates resources collected from all citizens to provide sport to all citizens. There are many arguments for and against government's providing sport services, including the concept of positive and negative externalities. In some cases, government has sought means by which it can turn over its responsibilities, perhaps through privatization or through subsidies to community organizations.

Community-based organizations supply a variety of sport experiences to people. These are nonprofit organizations that seek to fill need not met by either government or private enterprise. Much sport is provided through private enterprise, where the goal is generally profit maximization. Corporate ownership is responsible for much of the business activity in the sport industry. Benefits and costs exist for both public and private ownership of firms. Merger and acquisition activity also has benefits and costs that must be considered before a firm participates in such behavior.

Western City (at the beginning of this chapter) is an illustration of the issues involved in choosing how to supply sport. Each of the options presented by council members has costs and benefits that must be considered in making decisions.

Chapter Questions

1. What are externalities?
2. What are two arguments in favor of government's supplying sport? What are two arguments against?
3. Why do people participate (directly or indirectly) in community-based sport organizations?
4. How does a firm's ownership structure affect the firm's objectives and operations? Why would a municipal government consider privatizing its sport services?
5. Chris Branvold is the General Manager of the Colorado Rockies. The Assistant Director of Baseball Operations has come to him and informed him that three of the club's minor league affiliates are up for sale. Chris has been thinking that there might be advantages to buying the minor league clubs but worries that the disadvantages might be too great. What are the advantages and disadvantages? Would it work?

Learning Activities

1. Determine what sport and recreation services are provided in your home community. Who provides them? Why has this delivery system arisen? How well does it work? Does everyone get served?

2. You are a news reporter, covering a debate in the local community. Arguing that the community provides other children with summer leagues in which to participate, a group of parents who have children with disabilities has demanded that the mayor and supervisors offer a summer Challenger Baseball League for their children. The mayor and supervisors say there isn't enough money in the budget to support such a program. Write an article that reviews the debate and the economic issues that underlie it.

3. Wong Company is a major builder of recreational soccer complexes throughout the South. The company has been successful and has a lot of cash available for growth. Company president Rosanne Wong wants to expand operations and needs advice as to what might benefit the company. She has come to you as a consultant on mergers and acquisitions. Write a memo to her suggesting the direction she might consider. What might be some good targets for a merger or acquisition? Why would this be logical for Wong Company?

Chapter Seven

THE SPORT INDUSTRY: A CRITICAL CENTER OF ECONOMY

Introduction

The sport industry has been viewed as a critical center in the United States economy. Using the Gross National Sports Product (GNSP) to determine the size of the sport industry in the United States, *Sports, Inc.* reported in 1987 that sport was a $50 billion industry (Sandomir, 1987). Using 1995 data, Meek conducted a similar study in 1997, which indicated that the sum of the output and services of the sport industry, measured by the Gross Domestic Sports Product (GDSP), was approximately $152 billion. The same study also found that the sport industry was ranked 11th in size when compared to other industries in the United States (see Table 7-1 for details). A recent special report, compiled by the *Street & Smith's SportsBusiness Journal* (*SBJ*), entitled "The Sports Business at the End of the Millennium," substantially increased the figure to $212.53 billion based on the 1997 data (Broughton, Lee, & Nethery, 1999b). The report considered the sport industry as one of economic behemoths, and it is bigger than the automobile industry, bigger than all the public utilities put together, and bigger than agriculture. The *SBJ* recalculated the 1997 data and believed that the size of the sport industry should be $182.83 billion instead (Broughton, 2002). The figure was $29.7 billion less than the original estimate in 1999. In 2002, the *SBJ* released a new estimate which claimed the sport industry is a $194.64 billion industry measured in 15 spending categories (King, 2002; see Table 7-2 for details).

> ### The Sport Industry: A Critical Center of Economy
>
> *Devon Lee, chief executive officer of the Jacksonville Footwear Corporation, was recently invited to give a speech at a meeting sponsored by the Chamber of Commerce for the Greater Jacksonville Area. In his presentation, he pointed out that the sport industry is a $193 billion industry and its impact was even greater than some conventional industries, such as the public utility industry. At the Q & A session, he was asked to explain how he came up with the number. Do you know how he was able to calculate it?*

Is the sport industry really that big? How did those studies estimate the size of the sport industry? This chapter will provide students with a detailed review of the issues related to determining and measuring the size of the sport industry so that they will gain a better understanding of how critical the sport industry is to the national economy. This chapter will also assess the contribution of the sport industry to the U.S. economy in terms of the annual number of jobs the industry creates.

Table 7-1. Top 25 U.S. Industry Ranking (Estimated 1995 Industry GDP; billions of $)

Rank Industry	Size
Real estate	850.0
Retail trade	639.9
Wholesale trade	491.0
Health service	443.4
Construction	227.6
Business service	275.3
Depository institutions	223.9
Utilities	205.3
Other service	194.9
Telephone and telegraph communication	155.7
Sports	**152.0**
Chemicals and allied products	141.0
Electronic and electrical equipment	138.5
Industrial machinery and equipment	123.3
Insurance carriers	115.4
Food and kindred products	113.3
Trucking and warehousing	100.6
Legal services	100.5
Printing and publishing	89.7
Motor vehicle and equipment	88.7
Fabricated metal products	86.0
Farms	85.0
Security and commodity brokers	75.6
Oil and gas extraction	62.7
Auto repair, services and parking	60.5

Source: Meek, 1997.

Table 7-2. The 15 Spending Categories Used by the *Street & Smith's SportsBusiness Journal* to Aggregate the Size of the Sport Industry in the United States

Categories	Expenditures (in billions of $)
1. Advertising	$ 27.43
2. Endorsements	0.90
3. Facility Construction	2.48
4. Gambling	18.90
5. Internet	0.24
6. Licensed Goods	10.50
7. Media Broadcast Rights	6.99
8. Medical Spending	12.60
9. Multimedia	2.02
10. Operating Expenses	22.98
11. Professional Services	15.25
12. Spectator Spending	26.17
13. Sponsorships	6.40
14. Sporting Goods	25.62
15. Travel	16.06
Total	$194.64

The Measurement of Gross Domestic Product

The value of the output of all final goods and services produced by any industry in a given economy is expressed as either the Gross National Product (GNP) or the Gross Domestic Product (GDP). Gross National Product is the total value of output owned by residents of a particular nation in a certain year. Gross Domestic Product, however, is the total value of output (i.e., the final goods and services) produced in the nation during a single year.[1] It is the market value of goods and services produced over time, including the income of foreign corporations and foreign residents working in the U.S., but excluding the income of U.S. residents and corporations overseas. GDP uses market prices because they are the values that people place on goods and services. GDP also measures all the goods produced over some time period, usually a year, whether they are sold or not. The difference between GNP and GDP is the net investment income that the country's residents receive from other parts of the world. After 1991, the Department of

---

[1]Final goods and services are those goods and services purchased for final use.

Table 7-3. Real Gross Domestic Product (1998)

GDP and Its Components	Symbol	Amount (billions of dollars)	Percentage of GDP
Personal consumption expenditures	C	8,229.9	70.1
Gross private domestic investment	I	1,927.3	16.4
Government purchase of goods and services	G	2,183.4	18.6
Net exports of goods and services	NX	-606.1	- 5.2
Gross domestic product	GDP	11,735	100

Source: U.S. Bureau of Economic Analysis, 2005. Web: *www.bea.gov.*

Commerce of the United States decided to use GDP to measure the aggregate economic activity, instead of GNP. The Department of Commerce of the United States uses several approaches to measure GDP. The one that has been widely adopted is called the expenditure approach or the final sales method (Auerbach & Kotlikoff, 1995). The Factor Income Approach is the second method used by the Department of Commerce of the United States to estimate GDP (Table 7-3 shows the Real GDP of the United States in 1998).

Measurement of GDP: The Expenditure Approach

The expenditure approach measures the value of production reflected by various types of spending on domestically produced goods and services within a specific interval of time. It includes four components in the estimate of GDP. They are personal consumption expenditures (C), gross private domestic investment (I), government purchase of goods and services (G), and net exports of goods and service (NX). The following is an expressive equation that reveals the relationship between GDP and these four components:

$$GDP = C + I + G + NX$$

PERSONAL CONSUMPTION EXPENDITURES

Personal consumption expenditures are household expenditures on goods and services produced by firms, such as beverages, exercise and sport shoes, athletic club memberships, and bikes. Personal consumption expenditures exclude purchases of households on real property (e.g., house, land), because house and land purchases are counted as a type of private investment. As such, they are included in the calculation in a separate category (i.e., gross private domestic investment). Personal consumption expenditures are the largest and are a relatively stable component of GDP. As Table 6-3 shows, American households spent $8,229.9 billion on goods and services in 2004, which accounts for 70.1% of the GDP (i.e., $11,735 billion) in that year.

GROSS PRIVATE DOMESTIC INVESTMENT

The expenditures of business firms on purchasing new capital equipment, newly produced physical structures (e.g., a new plant), and inventories are included in this category. The money that individual households spend on acquisition of new residential houses is also part of the gross private domestic investment. Specifically, gross private domestic investment analyzes two basic items: (1) net private domestic investment and (2) the consumption of fixed capital. The net private domestic investment is the part of gross investment that adds to the existing stock of physical structures and equipment. The consumption of fixed capital consists of depreciation and an allowance for accidental damage to the physical structures and equipment. In 2004, 16.4% of the GDP was contributed by the expenditures of business firms.

GOVERNMENT PURCHASES OF GOODS AND SERVICES

The component of government purchases of goods and services is also referred to as government consumption expenditures and gross investment. It calculates the goods and services purchased by all levels of government, from the federal government to local municipalities. The government consumption expenditures may include the costs and expenditures of providing services and law enforcement. Transfer payments, which are the payments by government to persons for the service they do not render, are not included in the calculation of this particular GDP component because they do not involve the production of goods and services. Government purchases of goods and services are typically the second largest component of GDP. For example, governments at all levels consumed $2,183.4 billion, or 18.6% of the GDP in that year.

NET EXPORTS OF GOODS AND SERVICES

The difference between the value of exports of goods and services and the value of imports of goods and services is the net exports of goods and services. Exports are the goods and services produced in a country but purchased by foreigners. The value of a pair of baseball gloves that are produced in the United States and sold in Hong Kong is calculated as part of U.S. exports. On the other hand, imports are the goods and services produced abroad and purchased by U.S. citizens in the United States. When an American buys an Italian-made warm-up outfit in Athens, Ohio, what he or she pays is calculated as part of the U.S. imports. The net exports of goods and services have always been a negative component of GDP, as indicated in Table 7-4. That means Americans have imported more goods from other nations than they have sold to the rest of the world. In 2004, Americans imported $606.1 billion in more goods and services than they sold to other nations. Table 7-4 provides longitudinal data on the GDP of the United States from 1930 to 2004 (U.S. Bureau of Economic Analysis, 2005).

There are basic rules that need to be rigidly followed in measuring the value of the output of a particular economy. The most important rule is that a single dollar cannot be counted twice (Sandomir, 1987). It is extremely important to remember that when calculating GDP, the value of intermediate goods and services, and goods purchased for resale or for use in producing other goods should not be included. Only the final goods and services produced count toward GDP. For example, when someone buys a new fishing boat from a local marine shop, the value of the boat is counted as part of GDP. However, the amount of money the marine shop pays to the manufacturer for the boat is not included in the calculation of GDP because doing so would cause the value of the boat to be double-counted.

Table 7-4. Gross Domestic Product or Expenditure, 1930–2004 (in billions of dollars)

Item	1930	1940	1950	1960	1970	1980	1990	1995	2000	2001	2002	2003	2004
Gross domestic product	$91.2	$101.4	$293.8	$526.4	$1,038.5	$2,789.5	$5,803.1	$7,397.7	$9,817.0	$10,100.8	$10,480.8	$10,987.9	$11,735.0
Personal consumption expenditures	70.1	71.3	192.2	331.7	648.5	1,757.1	3,839.9	4,975.8	6,739.4	7,045.4	7,385.3	7,757.4	8,229.9
Gross private domestic investment	10.8	13.6	54.1	78.9	152.4	479.3	861.0	1,144.0	1,735.5	1,607.2	1,589.2	1,670.6	1,927.3
Exports of goods and services	4.4	4.9	12.4	27.0	59.7	280.8	552.4	812.2	1,096.3	1,035.1	1,006.8	1,048.9	1,175.5
Imports of goods and services	-4.1	-3.4	-11.6	-22.8	-55.8	-293.8	-630.3	-903.6	-1,475.8	-1,401.7	-1,433.1	-1,543.8	-1,781.6
Government[2]	10.0	15.0	46.8	111.6	233.8	566.2	1,180.2	1,369.2	1,721.6	1,814.7	1,932.5	2,054.8	2,183.9

Source: U.S. Bureau of Economic Analysis, May 26, 2005. Web: www.bea.gov .

[2]Government consumption expenditures and gross investment.

The factor income approach measures GDP or the value of production by adding together all of the incomes paid by firms to households for the services of the factors of production that they use, including labor hired, interest paid for borrowed capital, rent paid for land use, and profit. According to the National Income and Product Accounts for the United States, published by the Bureau of Economic Analysis of the Department of Commerce, factor incomes are split into five components:

1. compensation of employees (CE),

2. rental income (RI),

3. corporate profits (CP),

4. net income (NI), and

5. proprietors' income (PI) (Auerbach & Kotlikoff, 1995; Parkin, 1993).

An expressive equation that reveals the relationship between GDP and these five components is shown as follows:

$$GDP = CE + RI + CP + NI + PI$$

COMPENSATION OF EMPLOYEES

Compensation of employees refers to the total payments by business firms for labor services. The total payments then include the wages and salaries that employees receive in a certain period of time (e.g., weekly, bi-weekly, and monthly), the portion of income withheld for tax purposes, and all fringe benefits paid for by the employer. Social security, health insurance, and retirement are examples of the fringe benefits that employees usually obtain as part of their compensation. For example, as athletic director of the Southern Athletic Club in Decatur, Georgia, Karen Smith receives an annual salary of $35,000 from the club.

RENTAL INCOME

Rental income is the payment for the use of land and other rented structures. Rental payment for a house/apartment and the imputed rental payment for an owner-occupied house are two major components of rental income. The imputed income is the implicit benefits received by a homeowner who has used the house as a business office. By considering the rental payment for the house as a cost to the business, the owner, in fact, saves an equivalent amount of money as a result of using the house as an office. Thus, the saving should be calculated as part of the owner's income.

CORPORATE PROFIT

Corporate profit is the total net income or profit that all business firms make in a given economy over a certain period of time. The period could be a month, quarter, six months, or a year. For example, the net income of Callaway Golf Company in the first six months of 2005 was $36.8 million (Callaway Golf Company, 2005).

Measurement of GDP: The Factor Income Approach

NET INTEREST

Net interest is the difference between the interest payments received by households on loans made by them, and the interest payments made by households on their own borrowing. The interest that households receive from their investments in bonds and the interest payments that households owe to financial institutions on their credit card balances are examples of various types of interest with which households commonly deal. For example, if a person receives an interest payment of $200 annually from an investment in a 20-year municipal bond, but pays $300 interest each year to a bank for a car loan, the net interest in this case is negative $100.

PROPRIETORS' INCOME

Personal income is a mixed index. A proprietor is an individual who owns and operates a business and who supplies labor, capital, land, and buildings to his or her own business. Proprietors' income is a category that mixes all four of the above elements because it is difficult to divide the income earned by a proprietor into such elements as compensation for use of labor, payment for use of capital, rental payment for use of land and buildings, and profit.

The Measurement of the Size of the Sport Industry

Using the framework of how GDP is measured, people can determine GDP in the sport industry, which is labeled as the Gross Domestic Sports Product (GDSP). Gross Domestic Sports Product is the sum of the value of the final goods and services produced domestically by the sport industry. The measurement of GDSP is far more complex than that of GDP for two reasons. First, the scope of the phenomenon of what we call "sport" can be very limited or inclusive depending on how we define the concept "sport." For example, should we consider fishing a sport? If yes, the magnitude of GDSP would be much higher than when they are left out. Specifically, American anglers, or fishing enthusiasts (16 years of age or older) spent about $37.8 billion annually, based on the information provided by the American Sportfishing Association, which claimed that it would be the 13th largest Fortune 500 company in the United States if sport fishing were considered a corporation in terms of revenue it generated, bigger than such global giants as Texaco and Dupont. Approximately $570 million was spent for fishing licenses, permits, and fees, and $15.4 billion for travel-related cost.

The second difficulty in measuring GDSP is that there is no sole category of expenditures in sport defined by government economic statistics. The economic significance of sport has been counted only as part of the contributions rendered by the recreation and entertainment industry. As mentioned in Chapter 1, the NAICS groups economic activities based on their similarity in production. The sport industry is not recognized as a stand-alone industry. Those firms and organizations that are included in the sport industry model proposed by Li, Hofacre, and Mahony (2001) are scattered across eight NAICS sectors. For instance, sporting goods manufacturers are included in the Manufacturing sector and intercollegiate athletic organizations are part of the Education Service sector. Only professional sport teams, sport event promoters, facilities, etc. are encompassed in the art, entertainment, and recreation sector. No comprehensive output or expenditure data are available from the federal government.

Numerous attempts with the use of different methodologies have been made to estimate the size of the sport industry (i.e., GDSP) in the United States over the past two decades (Broughton, Lee, & Nethery, 1999b; King, 2002; Meek, 1997; Sandomir, 1987). However, due to the unavailability of data from the government, scholars had to piece information together from a variety of different sources. This has created a major methodological issue, that is, it was impossible to compare the size of the sport industry over the span of those studies. The accuracy of data and the potential in violation of the rules used in estimating GDP, such as a single dollar cannot be counted twice, are other concerns. In the following section, a detailed discussion is provided in terms of how GDSP is measured theoretically. It is hoped that the discussion will provide concerned sport management professionals a framework to examine issues related to the size of the sport industry in the United States.

GDSP is typically measured with the use of the Expenditure Approach. As discussed previously, there are four components that are directly derived from GDP: personal consumption expenditures (C), gross private domestic investment (I), government purchase of goods and services (G), and net exports of goods and service (NX). Correspondently, there are four basic categories in the measurement of GDSP. That is, personal sport consumption (PSC), gross sport investment (GSI), government sport purchases (GSP), and net sport exports (NSE). The conceptual relationship between GDSP and the four categories of sport expenditures is expressed in the following equation:

$$GDSP = PSC + GSI + GSP + NSE$$

PERSONAL SPORT CONSUMPTION

Personal sport consumption refers to the expenditures of households on goods produced by sporting goods companies and on services rendered by service-oriented sport businesses. Examples of sporting goods include sports and exercise equipment, sporting apparel, and athletic shoes. The money paid for the membership to an athletic club, for a round of golf in a public golf course, and for the admission to a minor league hockey game exemplifies consumer spending for sport services. Personal sports consumption is highly inclusive as it covers the money that people spend on a variety of things. According to Meek (1997), the expenditures of consumers on sports can be summarized into three main categories: entertainment and recreation; products and services; and non-sport-related advertising expenditures. (The authors believe that this category is a standalone element of GDSP and that should be discussed in a separate section.) In 1995, sports consumers spent $144,848 million on sport. This is the largest component of GDSP. In the latest study conducted by the SBJ for estimating the size of the sport industry (King, 2002), several of the fifteen categories of expenditures were related to personal sport consumption of Americans, the sum of which was approximately $80.57 billion.

Table 7-5. Selected Attendance at Major Spectator Sports in the United States from 1990 to 2000 (in thousands)

Sports	1995	1997	1998	1999	2000
Major League Baseball	51,288	64,921	71,930	71,558	74,316
Basketball					
NCAA (men)	28,548	27,738	28,032	28,505	29,025
NCAA (women)	4,962	6,734	7,387	9,010	8,698
NBA	19,883	21,677	21,801	13,450	21,503
Football					
NCAA	35,638	36,858	37,491	39,483	39,059
NFL	19,203	19,050	19,742	20,763	20,954
NHL	9,234	17,641	17,265	17,152	18,831

In order to determine accurately what spending by households would count as personal sport consumption, a theoretical framework or system needs to be established. Meek (1997) groups American households' sport consumption into two major categories: spending on entertainment and recreation, and spending on sporting goods and services. The SBJ allocated such sport spending into five areas: spectatoring, gambling, spectator travel, medical spending, and licensed goods (King, 2002).

This book organizes personal sport consumption along the two basic domains of sport: *sport spectatorship/viewership* and *sport participation* (Durand & Bayle, 2002). Sport spectatorship/ viewership is a collective term used to describe American holders' involvement in sports activities as spectators and viewers. Sport participation, on the other hand, is used to depict their spending behavior for the sake of participation in sport activities. Table 7-5 details sport consumers' selected attendance at major spectator sports in the United States from 1990 to 2000 (in a thousand) and Table 7-6 shows the participation in the ten most popular sports activities in the United States in 2000 (U.S. Census Bureau, 2002).

Table 7-6. Participation in Ten Most Popular Sports Activities in the United States in 2000

Activity	All Persons Number	Rank	Sex Male	Female
Aerobic Exercising	28,518	9	6,575	22,057
Bicycle Riding	43,135	6	22,174	20,962
Billiards	32,548	8	19,281	13,267
Bowling	43,133	7	21,046	22,086
Camping	49,881	3	25,610	24,271
Exercise Walking	86,296	1	28,668	57,627
Exercise with Equipment	44,820	4	20,439	24,380
Fishing—Fresh Water	44,389	5	29,223	15,161
Swimming	60,758	2	26,404	34,353

Source: U.S. Census Bureau. (2002), Web: *http://www.census.gov/prod/2001pubs/statab/sec07.pdf*

Table 7-7. Personal Consumption Expenditures on Spectator Sports[3] (1985–1995) (in millions of current dollars)

Sport	1985	1986	1987	1988	1989	1990	1991	1992	1993	1994	1995
Professional Baseball	325	350	385	426	469	489	562	592	781	648	691
Professional Football	263	259	263	293	323	348	373	398	408	414	443
Professional Basketball	217	248	286	192	240	268	281	299	310	332	365
Professional Soccer	4	5	9	3	7	10	10	11	24	25	25
Professional Hockey	188	204	226	138	151	162	171	185	207	197	194
Dog and Horse Racing	312	316	327	345	398	381	391	346	335	300	281
College Football	139	149	160	165	182	196	206	206	206	226	230
College Basketball (men & women)	123	131	141	151	164	180	191	196	189	182	216
High School Athletics	1,222	1,157	1,123	1,387	1,670	1,684	1,803	1,948	2,176	2,404	2,575
Other Sports	487	464	445	470	543	520	534	473	457	478	518
Total	3,279	3,284	3,366	3,569	4,147	4,238	4,522	4,656	5,093	5,206	5,537

Source: U.S. Census Bureau (1997). *Statistical Abstract of the United States, 1997*, Web: http://www.census.gov/prod/www/statistical-abstract-1995_2000.html.
[3]The spending figure consists of admission to all professional and amateur spectator sports events.

Sport Spectatorship/Viewership

Paying admission to attend a sports event, purchasing printed materials in sports (e.g., books, magazines), and subscribing to a pay-per-view sport programming and online sporting news are examples of sport spectatorship. There are many costs associated with attending sports events. Monies spent on tickets, parking, transportation, and concessions fall under this category. The expenditure of American households on spectator sports over the last decade is summarized in Table 7-7. The figures in Table 7-7 indicate that consumers have gradually spent more money on attending various spectator-oriented sporting events. They include the traditional athletic events like professional and collegiate football, basketball, and baseball games, as well as the non-traditional events, such as auto, horse, and dog racing.

In addition to attending spectator sports events, American consumers also spend millions of dollars to receive pay-per-view sports events at home. Pay-per-view is a $1 billion-a-year industry. A variety of sports programming is available for viewers, ranging from pro sports to college basketball March Madness. While more than 60 million households in the United States have cable TV connections, 35 million of them pay for converter boxes that enable them to watch pay-per-view events. Although the cost for viewing an event averages about $50, consumers are still willing to pay these large sums if the event is in high demand—about 1.8 million viewers subscribed to the Mike Tyson-Lewis fight (Bernstein, 2002).

Sport Participation

This category includes anything that American households pay for in order to participate in a sport activity, like the entry fee to a 5K road race and the equipment purchased for rollerskating. This category of expenditures can be broken down into five types of activities: spending on participation in sport-related activities; acquiring memberships to health, fitness, and sports clubs; purchasing sporting goods for participation; purchasing sport-related computer and video games to play; and partaking in sport gambling.

1. Spending on participation in sport-related activities. The registration fee paid for a sports activity refers to the spending on sports events and activities, such as the registration fee paid for a 5K road race. For example, the American Sportfishing Association reports that there are over 35 million anglers in the United States spending $37.8 billion on their sport a year, which produces a total economic output of $108.5 billion (American Recreation Coalition, 1998). Overall, 88.8 million Americans participated in sports and fitness activities on a frequent basis in 1996 (Sporting Goods Manufacturers Association, 1998). Visiting sports halls of fame, touring sports facilities, and attending special banquets with sports celebrities are another form of participation in sport-related activities.

2. Acquiring memberships to health, fitness, and sports clubs. According to the International Health, Racquet and Sportsclub Association, or IHRSA (2005), there are approximately 26,836 commercial health and sports club industry in the United States. Together, they make an enormous contribution to the U.S.

economy. Specifically, the commercial health and sports club industry provides health and fitness services to over 39.4 million club members and employs approximately 198,000 full-time employees and another 748,000 part-time employees. Just in 2003 alone, the U.S. commercial health and sports club industry generated $14.8 billion in revenue. In other words, American households spent the same amount of money on club memberships, private instructions, and other related products and services in that year.

Table 7-8. Sporting Goods Sales, by Product Category, 1990 to 2002 (in millions of dollars, except percent)

Selected Product Category	1990	1995	1997	1998	1999	2000	2001	2002
Sales, all products	50,725	59,794	67,333	69,848	71,161	74,442	74,337	77,917
Percent of retail sales	N/A	2.6	2.7	2.6	2.5	2.4	2.4	2.4
Athletic and sport clothing	10,130	10,311	12,035	12,844	10,307	11,030	10,217	9,979
Athletic and sport footwear	11,654	11,415	13,319	13,068	12,546	13,026	13,814	14,107
Aerobic shoes	611	372	380	334	275	292	281	239
Basketball shoes	918	999	1,134	1,000	821	786	761	789
Cross training shoes	679	1,191	1,450	1,402	1,364	1,528	1,476	1,421
Golf shoes	226	225	239	220	208	226	223	243
Gym shoes, sneakers	2,536	1,741	1,980	2,010	1,936	1,871	2,004	2,042
Jogging and running shoes	1,110	1,043	1,482	1,469	1,502	1,638	1,670	1,733
Tennis shoes	740	480	545	515	505	533	505	503
Walking shoes	2,950	2,841	3,236	3,192	3,099	3,317	3,280	3,415
Athletic and sport equipment	14,439	18,809	19,033	19,192	20,343	21,608	21,594	21,748
Archery	266	287	270	255	262	259	276	276
Baseball and softball	217	251	290	304	329	319	316	306
Billiards and pool	192	304	242	347	354	516	528	543
Camping	1,072	1,205	1,153	1,204	1,265	1,354	1,371	1,415
Exercise equipment	1,824	2,960	2,968	3,233	3,396	3,610	3,889	4,336
Fishing tackle	1,910	2,010	1,891	1,903	1,917	2,030	2,058	2,024
Golf	2,514	3,194	3,703	3,658	3,567	3,805	3,871	3,339
Firearms and hunting	2,202	3,003	2,562	2,200	2,437	2,274	2,206	2,470
In-line skating and wheel sports	150	646	562	509	473	1,074	726	494
Skin diving and scuba	294	328	332	345	363	355	348	331
Skiing, alpine	475	562	723	718	648	495	515	528
Tennis	333	297	319	318	338	383	371	397
Recreational transport	14,502	19,259	22,946	24,743	27,965	28,779	28,712	32,083
Bicycles and supplies	2,423	3,390	4,860	4,957	4,770	5,131	4,725	4,961
Pleasure boats	7,644	9,064	10,208	10,539	11,962	13,224	14,558	15,382
Recreational vehicles	4,113	5,895	6,904	8,364	10,413	9,529	8,598	10,960
Snowmobiles	322	910	975	883	820	894	831	780

Source: U.S. Census Bureau, *Statistical Abstract of the United States, 2005*. Web: http://www.census.gov/prod/www/statistical-abstract 2001_2005.html.

3. Purchasing sporting goods for participation. In 2002, Americans spent about $80 billion on sporting goods (U.S. Census Bureau, 2005). The expenditures on sporting goods include spending on sports and exercise equipment, outfits/apparels, souvenirs, and novelties. Table 7-8 shows how much American households spent on sporting goods (reflected by the sales figures) from 1990 to 2002. According to the Recreation Market Report presented by the Sporting Goods Manufacturers Association (2005), the sales of sports equipment, apparel, footwear, and recreational transport hit $66.14 billion in 2000. Specifically, the sales of sports equipment, accounted for 26.24% ($17.36 billion), sports apparel for 34% ($22.49 billion), athletic footwear for 13.58% ($8.98 billion), and recreational transport for 26.19% ($17.32 billion).

The water-based sporting goods market in the ten-year period between 1985 and 1995 exhibited a steady upward pattern, and this same pattern has remained in the early years of the 21st century. It is evidenced by the amount of consumer spending on such water-based recreational sports equipment as purchasing and rentals of boats as well as other water sport-related equipment (e.g., fishing tackle). In 1995, Americans spent more than $7.47 billion on water-based recreational sports equipment, a 4.2% increase from 1990. Table 7-9 provides detailed information about consumer spending on water-based recreational sport (in million of dollars) from the period of 1985–1995.

Table 7-9. Consumer Spending on Water-Based Recreational Sport, 1985—1995 (in millions of dollars)

Type of Spending	1985	1987	1990	1993	1995
Purchase of Boat without Motor and Boat Trailers	321	516	1,207	1,763	380
Purchase of Boat with Motor	4,908	5,615	3,508	3,655	4,568
Rentals of Boats and Trailers	162	107	110	151	203
Docking and Landing Fees	418	506	388	802	463
Purchase of Fishing Equipment	1,378	772	846	699	876
Purchase of Other Water Sport Equipment	914	954	1,110	1,060	977
Total	8,101	8,010	7,169	8,130	7,467

Source: Cordell, H. K., McDonald, B. L., Teasley, R. J., Bergstrom, J. C., Martin, J., Bason, J., & Leeworthy, V. R. (1999). Outdoor Recreation Participation Trends. In H. K. Cordell (ed.), *Outdoor Recreation for 21st Century America—A Report to the Nation: The National Survey on Recreation and the Environment.* State College, PA: Venture Publishing, Inc.

4. Purchasing sport-related computer and video games to play. The computer and video game industry takes in $10 billion per year worldwide (Entertainment Software Association, 2004). In 2004, the sales of computer and video games in the United States were $7.3 billion. Of the amount, 5.4% came from the sales of sport-related computer and video games. During the same period, $287 million worth of game units were purchased by American households.

5. Partaking in legal sports gambling. Gambling costs are the last category of personal sports consumption. Money that consumers spend on various gambling activities, including wages paid for betting on the results of sports competi-

tions, such as horse racing, and money spent on sport-related lotteries or lotteries that are sold and earmarked specifically for the sake of sports development is included here. Many Americans are deeply obsessed with gambling, and they spend millions of dollars each year on gambling activities. According to a congressional report, the State of Nevada in 1990 took in about $1.8 billion from its state-licensed sports wagering activities and the State of Oregon received $14.5 million from the state's sport lottery sales in its first two years of operations (Mills, 1992).

Gross Sport Investment (GSI)

Gross Sport Investment consists of (1) the expenditures of sport businesses on purchasing durable/capital equipment, and on restocking inventories, and (2) the expenditures of individuals on acquisition of big ticket items in sports. Sail boats and luxury race cars are examples of big ticket items.

Expenditures of Sport Businesses

As with their counterparts in other industries, sport businesses constantly invest a large sum of their operating revenue on purchasing needed durable/capital equipment, on inventorying, and on building new facilities. The following section will examine these various categories of gross sport investment.

Sport equipment is the first category of expenditures for sport businesses. Sport equipment in the sense of gross sport investment differs from the sport equipment discussed in the personal sport consumption, where it is used by sport participants to engage in a sport activity. Here it refers to the equipment that is essential for a sport business to conduct its operations. Each year, American sport businesses and organizations spend millions of dollars on various kinds of equipment. These expenditures range from buying a scoreboard for a minor league baseball team to paying for a treadmill for a sports club. The expenditures of sport businesses on business inventories, the second category of gross sport investment, are usually determined by focusing on those segments of the sport industry that involve production, distribution, and sales of goods. These include sporting goods manufacturers (e.g., Nike, Reebok, New Balance, and Wilson), distribution warehouses (including those affiliated with the producers and independent ones), and retail sporting goods stores (e.g., Foot Locker, the world's largest retail source for athletic footwear and apparel).

Private participation in sport facility construction has been a growing trend in the last two decades. There are two methods of private participation: (1) private dollars are used exclusively to build a sports facility and (2) private dollars are joined with monies from the public sector to share the construction cost of

Photo by Ben Shafer, courtesy of stock.xchng iv

a sports facility. The first means is commonly seen in golf course and athletic club construction. The amount of funds involved usually is relatively small and the ownerships of those facilities are able to come up with the construction funds through their own contributions or a bank loan. More golf courses have been built in the United States in the past eight years than have been opened in England in the past four hundred (Golf Research Group, 1997). According to the U.S. Census Bureau (2005), there were about 12,346 golf facilities in the United States in 1985. In 2002, there were 15,899 golf facilities in the country. The booming of golf facilities in this country is attributed to the strong public demand for this type of recreational sport. During the same period of time, the number of people who play golf increased from 17.5 million in 1985 to 26.2 million in 2002, a roughly 50% increase (U.S. Census Bureau, 2005). It has happened a few times in the 1990s and early the 21st century, when a sports franchise decided to build a sports facility with funding exclusively from private sources. The Staples Center and the AT&T Park, just to name a few, are examples of private dollars used exclusively to build a sports facility in professional sport.

The second method of private participation in sports facility construction is to share the development cost. In many cases, in order for a professional sports franchise to have the public support for either renovating an existing facility or building a new one, the team ownership must provide a portion of the needed construction fund. In the 1990s, many sports stadiums and arenas were funded jointly by local governments and sports franchises, such as the Minute Maid Park for the Houston Astros and Comerica Park, home of the Detroit Tigers.

Expenditures of Individual Sports Investment

There are two basic types of individual sports investment: (a) money spent on long-term big ticket items and (b) funds used to buy sports-related stocks. The sport-related long-term big ticket items include the individuals' purchase of luxury race cars and sail boats, which usually have a relatively long useful life. Gross Sport Investment in 1997 was estimated around $11,815.6 million (Meek, 1997). According to the U.S. Census Bureau (2003), Americans spent approximately $13.8 billion in sporting boats in 2002. The same trend was also seen in the total number of sporting boats owned by Americans. In 1990, fewer than 16 million Americans owned a sporting boat. Ten years later in 2000, about 1.2 million more Americans became owners.

GOVERNMENT SPORT PURCHASES

Government sport purchases refers to the goods and services purchased by all levels of government (mainly the state and local governments) for sport development and for provision of services to fulfill the needs of citizens for sport activities. Government spending on sport is found mainly in one of three areas: (a) construction and maintenance of publicly owned sports facilities; (b) purchases and maintenance of sports equipment for local parks and recreation departments; and (c) bidding for organization of various sports events.

The construction and maintenance of publicly owned sports facilities includes the money spent by all levels of government, from federal to local, on constructing public assembly facilities that may be used for various sports functions (e.g., arenas, civic centers, stadiums, recreational sports complexes) and on remodeling or renovating existing sports facilities. In the past decade alone, it is estimated that 30 new public assembly facilities have been built for the use of professional sports teams at a cost of more than $4 billion (Bernstein, 1998). It was estimated by the *SportsBusiness Journal* that more than $660 million public funds were spent on sport facilities to be used by professional sports franchises in 2005. It accounted for about 82% of the total funds needed to build those facilities (Fish, 2005). Even though public funding for new facilities has become a controversial issue, many government officials still strongly embrace the argument that new stadiums will create jobs and attract professional sports teams to their communities and that the presence of a professional sports team will significantly boost the economy of the involved community. Accordingly, officials have done many desperate things to lure a professional sports team or to keep it in their community. Using public funds to build and maintain sports facilities has become a common practice among those politicians. For example, in November 1996, voters in Houston, Miami, and Detroit approved bond issues worth almost $1 billion to construct new stadiums that would either keep their pro teams or lure new ones (Laing, 1996). In addition to spending a certain portion of its funds appropriated by local governments (i.e., the city council or county commission) on sports facilities, local public sports agencies, such as park and recreation departments, also use part of their budgets for purchasing and maintaining sports equipment (e.g., football and baseball helmets, basketball goals).

Sports events have been viewed as an economic catalyst that can generate a considerable amount of economic impact on the economy of a region, whether it is a metropolitan area or a relatively small community (see Chapter 7 for details about how to determine the magnitude of economic benefits brought about by a sports activity to a particular locale). All levels of government in the United States spend a portion of their tax revenues each year on bidding for sports events through a conduit like a sports commission or authority. For example, the County Commission of Palm Beach in Florida in 1999 designates 5% of the first three pennies raised from the 4% bed tax or so-called hotel occupancy tax to be allocated to a tourism development fund. This equals $172,000 a year (telephone communication, 1999).

NET SPORT EXPORTS

Net sport exports are the difference between sport exports and sport imports of a nation in a particular year. Due to the strong value of the dollar against that of foreign currencies, U.S. net sport exports have been negative in recent years. Sport exports refer to the amount of sales of sporting goods in foreign nations that are manufactured in the United States. The categories of such goods may include sportswear, footwear, fishing gear, bicycles, gym and exercise equipment, equipment and accessories for winter sports, water sports, track and field, camping, hunting guns, race cars, and so on. The world demand for certain American sporting goods has been in a state of constant growth because U.S. brands have an appealing image, especially among the younger population. This growth trend is demonstrated in Table 7-10. According to the Sporting Goods Manufacturers

Table 7-10. U.S. Sporting Goods Exports[4] (1989–2004)

Year	Value of Export (in billions)	% Change from Prior Year
1989	0.96	+38.1
1990	1.10	+14.4
1991	1.19	+ 8.1
1992	1.36	+14.4
1993	1.54	+12.9
1994	1.78	+15.5
1995	2.16	+21.4
1996	2.27	+ 5.3
1997	2.43	+ 6.8
1998	1.95	- 17.0
1999	1.80	- 7.7
2000	1.87	+ 4.4
2001	1.96	+ 4.3
2002	1.82	- 7.1
2003	2.00	+ 9.7
2004	2.11	+ 5.6

Source: Sporting Goods Manufacturers Association (2005). Press Release. Web: *www.sgma.com*.

[4]The statistics excluded the amount of exports in sports apparel, camping equipment, and other recreational equipment.

Table 7-11. U.S. Sporting Goods Imports (1989–2004)

Year	Total Imports (in billions)	% Change from Prior Year
1989	4.99	+ 2.4
1990	5.75	+15.2
1991	5.95	+ 3.6
1992	6.62	+11.2
1993	6.88	+ 4.6
1994	6.52	- 5.3
1995	6.80	+ 4.4
1996	7.22	+ 6.1
1997	7.86	+ 8.9
1998	7.61	- 3.2
1999	7.56	- 0.7
2000	8.09	+ 7.0
2001	8.05	- 0.5
2002	9.01	+11.9
2003	9.70	+ 7.7
2004	10.43	+ 7.5

Source: Sporting Goods Manufacturers Association (2005). Press Release. Web: *www.sgma.com*.

Association (2005), American sporting good companies exported approximately 960 million-dollars-worth of goods in 1989. Fifteen years later, the amount of sporting goods exported jumped to $2.11 billion in 2004, a 120% increase from 1989. The estimate did not include the amount of exports in sports apparels and other recreational sports equipment. The actual amount of exports would have been higher if sports apparel and recreational sport equipment were included in the calculation.

Approximately 77 percent of the sporting goods exported by American companies in 2004 were sold in such five countries alone, China, Taiwan, Canada, Mexico, and South Korea. China's share was the greatest, accounting for 58.9% (Sporting Goods Manufacturers Association, 2005). The increase in exports in American-made sporting goods is mostly due to the international expansion effort of U.S. sporting goods companies. They have been very aggressive in expanding into international markets and have fought for greater market shares. In addition to receiving revenues from sales of exported sporting goods, the American sport industry also takes in licensing fees from foreign companies that use the trademarks of American professional sports teams and leagues. According to Meek (1997), the United States obtained about $1 billion from licensing fees internationally.

Sport imports refer to the amount of sales in the United States of sporting goods that are manufactured in other nations. Table 7-11 shows U.S. sport imports from 1989 to 2004. As the table indicates, American companies bought about $4.99 and $10.43 billion worth of foreign-made sporting goods, respectively, in 1989 and 2004. According to the Sporting Goods Manufacturers Association (1997), China, Taiwan, and South Korea are three top contributors or import leaders. Together they provide about 54% of U.S. sport imports.

As mentioned above, the difference between sport exports and sport imports is net sport exports. According to data provided by Sporting Goods Manufacturers Association (2005), sport imports in the United States outnumber sport exports. The difference between sport exports and sport imports demonstrated an upward trend in the period from 1989 to 2004, from $4.03 billion in 1989 to $8.32 billion in 2004, an increase of 106%. The average difference over the past 15 years was $5.67 billion. The economic crises experienced by many countries in Asia, Europe, and South America have contributed greatly to the increase in sport imports in the United States in this decade. As long as the value of U.S. dollar is comparatively strong, the momentum of the sport imports will be high. Accordingly, net sport exports will continue to be on the negative side.

EXPENDITURES OF NON-SPORT BUSINESSES: A FIFTH COMPONENT OF GDSP?

Meek (1997) argues that a fifth category of GDSP, the expenditures of non-sport businesses (ENB), be added to the equation. The essence of the argument is that the expenditures of those non-sport businesses on sport sponsorships, advertisements, licensing rights, etc. should be attributed to the sport industry. The SBJ's 2002 estimate of the size of the sport industry also included several categories of expenditures by non-sport businesses in its calculation, such as sponsorships, advertising, etc. (King, 2002). Should such expenditures be treated as the fifth component of GDSP? The proponents insist that when we are discussing how critical the sport industry is to the nation's economy, it conceptually makes sense to include ENB in the equation, as many American businesses annually spend a portion of their budgets to advertise in sports-related events and to sponsor sports teams, events, and facilities. According to IEG (2003), the spending of corporations in the world on sponsorship in the areas of arts, attractions, causes, entertainment, festivals, and sports was about $24.9 billion in 2003. In North America alone, more than $9 billion was spent in sport sponsorships and it is ranked higher than all other major categories, such as entertainment tours and attractions, and festivals, fairs, and annual events (IEG, 2003). Global business giants, like Coke, Kodak, Gillette, Anheuser-Busch, UPS, and Visa, have continued their efforts to develop further bonds with sports, and to "create corporate power bases that derive their strength from the continuing popularity of sports as big business" (Burton et al., 1998, p. 8). The sum of sponsorships and advertising was $33.83 billion in the SBJ's model, or 17.38% of the estimated size of the sport industry ($194.64 billion). Other than spending millions of dollars on sport-related advertising and sponsorships, some American non-sport businesses invest part of their wealth to purchase Personal Seat Licenses (PSL) and luxury suites in various sports facilities.

Opponents believe that it is methodologically flawed to treat the expenditures of non-sport businesses on sport as the fifth component of GDSP, since the expenditures are the income of the firms and organizations in the sport industry from non-sport businesses. As discussed previously, the determination of GDSP can be done with the use of either the expenditure approach or the income approach. They should not be mixed in the calculation. However, for the sake of discussion of the economic significance of the sport industry, it can be examined alone and treated as a separate factor.

Jobs in the Sport Industry

The sport industry, to a certain extent, is labor intensive. In 1992, more than half a million people were employed by privately owned sports establishments (see Table 7-12 for details). This figure only indicates a small portion of the jobs created in the sport industry. If we assume that every $40,000 in consumer spending creates a job, $152 billion in GDSP (Meek, 1999) then translates into 3.8 million jobs. If the size of the sport industry was $194.64 billion, as the SBJ estimated in 2002, this would translate into 4.87 million jobs.

Table 7-12. Contributions of Sports Establishments[5] to the Economy of the United States (1992)

Types of Sports Establishments	Number	Receipts[6]	Employment[7]
Professional Baseball Clubs	141	827,388	8,233
Professional Football Clubs	35	528,356	4,129
Other Professional Sports Clubs	137	930,076	7,595
Sport Marketing and Event Management	772	1,210,376	14,167
Bowling Centers	6,093	2,845,043	95,701
Gymnasiums and Athletic Clubs	7,519	2,943,457	95,975
Physical Fitness Facilities	9,216	3,823,566	129,925
Public Golf Courses	3,780	2,338,748	42,348
Membership Sports and Recreation Clubs	7,275	5,018,717	124,632
Auto Racetracks	511	412,174	4,296
Horse Racetracks	130	2,210,666	28,252
Dog Racetracks	59	641,355	12,182
Roller Skating Rinks	1,636	336,465	16,720
Ice Skating Rinks	195	124,257	3,464
Total	37,499	24,190,644	587,619

Source: *1992 Census of Service Industries (taxable firms)—U.S.*, U.S. Census Bureau.

[5] An establishment is a single physical location at which business is conducted. The list does not include sports organizations related collegiate athletics, such as individual athletic departments and conferences, and other nonprofit sports organizations.

[6] Receipts refer to what customers pay for receiving the services rendered by those sports establishments. The number is in thousands.

[7] Employment refers to the number of people who are on the payroll of those sports establishments.

Summary

Because it is among the biggest industries in the United States in terms of the amount of sales, the sport industry is clearly a critical component in the U.S. economy. The Gross National Product (GNP) and the Gross Domestic Product (GDP) are two concepts that are used to measure the economic status of a nation. GDP consists of four components: personal consumption expenditures, gross private domestic investment, government purchases of goods and services, and net exports. Gross Domestic Sport Product (GDSP) is an industrial category of GDP, and it has four components. They are personal sports consumption, gross sport investment, government sport purchases, and net sport exports. The expenditures of non-sport businesses on sport has been proposed as the fifth component of GDSP and included in the estimate of GDSP in some studies. Other than just analyzing the amount of sales in the sport industry to determine its significance to the U.S. economy, the number of jobs it creates for the nation should also be given a close look to truly appreciate its economic importance.

Chapter Questions

1. Why is the sport industry viewed as a critical center of the economy?
2. Define both GDP and GNP and explain the difference between them.
3. Elaborate on each of the four components of GDP.
4. What is the basic rule that must be used in measuring GDP?
5. Discuss how to measure GDP using the so-called Factor Income Approach.
6. Explain why it is more complicated to estimate GDSP than GDP.
7. How many components compose GDSP?
8. What factors of personal expenditures must be considered in order to accurately estimate the amount of personal sports consumption?
9. What are the elements that contribute to the estimate of gross sport investment?
10. Explain what costs the government incurs in providing sport services that are included in the calculation of government sport purchases.
11. Using statistical data, explain why sport imports outnumber sport exports in the United States.
12. Why are the expenditures of non-sport businesses on sport part of the GDSP calculation formula? Explain.
13. Discuss how economically critical the sport industry is in terms of the number of people it employs.
14. Explain the importance and significance of sport globalization to the growth of the sport industry in the United States.

Learning Activities

1. Using the given numbers, calculate the GDSP of a nation.
2. Visit the web sites of the Bureau of Economic Analysis (www.bea.doc.gov), the Sporting Goods Manufacturers Association (www.sportlink.com/press_room/index.html), and the U.S. Census Bureau (www.census.gov) to obtain information on consumer expending on sports activities. Use the data to calculate the personal sport consumption in a certain year.

Chapter Eight

Economic Impact of Sport

Introduction

Economic Impact of Sport

The Grand Prix at XYZ Harbor will be held on Tybee Island on March 26. This will be the first time since 1920 that another race event comes back to the City of XYZ. Before the City decided to endorse and sponsor the event, local media debated heavily whether the city should spend taxpayers' money to renovate the long-abandoned race track. Proponents believe that the event can attract a large number of visitors and bring a considerable number of tourism dollars to the community. Although the city council finally decided to endorse the event and spend $1 million to upgrade the facility, most council members were not sure if it was a worthwhile endeavor. Accordingly, a sport management professor from a local university was asked to head a research team that would conduct an economic impact study on the event to provide City government with some justifications of the City's investment. What kind of information should the research team collect in order to make a proper estimate of the magnitude of the economic impact caused by the event?

Economic impact of sport refers to "the net change in regional output, earnings and employment that is due to new dollars flowing into the region from outside the region" (Humphreys & Plummer, 1995) as a result of hosting a sport tourism event or providing a sport or leisure activity (Turco, 1995). It is one of the topics extensively debated by sport economists in the last two decades. The debate focuses on whether or not a community will benefit economically (i.e., the net change in the economy of the region will be positive) through hosting a sport event or through subsidizing the construction of sports facilities to be used later by professional sports franchises. To understand the arguments of both sides of this debate, the sport management student must develop a working knowledge of what economic impact is and how such impact is measured. The following sections provide information about the theoretical foundation of economic impact research and the procedural steps in conducting an economic impact study in the sport industry.

Theoretical Foundation of Economic Impact Studies

The question of how to accurately measure the size of the economic impact of an event or facility on a community is one that economists have examined for more than 200 years (Yeh, 1997). Examinations have included attempts to use various mathematical models to quantify the size of effect, one of which was the famous input-output model developed by Leontief in the 1930s (Leontief, 1985).

THE INPUT-OUTPUT TECHNIQUE

The input-output model (I-O model) is a mathematical model used to estimate monetary flows between industrial sectors (e.g., the sporting goods manufacturers purchase all kinds of fabrics from the mills and factories in the same region that produces those fabrics to make sports and athletic apparels) in quantitative terms

(Slesinger, 1972) and measure the "interdependence among economic activities within a region" (Pomery, Uysal, & Lamberte, 1988, p. 282). This model is based on the notion that the production of output requires inputs. The inputs can be semi-manufactured goods, raw materials, or inputs of services supplied by the households or government. Having acquired inputs from other sectors, households, and government, a sector produces output and sells this either to the other producing sectors, to the final users such as households or government, to the residents of the other regions, or to other firms for investment purposes (Leontief, 1985). Let's use an example to illustrate this economic notion. The City of Savannah wants to build a new baseball stadium for the Savannah Sand Gnats, and a construction company is hired to do the project. To build the facility, the company needs to purchase a variety of semi-manufactured goods and raw materials, such as bricks, sand, steel, and cement from suppliers. It also needs to hire skilled workers (i.e., to purchase their services). If the company fails to acquire the needed construction materials and skilled workers from Chatham County, where Savannah is located, it has to seek them from other regions.

The essence of the I-O model is the double accounting principle. This means that the gross regional production can be accounted for by adding up the costs of raw materials (e.g., number of logs used to make baseball bats, number of tons of cement used in the stadium construction), intermediary inputs (e.g., strings purchased and used in assembling badminton racquets), as well as the labor and capital costs (e.g., salaries and wages paid to workers involved in producing those sporting goods and money invested by the owner of the sporting goods manufactory in machines and buildings). The gross regional production can also be accounted for by tracking the flows of output from sectoral sources to the destination of intermediary and final use (Leontief, 1996). In other words, the number of baseball bats and badminton racquets purchased by consumers or final users can also be used in calculating the gross regional production.

The application of the I-O model involves the use of a so-called I-O table that records various transactions among industrial sectors in a particular region. The table shows data collected from the sales and purchases of these sectors over a designated period, usually a calendar year. Table 8-1 is a simplified example of the I-O table (Yeh, 1997).

The inter-industrial purchases of the agricultural industry, the manufacturing industry, and the service industry, as Table 8-1 shows, compose both the intermediate inputs and outputs. The intermediate inputs are provided by various sectors within each of these three industries that sell intermediate products to other sectors within the same industries in a defined economy. On the other hand, the intermediate outputs are produced when inter-industrial purchases of intermediate or final products occur among sectors across these three industries. The primary inputs also include three components.

The first one involves the resources provided by household (e.g., the services rendered by workers) and the payments (i.e., salaries and wages) in return given back to them (P). The next component relates to the resources provided by government sectors and the payments received by them accordingly (T). For example, the City

Table 8-1. Simplified Input-Output Table

	Output						
	Intermediate Output			Final Output			Total Output
	Agriculture	Manufacturing	Service	Household Consumption	Government Purchase	Export	
Input							
Intermediate Inputs		[I]			[II]		
Agriculture	X_{11}	X_{12}	X_{13}	C_1	G_1	E_1	X_1
Manufacturing	X_{21}	X_{22}	X_{23}	C_2	G_2	E_2	X_2
Service	X_{21}	X_{23}	X_{33}	C_3	G_3	E_3	X_3
Primary Inputs							
P	P_1	P_2	P_3	PC	PG	PE	P
T	T_1	T_2	T_3	TC	TG	TE	T
I	I_1	I_2	I_3	IC	IG	IE	I
Total Inputs	X_1	X_2	X_3	C	G	E	X

of XYZ built a multipurpose convention/sport facility, which, in return, generates revenues (i.e., the payment received the government) for the City. Import of intermediate and final products is the third type of primary inputs to a defined economy. The primary inputs provide resources for intermediate or final demand in a defined economy. Consumption of households (C), government expenditures (G), and exports (E) make up the final outputs. A portion of the table shows the purchasing activities of these three sectors of the intermediate or final inputs (products) for final outputs (consumption) in a defined economy.

The information presented by an I-O table can be interpreted in three ways:

1. Exactly where an industrial sector obtains its inputs and where its product or output goes.

2. How the particular industrial sector links to others in the same region through its purchasing and sales activities.

3. How the resources from the input side flow to the output side and the payments flow from the output side to the input side.

The total inputs should always be equal to the total output; that is,

$$P + T + M = C + G + E$$
$$\text{or}$$
$$P + T = C + G + E - M$$

Where

$$P + T = \text{Gross regional income}$$
$$C + G + E - M = \text{Gross regional product.}$$

The I-O table is constructed in such a way that the rows record the output or sales distribution of an industrial sector and the columns show the purchases for each industrial sector of the regional economy. As a whole, the table highlights the relationships among industrial sectors in the region. Thus, the table includes information about all sales revenues, costs, and residual balancing items of profit, and it provides details about all the economic activities that have occurred in a region and the complete structure of its economy. The interdependence of all the industrial sectors can be expressed with a set of linear equations, the solution to which forms a matrix. Each element included in the matrix shows the direct, indirect, and induced changes in the output of a particular industry as a result of a change in the final demand of that industry (Pomeroy, Uysal, & Lamberte, 1988).

The solution of the I-O table can be expressed in a mathematical matrix notation

$$X = [I-A]^{-1} Y$$

Where

    X = total output necessary to support the final demand Y

Y = final demand

    $[I-A]^{-1}$ = a matrix of interdependency coefficients.

An I-O model usually consists of several of these matrices. From the matrices, multipliers are generated and used to measure the net change of economy in a given locale in three basic types of economic variables: output, earning, and employment.

MULTIPLIER AND MULTIPLIER EFFECT

As discussed above about the I-O model, industrial sectors in an economy are interdependent for inputs and resources. So any initial-round spending will stir up further rounds of respending of these initial dollars among industrial sectors within that economy. The initial round of spending in the context of sport generally comes from the spending of visitors to a sport event on such areas as lodging, food and beverage, and miscellaneous retails. Detailed discussion on how to measure the spending of visitors will be provided later in this chapter.

As Turco (1995) maintains,

> Visitors spending into an area does not stop as soon as the dollar has been spent . . . A portion of the dollar then re-circulates through the local economy before slowly leaking out to pay for basic purchases and supplies elsewhere. That portion of the respending that stays in the community is the multiplier effect and that portion that is lost to respending elsewhere is termed "leakage" (p. 1).

A multiplier can be understood as a "ratio of the total economic effect on a regional economy to the initial change" (Coughlin & Mandelbaum, 1991, p. 19), and it helps to trace the flows of respending of the money initially injected into the economy until its complete leakage out of the economy and to determine the interdependency among industrial sectors within the economy (Stynes, 1999a). In other words, a multiplier helps capture the secondary effect of the initial monetary injection. The larger a defined economy is, the more inter-industrial purchases among industrial sectors will be made within the economy, and therefore, the larger the multiplier will be. The multiplier is higher in a self-sufficient economy than in a small and specialized economy.

TYPES OF MULTIPLIERS

Three types of multipliers are used to estimate the magnitude of economic benefits as a result of a dollar injected from outside a defined economy. They are the output multiplier, the earning multiplier, and the employment multiplier. The output multiplier is also called the sales multiplier. An output multiplier estimates the total change in output of all industrial sectors in a defined economy by the addition of a dollar of final demand. The higher the interdependency among industrial sectors, the higher the multiplier will be. In other words, the degree to which the industrial sectors in an economy can satisfy each other's needs for intermediate or final products without relying on the industrial sectors outside this economy to furnish those intermediate or final products determines the size of the multiplier effect. An output multiplier of 2 means that an addition of $1 million in final demand will increase the total value of production or output in all industrial sectors of that particular economy by $2 million. The earning multiplier is sometimes referred to as the income multiplier. It indicates how much has changed in salaries and wages of households of a defined economy as a result of an additional dollar spent. The magnitude of this type of multiplier also depends on the degree of interdependency among industrial sectors in the given economy. The more self-sufficient it is, the higher the multiplier will be for the economy. An earning multiplier of 2.5 implies that $1 million spent may lead to the increase in wages and salaries of households in a defined economy by $2.5 million. The employment multiplier is used to estimate the change in employment (number of jobs created) in a defined economy due to the addition of new wealth. The interpretation of the employment multiplier differs in various I-O models. An employment multiplier of 12 could mean that for every $1 million spent, 12

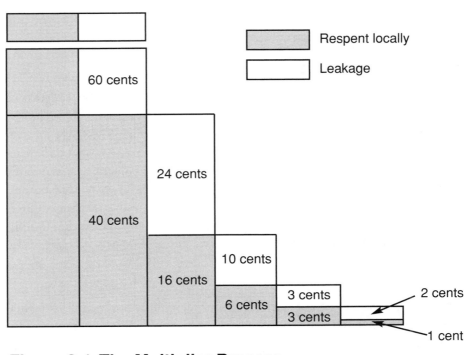

Figure 8-1. The Multiplier Process

full-time equivalent jobs are expected to be created in a defined economy. It could also mean that an increase in employment by one person in a particular industrial sector may create 12 full-time equivalent jobs in that economy overall.

Figure 8-1 illustrates the multiplier effect. As shown in Figure 8-1, for every dollar spent in a defined economy, 40 cents remain in it and 60 cents leak out of that economy through nonlocal taxes, nonlocal purchases, and income transfers. In the next round of respending, only 16 cents stay, and 24 cents go elsewhere. In the subsequent rounds of respending, the portion that remains in the economy becomes smaller and smaller until the money has completely left the economy. The change in total economic activity as a result of an additional dollar to the economy, thus, can be calculated as

$$\$1 + \$0.40 + \$0.16 + \$0.06 + \$0.03 + \$0.01 = \$1.66$$

The 1.66 is the multiplier. It means that $1.66 of total economic activity is created in that economy for each dollar of external input.

As far as whether households are included as part of the industrial system is concerned, two kinds of multipliers are respectively used. Type I multipliers exclude households in the interaction process among industrial sectors, and this type of multiplier considers households as part of the final demand. Type I multipliers treat the income or earning received by households as a leakage. If households become an integral part of the industrial system and their spending will be added to the total effect, the multiplier used is the Type II multiplier. The Type III multiplier is another type of multiplier that has been used in many economic impact studies. As a matter of fact, technically, the Type III multiplier is very similar to the Type II multiplier. The only difference is that the former treats households as exogenous and the latter considers households as a sector of the local economy.

The concepts of direct sales, indirect sales, and induced sales will be discussed in the following section.

ECONOMIC IMPACT MODELS

Derived from the input-output method, several economic impact models have been commonly used in measuring the size of economic impact of an event. The most common ones include the impact analysis for planning (IMPLAN), the regional input-output model system (RIMS II), and the travel economic impact model (TEIM). These models provide the researcher conducting an economic impact study with multipliers to be used to understand the effect on local output, earning, and employment. Researchers, however, must realize that some differences exist among these models and should exercise caution when trying to compare the results of impact studies that have used different models.

IMPLAN

The Forest Service of the U.S. Department of Agriculture has been instrumental in the construction of the IMPLAN model (Minnesota IMPLAN Group, 2000). Economic data from 528 intermediate industrial sectors, 12 final demand sectors, and six primary supply sectors are assimilated in the model in all U.S. counties.

Accordingly, this model can be used to generate economic data for regions (e.g., single counties, groups of counties, single state or group of states, and the entire United States) and compute input-output multipliers. The model was later extended by the Minnesota IMPLAN Group, Inc.

RIMS

Developed by the Bureau of Economic Analysis of the U.S. Department of Commerce, this model "contains a set of industry and area specific multipliers which allows one to determine the total impact of an exogenous change in spending on the local economy" (Division of Research, 1990, p. 4). Many economic impact studies conducted in the sport industry, including the one done to estimate the induced economic impact of the 1996 Atlanta Summer Olympic Games, have used this model to generate multipliers. According to the Bureau of Economic Analysis (1997), "the RIMS II multipliers can be estimated for any given region composed of one or more counties and for any industry, or group of industries, in the national I-O table" (p. 2). Two series of multipliers are provided by RIMS II. Series 1 multipliers are for 490 detailed industries, and Series 2 includes aggregated multipliers for 38 industries. Four tables are included in each series: Table 1 for final-demand output multipliers, Table 2 for final-demand earning multipliers, Table 3 for final-demand employment multipliers, and Table 4 for the summary of final-demand multipliers for output, earnings, and employment and direct-effect multipliers for earning and employment (Bureau of Economic Analysis, 1999).

REIM

The REIM model, developed by Regional Economic Models, Inc. of Amherst in Massachusetts, specifies commodity-trade and personal-income flows between regions. Forty-nine nonfarm private industrial sectors, three government sectors, and the farm sector are categories included in the model. REIM is constructed with the combination of an industry-based input-output component with an econometric component. Because of this feature, the model is relatively dynamic and can be used not only as an impact model, but also as a model for economic forecasting (Rickman & Schwer, 1993).

Estimating Economic Impact of Sport

Before attempting to estimate the magnitude of economic impact of a sport activity or service (e.g., a sport event) on a region, the researcher must develop a thorough grasp of the important concepts, issues, and procedures pertaining to how to properly conduct an economic impact study. Without such an understanding, it is impossible for him or her to render an accurate estimate. The following section will present these important concepts, issues, and procedures.

We can measure and examine the economic impact of a sport activity or service in two ways: the short-term impact and the long-term impact. All economic impact studies analyze the short-term effect, but only a few of them also consider the long-term benefits.

THE SHORT-TERM ECONOMIC IMPACT

The short-term economic impact mainly analyzes the expenditures of several groups of people associated with an activity, which may include the spending of the activity organizer and the spending of the activity participants, who include athletes, officials, media personnel, spectators, and other visitors. For some hallmark events (e.g., the Olympic Games), the short-term impact may also include the spending of various corporations in their promotion and marketing activities. The short-term impact is calculated through the determination of three subcategories of impacts: the direct impact, the indirect impact, and the induced impact. The sum of the direct, indirect, and induced impacts is the total short-term impact of a sport activity.

Direct Impact

The direct impact is the change in economic activity during the first round of spending by visitors. The direct impact is also referred to as "final demand"—the amount of direct economic activity generated by a sport activity or service. For example, money spent by the visitors to a regional golf tournament or the business sales to visitors by the involved industrial sectors signifies this type of impact.

Indirect Impact

The indirect impact is the changes in output, earning, and employment in other industrial sectors within the region due to their supplying of goods and services to the industrial sectors that receive money from visitors' initial round of spending. The industrial sectors usually affected by visitors' initial round of spending are hotels, restaurants, retail stores, and other entertainment-related businesses. During and/or after the event, these sectors restock themselves through some interindustrial purchases from other industrial sectors in the same region. For example, the hotel sector needs to restock its inventory in alcoholic products from various breweries. In short, the indirect impact examines the spending of the economic benefits felt by local businesses as an indirect result of the sport activity or event.

Induced Impact

The induced impact is the change in economic activity caused by local households who spend their income earned directly or indirectly from visitors as they purchase goods and services during a sport activity or event. For example, the employees of a local restaurant patronized by visitors during a golf tournament spend their income locally to buy groceries.

The sum of the indirect and induced impacts is sometimes collectively called the secondary or ripple effect of the sport activity or service. The sum of the direct impact, indirect impact, and the induced impact is the total impact of the sport activity or service on a given region or community.

When estimating the magnitude of the short-term economic impact for a hallmark event like the Olympic Games, the researcher should take account of the displacement or disturbance effect while calculating the total impact. The displacement effect refers to the reduction in tourism spending as a result of economic recession, strong and highly valued currency, negative publicity related to the travel and accommodation conditions of the host region, and altered vacation plans by visitors. For example, researchers examining the Los Angeles Summer Olympic Games subtracted some $331 million as displacement caused by the Games from the total economic impact.

THE LONG-TERM ECONOMIC IMPACT

The long-term economic impact refers to the long-term benefits (catalytic effects) that the host region would enjoy after a sport activity or event. Such an effect includes

1. The creation and development of new facilities,

2. The national and international recognition of the host city, state, and the nation due to extensive media exposure, and

3. The community benefits including local volunteerism, job creation and training, youth education programs, and funding for community economic development projects and cultural programs.

Table 8-2 shows the long-term economic impact of the 1996 Atlanta Summer Olympic Games on the City of Atlanta.

Table 8-2. Legacy of Olympic Venues (amounts in millions of dollars)

Facility	Total Investment	ACOG Share
Olympic Stadium	189	189
Georgia International Horse Park	90	28
Wolf Creek Shooting Complex	17	17
Stone Mountain Tennis Center	18	18
Lake Lanier Rowing Center	10	10
Georgia Institute of Technology		
Dormitories	194	47
Natatorium	24	21
Alexander Memorial Coliseum	1.5	1.5
Atlanta University Center	51	51
Stadiums—Morris Brown College/Clarke Atlantic University	37	37
Basketball Arena—Morehouse College	11	11
Tennis Facility—Spelman College	1	1
Drug Testing Center—Morehouse School of Medicine	1	1
Interdenominational Theological Center	0.8	0.8
Georgia State University		
Gymnasium Renovation	2	2
Clayton County International Park	3	0
TOTAL	**599.3**	**384.3**

Source: Atlanta Committee for the Olympic Games, HE Advisors and The Selig Center for Economic Growth, Terry College of Business, The University of Georgia (June, 1995).

Note: Values shown only include portion of project budget dedicated to construction/renovation of permanent facilities.

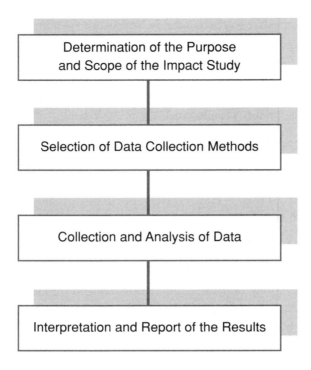

Determination of the Purpose
and Scope of the Impact Study

Selection of Data Collection Methods

Collection and Analysis of Data

Interpretation and Report of the Results

Figure 8-2. Steps in Conducting Economic Impact Studies

STEPS IN CONDUCTING ECONOMIC IMPACT STUDIES

Economic impact studies, like many other forms of research inquiry, require the researcher to follow a systematic and ordered sequence of activities. These steps include

Step 1: Determination of the purpose and scope of the impact study

Step 2: Selection of data collection methods

Step 3: Collection and analysis of data

Step 4: Interpretation and report of the results

Figure 8-2 portrays these four steps.

Determination of the Purpose and Scope of the Impact Study

The determination of the purpose and scope of the impact study is the most important step in conducting a sport economic impact study. This step involves three tasks: (a) determination of a cause of impact, (b) definition of a source or sources of impact, and (c) determination of an impact region.

The researcher first needs to determine what causes the net economic changes to the region. In some economic impact studies in recreation and tourism, "action" is used as the interchangeable term as the activity that causes economic change (Stynes, 1999b). Without clearly delineating the cause of the impact, it is impossible to properly collect the necessary information. The impact could be caused by

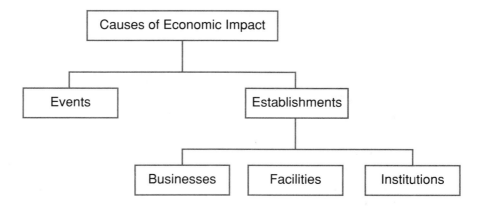

Figure 8-3. Causes of Economic Impact

a short-term sport activity or event, lasting from a day to a week. It could also be caused by a sport activity or event that lasts longer than a year. The Super Bowl, the NCAA Basketball Final Four, and the Indianapolis 500 are examples of short-term sports activities or events. On the other hand, the Summer and Winter Olympic Games are examples of sport activities or events that take longer than a year for the organizer to prepare and produce. The preparation usually includes the formation of various functional departments and units, intensive promotion of the event, and massive construction of facilities and infrastructures. The impact of this type of long-term activity or event may last a number of years.

An economic impact study can also be used to determine the magnitude of the net change in the local economy of a community caused by a sport-related establishment, such as a business enterprise, a facility, or an institution. Professional sports franchises have been considered instrumental in stimulating economic development in their host communities (Office of Business and Economic Research, 1995). A facility, such as a sports stadium, an arena, or a convention center, can also be an economic energizer for the local community within which it resides. Both types of establishments affect the net economic changes of a community by attracting tourist dollars. In addition, an athletic department, as part of an educational institution, can bring economic benefits to its host district. For example, it was estimated that the economic impact of the athletic programs at the University of Georgia on the economy of the Athens metropolitan statistical area (MSA) was about $44.6 million in 1998. Figure 8-3 helps to illustrate the various causes of economic impact.

As discussed previously, to actually determine the magnitude of the economic benefits brought about by an activity or event, researchers must collect information pertaining to the kinds of spending by various parties involved in the activity (Stynes, 1999b)—for example, the amount spent by visitors before, during, and after the event in the region where the activity is held and the amount of money spent by the government of the host community on the activity. In general, the information is listed in two categories: the primary source and the secondary source. Due to the difference in cause of impact, the information needed in making impact estimation varies from study to study. Nevertheless, some items, such as number of visitors, visitors' expenditures, length of visit, size of each visitor group, their demographic, and expenditures of organizers, seem to be generic and sought after in almost all impact research.

An impact region refers to a geographic area over which the economic impact will be measured. As mentioned previously, the impact brought about by the provision of a sport activity refers to the total economic change in a local community as a result of the activity. Therefore, the determination of the size of the community, or the so-called impact region, is considered another critical step in designing appropriate economic impact research, because the magnitude of the economic impact varies with the breadth of the region (Beck, Elliott, Meisel, & Wagner, 1995). The size of the impact region may have a considerable impact on the calculation accuracy of the total economic change caused by the injection of "new money" by visitors in that particular community.

An estimate of the overall impact can be accomplished by using various multipliers (e.g., output, earning, employment) derived from an input-output model. The application of such a model requires a clear definition of the geographic area or region. The greater the area, the more economic interactions and interrelationships among involved industries will exist; therefore, the output and earning multipliers will be higher, and subsequently, the impact will be greater. Studies examining the economic benefits of activities in recreation and tourism usually use a 30- to 60-mile radius to define the impact region (Stynes, 1999b). The U.S. Travel Data Center defines a visitor as "one who travels a minimum of 100 miles away from home within the United States or stays one or more nights in paid accommodations regardless of the distance away from home" (Frechtling, 1994).

Selection of Data Collection Methods

Once the purpose and scope of an economic impact study (i.e., the cause and source of impact and the impact region are determined) is clearly defined, the next step in the planning process of the study is to determine the most appropriate and comprehensive method or approach for data collection. As indicated previously, the investigator may wish to investigate several important sources of impact. Nevertheless, the decision regarding what data to collect and how to collect them should be based on what the researcher wants to accomplish in a particular impact study as well as on the availability of resources (Delpy & Li, 1998). The methodology adopted by the researcher dictates the kind of information to be collected. In general, there are two ways to estimate the magnitude of the economic impact: the survey methods and nonsurvey method (Behavior Research Center, 1993; Datapol, Inc., 1988; Division of Research, 1990; Fleming & Toepper, 1990; Murphy & Carmicheal, 1991; Schaffer & Davidson, 1975; Turco, 1993, 1995; Wang & Irwin, 1993).

The survey method is commonly used in economic impact studies in sport. It is a research technique in which data are collected from a sample of visitors, such as spectators and participants, by using a questionnaire. From the responses, researchers usually obtain information about visitors' expenditures and their demographic characteristics. Visitors' expenditures are considered the basic compo-

Table 8-3. Summary of the Merits and Shortcomings of Various Survey Methodologies

Methods	Merits	Shortcomings
Survey		
On-site interview	Opportunity for feedback	Cost
	High participation	Labor intensive
	High completion of survey	Projection bias
Telephone interview	Opportunity for feedback	Cost
	Absence of face-to-face contact	Sample bias
Self-administered survey	Recall and response bias	
On-site self drop-off survey	Low labor intensity	Low return rate
	No interviewer bias	Response and projection bias
Mail survey	Low labor intensity	Low return rate
	No interviewer bias	Recall and response rate
	A representative sample	Cost
Expenditure logs or diaries	Most reliable and accurate	High mortality rate
		Low response rate
Non-survey method		
Interview with event/facility or business managers/owners	Pre-event	Attribution error
	Low cost	Accessibility to private records
Public tax records	Low cost	Time delay
		Limited information

Source: This table is modified from the one developed by Turco (Turco, D. W. [1995]) "Measuring the Economic Impact of a Sporting Event," paper presented at the 1995 North American Society for Sport Management Annual Conference, Athens, GA).

nents in estimating the total economic wealth injected by the visitors into a particular community or region. In practice, the survey method consists of four data-collection approaches: on-site interview, telephone interview, self-administered survey, and expenditure logs. Table 8-3 summarizes the merits and shortcomings of various survey methods.

On-site interviews are conducted in some high-traffic areas (e.g., entrances and exits, spectator seating areas, concession stands). There, interviewers intercept visitors to collect the needed research data. Telephone interviews are often conducted after an activity or event. Based on the information obtained from registration, such as the home address and phone number, the interviewer randomly identifies some visitors and interviews them over the phone. The interviewees are asked to recall and provide information about their spending associated with the activity. Self-administered survey is implemented by placing questionnaires in several high-traffic areas, including the entrances and exits, concession stands, and information booths around the event site. A certain incentive is used to encourage visitors to complete the survey instruments. Expenditure logs and diaries are also utilized by researchers in various economic impact studies. Prior to the activity, the surveyor identifies and contacts a number of visitors to determine their willingness to participate in an economic impact survey. Again, an incentive is generally offered. Those who agree to cooperate are asked to keep track of their expenditures with a diary over the period of their visit to the region where the activity is held and to mail the diary back to the surveyor after returning home (Delpy & Li, 1998). The appendix to this chapter shows a sample questionnaire used to collect data on visitors' expenditures while attending a sport event.

Although the nonsurvey method, sometimes also referred as the eco-metric method, is adopted to determine the impact figure, various means are utilized to obtain data to use in estimating the generated benefits that accrue to economic areas in the form of payroll, employment, and taxes (Fleming & Toepper, 1990; Pomeroy, Uysal, & Lamberte, 1988; Stynes, 1999b). No surveys are needed. Instead, the data are mainly obtained from secondary sources of information (e.g., government sources and similar studies). One example of the nonsurvey method is the so-called LOCI model or the Local Area Impact Model developed by the Georgia Tech Economic Development Institute. The LOCI model incorporates two sets of secondary local data into impact calculation: community-related data and project-related data. The community-related data include

- Taxes (sales, personal and real property, business, alcohol, income);

- Utility information (water, wastewater, solid waste removal, electric, natural gas);

- Retail activity (effective buying income);

- Demographic information (disposable income, number in household, employment);

- Economic base information (discount rate, total personal income); and

- Tourism-related information (lodging excise tax rate, revenue and value added for tourism-related industries) (Kanters, 1999, p. 6)

The following are project-related data:

1. Information on the construction of the facility (materials, labor, percentage local purchases, development subsidies);

2. Operation of the facility (sales, percentage of sales subject to sales taxes);

3. Specific multipliers for income and employment calculated for the industry in question and the county under investigation (input-output model);

4. Utility rates and consumption;

5. Employee characteristics; and

6. Tourism information (number of visitors, duration of stay, average of daily expenditures) (Kanters, 1999, p. 7)

The tourism-related information is estimated through comparisons of the facility studies with those of similar facilities. The major advantage of the nonsurvey method is that it eases the difficulty in estimating the economic impact of hall-

Table 8-4. Methods/Approaches to Economic Impact Assessment

Level	Activity	Spending	Multiplier
1—Judgment	Expert judgment to estimate activity	Expert judgment	Expert judgment to estimate multipliers
2	Existing counts for the area or total estimates from a similar area or facility	Use or adjust spending averages from studies of a similar area	Use or adjust aggregate spending multipliers from a similar region/study
3	Estimate activity by segment or revise estimates by segment from another area	Adjust spending that is disaggregated within particular spending categories	Use sector-specific multipliers from published sources
4—Primary Data	Visitor survey to estimate number of visitors by segment or a demand model	Survey random sample of visitors to estimate average spending by segment and spending category	Use an input-output model of the region's economy

Source: Stynes, D. J. (1999). Economic impacts of tourism. *Bulletins on Concepts and Methods*, Department of Parks, Recreation, and Tourism Resources, Michigan State University, East Lansing, Michigan.

mark events, such as the Olympic Games, on the host region. Due to the scale of those events in terms of the number of participants, spectators, and other types of visitors, it is uneconomical and difficult, if not impossible, to use the survey methods for obtaining the needed expenditure data. Nevertheless, using the non-survey method requires the provision of detailed input information for accuracy in estimation (Wang & Irwin, 1993). Table 8-4 provides brief descriptions of four basic methods or approaches of data collection in economic impact analysis in terms of how to collect needed expenditure information and how to derive multipliers for analysis and estimation.

Collection and Analysis of Data

Because the survey method is the most frequently used in the economic impact research in sport, we will mainly discuss how to use this method in the data collection and analysis section. Information regarding the number of visitors to the region, the size of each visitor group, and, on average, the amount each visitor group has spent in such categories as lodging, food and beverage, local transportation, entertainment, admission to the event, and miscellaneous retails must be collected through a survey. Once the needed data have been collected, a series of computations are followed. First, the total expenditure of visitors in each spending category needs to be determined using the two formulas shown below (Turco, 1996):

$$\text{Total Categorical Expenditure} = \text{ADS} \times \text{Number of Groups} \times \text{Average Number of Days}$$

Where

$$\text{Average Daily Spending} = \text{The average daily spending of all visitor groups in each concerned category, such as lodging, food and beverage, etc.}$$

Number of Groups = The number of groups of visitors

Average Number of Days = The average number of days all visitor groups stayed in the impact region

Dividing the total number of visitors by the average group size, we can obtain the number of visitor groups. The average number of days that all visitor groups stayed in the impact region is determined by dividing the total number of days they stayed by the number of visitor groups. The sum of the total categorical expenditure of all concerned spending categories is the total direct impact.

Total Direct Impact = Σ Categorical Expenditures (Lodging, Food & Beverage, Retails, Entertainment, Local transportation, . . .)

Determining the secondary effects is the next step if the researcher is interested in the ripple effects of visitor spending, or the effects of the sum of the indirect and induced impacts. The ripple effects are determined by multiplying the total categorical expenditures with respective multipliers obtained either from an input-output model (e.g., IMPLAN) or from published studies done in the same region. As we know, the total economic impact is usually estimated in three areas: (a) total output, (b) total earning, and (c) total employment.

Total Output = Σ Categorical Expenditure $\times$ Respective Output Multiplier (Lodging, Food & Beverage, Retails, Entertainment, Local transportation, . . .)

Total Earning = Σ Categorical Expenditure $\times$ Respective Earning Multiplier (Lodging, Food & Beverage, Retails, Entertainment, Local transportation, . . .)

Total Employment = Σ Categorical Expenditure $\times$ Respective Earning Multiplier (Lodging, Food & Beverage, Retails, Entertainment, Local transportation, . . .)

The process may be understood better with an example. The calculation of the total visitor spending in a golf tournament held recently in Savannah yields a total spending of $4 million in lodging, $3.5 million in food and beverage, and $1.5 million in retail shopping. The secondary effects of visitor spending, or the sum of the indirect

Table 8-5. The Secondary Effects of the Spending of Visitors to the Savannah Open Golf Tournament

Expenditure Category	Total Spending	Indirect Effect[1]	Induced Effect[2]	Output Multiplier[3]	Total Output
Lodging	$4,000,000	$1,161,160	$1,623,452	1.699893	$ 6,799,572
Food & Beverage	$3,500,000	$1,029,102	$1,420,521	1.699893	$ 5,949,636
Retail Shopping	$1,500,000	$ 441,044	$ 608,795	1.699893	$ 2,549,840
Total	$9,000,000	$2,631,306	$3,652,768		$15,299,048

Notes: 1. The indirect effect coefficient is 0.294029.
2. The induced effect coefficient is 0.405863.
3. It is a Type II output multiplier.

and induced impacts of the spending on total output, are shown in Table 8-5. As Table 8-5 indicates, the total direct spending of visitors to the golf tournament is $9 million. As a result of considering the production changes resulting from various rounds of respending of the money by the affected industries (e.g., hotels, restaurants, and retail stores) and the changes in economic activity resulting from the spending of income by the employees of the affected industries, the total output or impact becomes over $15 million. The difference between the total direct spending and the total output, or approximately $6 million, is the secondary effect.

In addition to estimating the impact created by the spending of visitors in total output, total earning, and total employment of the affected region, the researcher should look at the local sales tax impact to obtain a comprehensive view on the effect of a sport activity or event. The local sales tax impact can be felt from three main areas: retail, lodging, and gasoline. Due to the difference in tax rates, the local sales tax impact in each of these three areas must be calculated separately. Their sum is the total local sales tax impact. The calculation usually follows such a formula:

$$\text{Revenue}_{Retail} = \text{Total Spending of Visitors in Retail} \times \text{Local Sales Tax Rate}$$

$$\text{Revenue}_{Lodging} = \text{Total Spending of Visitors in Lodging} \times \text{Local Hotel Occupancy Tax Rate}$$

$$\text{Revenue}_{Gasoline} = \text{Total Spending of Visitors in Gasoline} \times \text{Local Gasoline Sales Tax Rate}$$

$$\text{Total Local Sales Tax Impact} = \text{Revenue}_{Retail} + \text{Revenue}_{Lodging} + \text{Revenue}_{Gasoline}$$

For example, the visitors to the 1997 World Series champions of the North American Gay Amateur Athletic Alliance held in San Francisco spent roughly $658,000 on lodging, and the tax rate for hotel accommodation is 16%. So the tax revenue from the visitors is $105,280.

Turco (1995) suggests using the "return on investment" (ROI) to examine the financial return of spending by the government of a community on a certain sport activity or event if it is organized by a unit of the government, such as the parks and recreation department. The return on investment is estimated with the following formula:

$$ROI = (ER + LTR)/EE$$

Where

ER = Event Revenue
LTR = Local Tax Revenue Generated
EE = Event Expenditures

For example, the parks and recreation department of the City of Athens/Athens County in July 2003 sponsored a state softball tournament from which the department generated $34,000 in operating revenue. Visitors from all over the state brought in $2,400 tax revenue. For preparing the tournament, the parks and recreation department spent $32,000. The ROI in this case is 114%, or add $34,000 and $2,400 and then divide the sum by $32,000. The return on investment has been used by many local sport organizations as leverage for receiving discounted services from other local government units, such as police and emergency medical rescue (Turco, 1995).

Interpretation of the Data or the Total Impact

After completing tedious calculations to determine the magnitude of the impact on output, earning, and employment, the researcher must present this information in language that concerned individuals, such as local politicians and the management of a sports event, can understand. Those people usually do not have adequate training and or background to comprehend the abstract impact numbers. Interpreting the results is an important task that the researcher should not overlook. The interpretation should focus on total output, total earning, and total employment and should explain what they mean. Table 8-6 shows the economic impact of the 1990 MCI Heritage Classic on the Hilton Head area (The Division of Research, 1990).

As Table 8-6 indicates, the direct spending of the two spending categories is $13,652,878. The total output, total earning, and total employment effects are $18,988,183, $6,029,097, and 616, respectively. That means, as a result of the approximately $13.7 million spent by visitors (both the out-of-town attendees and the event sponsors' patrons) in Hilton Head Island as final demand, the total value of production or output in all industrial sectors of that economy increased by about $19 million, or a 1:1.39 ratio. That is, for every new dollar injected, the production of the industries on the island as a whole increased 39 cents in their output. The $6,029,097 is the change in wages and salaries of households in Hilton Head Island as a result of the spending of $13,652,878 by visitors. The $13.7 million is the new wealth injected into the area, which may have some impact on the earning of local residents. As the region gains more wealth, its residents may expect some increase in their income. The total employment effect implies that 616 full-time equivalent (FTE) jobs could be created in Hilton Head due to the addition of new money in amount of $13.7 million. These could be full-time, part-time, or seasonal jobs.

Table 8-6. Economic Impact of the 1990 MCI Heritage Classic on Hilton Head Island[1]

Spending Category[2]	Spending Level	Output Effect	Earning Effect	Employment Effect
Classic Tournament Attendees	$12,267,778	$16,742,110	$5,306,373	544
Sponsors and Patrons	1,385,100	2,246,073	722,724	72
Total	**$13,652,878**	**$18,988,183**	**$6,029,097**	**616**

Notes: 1. The results are obtained from the study entitled "The Economic Impact of the MCI Heritage Classic on the Economy of Hilton Head Island, South Carolina" conducted by the Division of Research, College of Business Administration at the University of South Carolina, Columbia, South Carolina.
2. This table includes only the spending of tournament attendees, and sponsors and patrons.

SIGNIFICANCE OF ECONOMIC IMPACT STUDIES

When an economic impact study should be conducted and why it should be conducted are two questions that have come to the attention of many concerned economists in the sport, tourism, and other related industries due to the growing in popularity of studies of this type. Commonly, economic impact studies in the sport industry are conducted for four reasons (Bernthal & Regan, 2004; Crompton, 1995; Delpy & Li, 1998; Turco, 1995):

1. To examine the cost and benefits of an economic endeavor or financial investment to determine if it is worthwhile. For example, the advocates in Tampa, Florida, who supported the use of public funds to build the Raymond James Stadium for the Tampa Bay Buccaneers may conduct an economic impact study to justify their position. Through the study, they could find such information as the increased number of visitors to the area and the increased local business sales. On the other hand, the City of Tampa and surrounding counties can also use the study to justify their decision in public subsidies by showing the amount of "new dollars" injected into the community as a result of building the facility.

2. To use the results of an economic impact study to influence legislators and lobby for more legislative support. It is common for a local park and recreation department to use the results of an economic impact study to justify its request for increasing local budget appropriation. The impact study may provide the department with information in terms of how many out-of-town teams visited and used its facility, how long the visiting teams stayed on average, and how much the local businesses have benefited from those visiting teams. Bernthal and Regan (2004) summarize this reason by stating that the local government can leverage the success, and therefore political and financial support of the event (p. 26), with the information provided by an economic impact study.

3. To raise public awareness of the importance of the sport industry. An economic impact study can help city or county government officials or the local business community develop an understanding pertaining to what the sport industry as a whole can do to the region's economy so that the government and the private sector can work together to use the sport industry to its full potential.

4. To provide sponsorship justification to both potential and existing sponsors (Bernthal & Regan, 2004). The information provided by an economic impact study can be used to persuade potential sponsors about the worthiness of developing an association with the event through a sponsorship. For example, the information collected from the impact study that is useful to any sponsor includes the number of event attendees and/or spectators, their demographics, etc. To the existing sponsors, the information serves the purpose of self-justification.

COMMON ERRORS IN SPORT ECONOMIC IMPACT STUDIES

Many errors have been found in sport economic impact studies. For example, in order to get the total output impact, some researchers simply multiply the total number of visitors by the output multiplier. The following section will specifically discuss several of the commonly detected errors (Crompton, 1995; Stynes, 1999b).

Not Clearly Defining a Cause or Action

The basic purpose of an economic impact study is to estimate the net change in the affected economy due to the injection of "new money." To properly attribute the change in economy, the cause of the injection should be determined first. In determining the reason for the change, the researcher must decide if the study only focuses on the spending by visitors or also on the spending of the event organizer for capital improvement and on the spending by government, etc. This is especially true when the impact study is done for a hallmark event like the Olympic Games. The organizer, such as the Atlanta Committee for Olympic Games (ACOG), usually spends a considerable amount of money on construction or renovation of sport facilities (capital improvement). Part of the funds used for that purpose might be obtained from outside the designated region (e.g., a bank loan or prepaid sponsorships).

Not Clearly Defining an Impact Region

One crucial step in conducting an economic impact study is to define the impact region. As we know, the major purpose of an economic impact study is to estimate the economic benefits that accrue to a host community by visitors. So the definition of a region would provide a researcher with clues to determine who are visitors and who are local residents so that the researcher can separate visitor spending from local resident spending. Without clearly defining the impact region, such a separation would become an impossible task. The inclusion of local spending inflates the impact attributed to a sport activity. Defining the size of a region is another related issue. The smaller the region, the more likely it is for some local residents to be regarded as visitors.

Using Inappropriate Multipliers

Multipliers have been used by various economic impact studies inappropriately in many ways. The most common error is to adapt a statewide multiplier to a local region, which may inflate the ripple or secondary effect because the statewide multiplier is always bigger (sometimes substantially bigger) than that of a particular locale within the state, and the economy of a state is always larger than that of the locale. As mentioned earlier, the larger a defined economy, the more inter-industrial purchases will occur among industrial sectors within the economy. The more interactions there are among industrial sectors, and the more self-sufficient the economy is (less leaking of the injected money), the larger the multiplier. The multiplier is always higher in a self-sufficient economy than in a small and special-ized economy.

Misinterpreting Employment Multipliers

Many economic impact studies attempt not only to estimate the total spending by visitors and its direct effect on the concerned region, but also to convert the esti-mate on total spending by visitors to income and employment. This conversion may yield such approximation in terms of how much income is generated and how many employment opportunities are created as a result of organizing a sport activity or providing a sport service. For example, the multiplication of the total spending by visitors with an aggregated employment multiplier suggests that an annual sport event may create 100 jobs in the economy. This number, however, needs to be interpreted very carefully. These jobs are not full-time equivalents, but seasonal and part-time. The demand for labor for an event of this type is usually met by the local existing labor force or by volunteers. Local residents may work overtime or use their vacation hours to work for the event. Exaggeration of the number of "full-time equivalent" jobs created by a sport activity has been seen as another common error.

Not Isolating Spending by Visitors from Spending by Local Residents

In estimating the impact magnitude of a sport activity or event to the economy of a host community, some studies have included the spending of local residents in their calculation. This inclusion inflates the economic benefits brought about by a sport activity because the monies spent by local residents in the impact region are not "new dollars" to the region. If the residents had not spent the money on the activity, they would have used it in other ways or for other forms of entertain-ment in the region. If a study wants to determine the economic significance of a sport activity, the spending of local residents with the event can be obtained. The data, however, should be interpreted separately.

Including All Spending by Visitors in Impact Calculation

If an economic impact study includes the spending by visitors on purchases made outside the impact region, such as the spending on side-trips out of the designated region during an event, the impact figure would be incorrectly inflated. For exam-ple, a family of four from Michigan attended the MCI Classic-Heritage of Golf Tournament held in Hilton Head Island for a week. While staying in Hilton Head, they took a side-trip to Savannah and spent a day there. The expenditure incurred from the Savannah trip should be excluded from the calculation of the family's total spending attributed to the tournament. Another mistake often made related to the inclusion of all spending by visitors is including in the calculation some money that visitors pay for the trip to the region where the activity is held. The money in most cases will not be allocated back to the impact region. A good example is the package deal for an event that includes a round-trip airline ticket, a couple nights of hotel accommodation, and a ticket to the event. It is very difficult, if not impossible, to determine how much or what portion of the money will be paid by the travel agency to affected businesses in the designated region. Inclusion in entirety of the payment for the package again exaggerates the actual benefit received by the region. The error most commonly committed by researchers in economic impact studies is to include all retail spending without taking consideration of the price paid by the retailer to get the goods from outside the region. For instance, while attending the MCI Classic-Heritage of Golf Tournament, a visitor bought a t-shirt from a local retailer for $50. The retailer, in fact, only paid $20 to get the shirt from a wholesaler in Atlanta. So the actual injection of "new dollars" is the difference of the retail price and the wholesale cost, or $30. It is believed that only 60–70% of visitors' spending can be considered as final demand in a region (Stynes, 1999b).

Summary

In this chapter, we provided information about how to properly conduct an economic impact study. The theoretical foundation of economic impact studies—the input-output technique—was first discussed and examined, followed by a detailed description of the procedural steps in terms of how to execute an economic impact study. These steps include (a) determination of the purpose and scope of the impact study, (b) selection of data collection methods, (c) collection and analysis of data, and (d) interpretation and report of the results. In this chapter, we also explained why researchers conduct economic impact studies as well as the common errors committed in executing economic impact research.

Chapter Questions

1. Discuss the nature of the I-O technique and explain why it is the theoretical foundation of economic impact research.
2. Discuss the multiplier effect.
3. List three types of multipliers that are commonly utilized in economic impact research and explain what each of them means.
4. List and define three components of the short-term economic impact.
5. Compare and contrast the merits and shortcomings of the four types of survey methods used in the economic impact studies in sport.
6. Explain how to determine the induced and total impacts.
7. Why conduct an economic impact study? Give at least three reasons.

Learning Activities

1. Return to the beginning of the chapter, and reread the scenario. Assume you are the professor who is in charge of the research project. What kind of information would you collect?
2. Conduct an economic impact study on one local sports event that may have "non-resident" participants and/or spectators to determine the magnitude of its economic impact on the local community.
3. Compile several economic impact studies done for sports facilities and events, and make comparisons in methods, sources of information, and multipliers used in their studies.

Appendix

XYZ PGA Golf Tournament/Economic Impact Survey

Hello, my name is (Surveyor Name) . I am helping the organizer of the *XYZ PGA Golf Tournament* determine the economic impact of the event on the economy of the City of XYZ. May I ask, are you from XYZ? (If the interviewee says no, you may continue your interview with this question: Can I take five minutes of your time to ask you some questions? If the answer is yes, you may stop the interview and say, Thank you very much.)

1. Where are you from? _____ , _____
                             Name of the Place   State

2. How many nights have you stayed in XYZ? _____

3. Are you going home today? Yes _____   No _____

If no, how many more nights will you stay in XYZ? _____

4. Is the event your primary reason to visit XYZ?
     Yes _____ No _____ (please specify the reason _____)

5. What is the total number of people in your travel party including yourself?

_____

6. While staying in XYZ, how much on average did your travel party spend per day in each of the following categories?

Lodging . . . . $ _____
Food & Beverage . . . . $ _____
Miscellaneous retails . . . . $ _____
Entertainment . . . . $ _____
Local transportation (e.g., gas and taxi, etc.) . . . . $ _____
Other miscellaneous expenses . . . . $ _____

7. Demographics

Thank you very much for taking the time to answer my questions.

Chapter Nine

LABOR MARKETS AND SPORT

Introduction

Labor, capital, and land are three factors of production. They are used as inputs into production activities, and they generate income for their owners. Professional athletes, sales representatives of sporting goods retail stores, and employees of sports facilities are examples of labor, and they are critical contributors to the economy of the sport industry. This chapter examines labor as a factor of production in the sport industry. First, an overview of the market for labor and related important concepts will be provided. In the second half of the chapter, specific labor issues in the sport industry with particular emphasis on professional sports will be addressed.

The Demand for Labor

Labor is demanded as a factor of production to help produce goods and services. The demand for labor is a derived demand. The demand for labor is derived from the demand of consumers for the goods and services labor can produce. Health clubs demand aerobics instructors because of consumer demand for aerobics classes. An increase in the demand for aerobics classes will increase the demand for aerobics instructors.

The productivity of labor for producing those goods and services consumers desire is a second critical determinant of the demand for labor. The productivity of labor is influenced by the education and training of labor, technology, and the use of other factors of production. The use of capital will increase the productivity of labor. For example, a computerized production line for athletic shoes will increase the productivity of workers. By using machinery, a worker is able to assemble more shoes in a period of time than working without machinery.

Workers with education and training are likely to be more productive than workers who have not had access to education and training. Education and training enable workers to better use the available resources. Workers on a computerized production line for shoes must be trained in the use of the machinery. The technology of the capital available to workers will influence the productivity of labor. Advances in computer technology have increased the efficiency of shoe production by improving the operation of the assembly line, increasing worker productivity.

For a profit-maximizing firm, the demand for labor depends upon the marginal revenue product of labor. The marginal revenue product of labor is the change in revenue from hiring one more unit of labor. Marginal revenue product of labor depends on consumer demand for the product labor produces and the productivity of labor. For example, employing another worker in the shoe assembly line of a sporting goods factory will result in more shoes produced per hour, and these shoes in turn can be sold to generate revenue.

The demand for labor is the relationship between the wage rate and the number of workers a firm wishes to hire. The demand for labor shows the highest wage rate a firm would pay for an additional unit of labor. The most a firm will pay for another unit of labor is the worker's contribution to the firm's revenue. Since the additional revenue from another unit of labor is the marginal revenue product of labor, marginal revenue product of labor determines the highest wage a firm would pay for another unit of labor and the demand for labor. If hiring a third worker for the shoe assembly line would increase a firm's revenue by $50 a day, the most the firm would be willing to pay that worker is $50 a day.

Table 9-1 shows how to calculate the marginal revenue product of labor. Assume the XYZ Sporting Goods Factory has recently developed a new line of bicycles called "Rock" and can sell as many as it makes to the sporting goods retail stores nationwide at a price of $80 a bicycle. The first three columns provide information on the productivity of labor at making bicycles. The marginal product of labor (shown in column three) is the change in output from hiring an additional unit of labor. The first worker increases total output (shown in column two) by five bicycles, the second worker increases total output by four bicycles, the third by three bicycles, the fourth by two bicycles, and the fifth worker by one bicycle.

Column four shows the total revenue the firm earned from selling bicycles. Total revenue is the product of the number of bicycles produced and sold multiplied by

Table 9-1. Marginal Revenue Product and Average Revenue Product at XYZ Sporting Goods Factory

Quantity of Labor (L) (number of workers)	Output (Q) (bicycles assembled per hour)	Marginal Product (MP) (bicycles assembled per worker)		Total Revenue (TR) (dollars)	Marginal Revenue Product (MRP) (dollars per worker)	Average Revenue Product (ARP) (dollars per worker)
0	0			0		
		 5			 400	
1	5			400		400
		 4			 320	
2	9			720		360
		 3			 240	
3	12			960		320
		 2			 160	
4	14			1120		280
		 1			 80	
5	15			1200		240

$80. For example, $1,200 would be the total revenue if 15 bicycles were assembled and sold.

The marginal revenue product of each worker in the bicycle assembly line is shown in the fifth column. It is the increase in total revenue from hiring another worker. As more workers are hired, the marginal revenue product of labor decreases. This decrease occurs because the marginal product of each additional worker falls. Each worker causes the production of bicycles to increase by less than the previous worker (see column three.). In general, as more variable input (such as labor) is added to production, the marginal product of that input will decline. The decline in marginal product as more input is added will cause a decline in marginal revenue product.

The marginal revenue product can also be calculated by multiplying marginal product (MP), shown in the third column, by marginal revenue (MR). Marginal revenue is the change in revenue from selling another unit. Since each bicycle can be sold for $80, the sale of each bicycle increases revenue by $80, so price equals marginal revenue for this firm. Multiplying the marginal product of the second worker, four bicycles, by the marginal revenue of $80 yields marginal revenue product of $320. The same answer can be derived by calculating the change in total revenue caused by the second worker.

If instead of changing labor by one unit at a time we are able to change the amount by any fraction of a unit of labor, we can diagram the marginal product of labor as a line. Since we expect the marginal product of labor to eventually

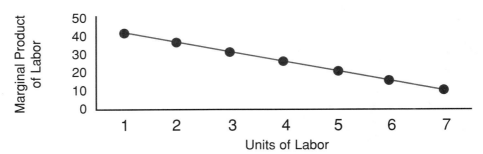

Figure 9-1. Marginal Product of Labor

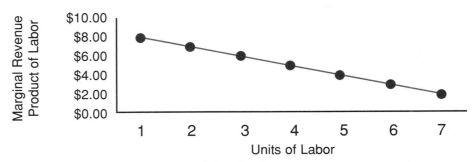

Figure 9-2. The Demand for Labor

Each unit of output may be sold for a constant price of $.20. $MRP_L = MP_L * \$.20$.

decline as more labor is used in the production process, the marginal product of labor may be represented as a downward sloping line as in Figure 9-1. If the marginal product of labor may be shown as a downward sloping line, so can marginal revenue product of labor, because marginal revenue product of labor is marginal product of labor times marginal revenue. Figure 9-2 shows the marginal revenue product of labor, which is also the demand for labor because the marginal revenue product of labor determines how much a firm is willing to pay for labor. At a wage rate of $4, the firm is willing to hire 5 workers. At a wage rate of $3, the firm will hire 6 workers.

Labor Productivity

It is important not to confuse labor productivity with the amount of effort workers are exerting. For example, the productivity of a grounds crew at a stadium depends on their education and training and the amount of capital they use. A worker assigned to mow the grass of a baseball field with a push lawnmower will work harder but be less productive than one mowing the field with a riding mower.

An increase in labor productivity may increase or decrease the demand for labor. This may be explained in terms of marginal revenue product. While the increase in productivity causes the marginal product of labor to rise, increasing marginal revenue product, the increase in productivity decreases the cost of production, putting downward pressure on price and marginal revenue, and thus decreasing marginal revenue product. What happens to the demand for labor depends on the size of the increase in marginal product and the decrease in marginal revenue.

A computerized assembly line for athletic shoes increases the productivity of labor. The increase in labor productivity reduces the cost of production, causing the price of shoes to fall, and thus decreasing the value of the output a worker produces at the shoe company. This decrease can be offset by the increase in the number of shoes a worker is now able to produce. If the increase in the number of shoes produced by a worker more than offsets the lower revenue from each additional shoe, due to the lower price the demand for labor increases. If the increased output does not completely offset the drop in revenue from the lower price, the demand for labor falls.

An alternative approach to understanding the impact of changing labor productivity on demand follows. The increased labor productivity of a computerized assembly line for athletic shoes reduces the demand for labor if output remains the same. However, the increased productivity reduces the cost of production, causing price to decrease; the lower price enables the firm to sell more output. The increase in output may cause the firm to hire more workers even though each worker can now produce more shoes than before the computerized assembly line.

Labor Supply

The supply of labor is the relationship between the wage rate and the amount of labor available for hire. In general, we expect higher wage rates to increase the amount of labor available for hire. The concept of opportunity cost is useful in understanding why we expect a direct relationship between the wage rate and the amount of labor available in the labor market.

Opportunity cost is the value of the best alternative given up when a decision is made. When people choose to offer to work in the labor market they are offering to give up the best alternative use of their time. Alternative uses of time include leisure activities and non-market work. Non-market work refers to activities such as cleaning your own house, watching your own children, etc. Non-market work produces goods and services people value. People also value leisure activities.

A person will be willing to work in the market when the return on market work exceeds the value of the best alternative. The higher the market wage rate, the more likely it is to exceed the value of the best alternative use of time, and the more willing people will be to offer to work in the labor market. The decision to offer to work in the labor market can be viewed in terms of an individual deciding how many hours to work. Higher wages will cause most individuals to be willing to work more hours.

At higher wages the total amount of labor available for hire increases so the supply of labor can be represented by a line with a positive slope. Figure 9-3 shows the supply of labor. Changes in the value of non-market work and leisure will change the amount of labor supplied by individuals. For example, having children increases the return to non-market work, causing some individuals to reduce the number of hours they are willing to work.

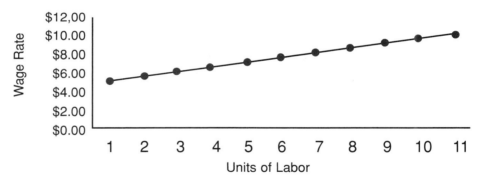

Figure 9-3. The Supply of Labor

Labor supply in the sport industry will differ from some other industries because of the significance of non-wage factors in the decision to offer to work. In addition to the monetary return from wages, some individuals derive pleasure from working in the sport industry. If people derive pleasure from being employed in the sport industry beyond what they would feel from employment in other industries, they will be willing to offer more hours of labor for a given wage rate, increasing labor supply in the sport industry.

This increase in labor supply will tend to reduce monetary wages in the sport industry. The people employed in the sport industry will tend to be those who derive satisfaction from it beyond their wages. Given lower wages in the sport industry because of the increased supply, those who do not derive satisfaction from working in the industry will decide to work in industries that offer higher monetary wages.

An example of a labor supply decision that can be analyzed using opportunity cost is the decision of an underclassman college football player to offer his services for sale to the National Football League in the player draft. A player weighs the expected return on non-market work, playing college football for another year compared to market work, playing for pay in the NFL. The greater the return on playing college football for another year, the more likely the player is to wait another year to enter the NFL. Part of the return to playing another year of college football to some players is the potential rise in draft position (and salary) in the NFL the following year. A factor reducing the return to another year of college football is the possibility of injury that would lower draft position (and salary) in the NFL the following year.

Labor Markets

The characteristics of labor markets vary. As a result the process of wage and employment determination differs across labor markets. Three types of labor markets are competitive, monopsonistic, and bilateral monopoly. In a competitive labor market, there are many buyers and sellers of labor. In a monopsonistic labor market, a single buyer of labor is present. In a bilateral monopoly, a monopolist seller of labor (a union) faces a monopsonistic buyer (a professional sports league).

COMPETITIVE LABOR MARKETS

In competitive labor markets the market wage rate is determined by the interaction of the demand and supply of labor. In a competitive labor market firms can hire as many workers as they want at the market wage rate. A firm will hire workers up to the point where the marginal revenue product of labor equals the wage rate. If the marginal revenue product of labor exceeds the wage rate, hiring more labor increases profit because revenue is rising faster than cost. Workers are paid their marginal revenue product in a competitive labor market because competition among firms will push the wage rate to the marginal revenue product of labor.

In a metropolitan area, a health club is likely to face a competitive labor market for aerobics instructors. There are likely to be many people willing to work as aerobics instructors in a city and many health clubs willing to hire them. Given the number of potential buyers and sellers, no single employer or employee determines the going wage rate for aerobics instructors.

Both potential buyers and sellers take the market wage rate as a given. For example, if the market wage rate is $15 an hour, a health club manager will compare that cost with the expected revenue from hiring another hour the services of an aerobics instructor. An aerobics instructor weighs the $15 an hour against the best alternative use of his/her time.

MONOPSONISTIC LABOR MARKETS

In a monopsony there is a single buyer. In a monopsonistic labor market there is only one employer of labor. Under monopsony workers do not receive their marginal revenue product because there is no competition bidding up wages. Workers may earn a wage just high enough to make them willing to provide their services to the firm. This wage, the reservation wage, must be high enough to compensate the worker for the opportunity cost of working for the firm.

In the absence of competing leagues or meaningful free agency, the National Football League (NFL) has acted as a monopsonist in hiring high-caliber football players. The NFL through the college player draft assigned a player to a particular team. Once assigned to a particular team, the player's choices were to sign a contract with the team or not play football in the NFL. The team did not have to pay the player his marginal revenue product because there was no competition for his services.

BILATERAL MONOPOLY

In a bilateral monopoly, a monopoly seller faces a monopsonistic buyer. The buyer is a firm that hires workers and the seller is a labor union representing the workers. The goal of a labor union is to maximize economic gains of its members. Unions attempt to increase workers' compensation (e.g., wages, fringe benefits, retirement pay), to improve working conditions (e.g., a healthy and safe working environment), and to expand job opportunities (e.g., job security) through collective bargaining.

The National Labor Relations Act passed by the U.S. Congress in 1935 forms the legal basis of union representation and collective bargaining. The Act grants workers the following three rights:

1. The right to self-organization, to form, join, or assist labor organizations;

2. The right to bargain collectively through representatives of their own choosing; and

3. The right to engage in "concerted activities" for employees' mutual aid or protection (Staudohar, 1989, p. 11).

With these three rights, workers through unions may collectively bargain with management and use strikes or other pressure tactics to gain a better position in the collective bargaining process.

A management strategy that can be used to gain a better position in the collective bargaining process is a lockout. In a lockout, a firm stops its operation and refuses to continue to hire its workers. An example of a lockout in professional sports was the National Hockey League (NHL) lockout of its players that resulted in the canceling of the 2004–2005 season.

In bilateral monopoly, the results of the collective bargaining process determine whether wages are closer to the reservation wage or to the marginal revenue product of labor. The labor markets for players in the four major sports leagues in the United States can currently be described as bilateral monopolies.

In the professional sports industry, players are workers. They are employed by a specific team or a league, or they are self-employed. In the next section two situations in professional sports are examined: (a) athletes as employees and (b) athletes as entrepreneurs. The first occurs most commonly in professional team sports, where a player signs a contract to play for a team or league for a number of years. The second condition, the athlete as an entrepreneur, usually occurs in professional individual sports, such as tennis, golf, track and field, and figure skating.

Most professional sports leagues in North America have some monopsonistic power over their players regardless of their business structure. Many of these leagues are the sole buyers and users of the service rendered by players. For example, if a college football player wants to play professional football at the major league level in the United States, he has to sell his service to the NFL. A female college basketball player has no choice but to make herself available to the WNBA if she wants to play professional basketball in North America. Professional sports leagues establish rules to enhance their monopsonistic position.

LEAGUE RESTRICTIONS TO ESTABLISH CONTROL OVER THE PLAYER LABOR MARKET

According to the reserve clause adopted in Major League Baseball (MLB) in 1879, once a team drafted a player, the player had to negotiate his contract and salary with that team. The team owned exclusive rights to the services of the player. The player could not sell his services and enter any contractual agreement with other teams unless he was traded or sold to other teams or dropped by the team that initially owned his contract.

Since a player could not sell his services to other professional baseball teams in MLB, players earned less than their marginal revenue product. Rather than facing a competitive labor market for their services players faced a monopsonistic employer. The ability to pay players less than their marginal revenue product led to the adoption of the reserve clause by other professional sports leagues in the United States and abroad. Under the retain and transfer system in English football, soccer players, like MLB players, were not allowed to sign contracts with any team other than the one which owned their rights.

The reserve clause (and its equivalents) prevented competitive bidding for players once they had signed a contract with a team in a professional sports league. They did not prevent teams from competing for players who had yet to sign with team in the league. Without a mechanism to prevent teams from competing to sign players to an initial contract, teams may have been forced to pay players their expected marginal revenue product in the league. To avoid paying incoming players their marginal revenue product, leagues established draft systems to allocate the rights to sign athletes entering the league.

According to the typical draft system, the franchises that had the worst records in the previous season are entitled to a better position in the amateur draft. The process goes on, and the best team picks the latest (a team's draft position sometimes is also subject to trades). The number of rounds in the draft varies by sport. The greater the number of rounds, the fewer athletes that can offer their talents to the league in a competitive labor market. Once a team drafts a player, other teams in the same league are prohibited from soliciting the player for his or her service under the draft rules and agreement among teams in the league.

PLAYER ALLOCATION RULES AND COMPETITIVE BALANCE

Professional sports leagues have claimed the main reason for player allocation rules such as the reserve clause and an amateur draft system is to promote competitive balance. Economists have questioned this rationale for restrictions on competition for players. For some sports, such as football and baseball, the immediate impact of a drafted player is minimal on the competitiveness of the team because of the large number of players on a team. Even if a new player can make a difference, the effect of the draft on competitive balance is lessened because the worst team's advantage exists only for the first player chosen. The best team picks a player before the worst team picks again (Sanderson & Siegfried, 2003).

A draft system may have more of an effect on competitive balance in basketball and hockey, where, because of smaller team size, a talented player sometimes can make a difference in a relatively short time. Tim Duncan, the first overall draft pick by the San Antonio Spurs in 1997, was instrumental in the team's 1999 NBA championship. Even if a draft system initially promotes competitive balance, its effects will be undone over time because of the incentives that exist for teams to trade players to markets where they are more valuable.

According to the Coase theorem, if property rights are well defined and the costs of buying and selling those rights are not prohibitive, resources will eventually gravitate to their most valuable use, no matter who is given the rights initially (Coase, 1960). The Coase theorem implies players will be transferred to those teams where they can produce the most revenue. If the Atlanta Hawks draft and sign a player and pay him a lower salary than the player could earn from the New York Knicks, both the Hawks and Knicks could benefit from a trade or sale of the player from the Hawks to the Knicks.

The Coase theorem has been the subject of many empirical studies using the movement of baseball players before and after the introduction of free agency. Under free agency, players with seniority are no longer bound by the reserve clause and may sell their services to the highest bidder. As would be expected from the Coase theorem, "[m]ost of these studies concluded that the transfer of property rights from teams to players did not affect the distribution of playing talent" (Sanderson & Siegfried, 2003, p. 270). The limiting of the reserve clause has led to higher player salaries, as would be expected when competition is introduced into what was a monopsonistic market.

RIVAL LEAGUES AND THE MARKET FOR PLAYERS

The labor market for players becomes more competitive when a rival league emerges to challenge an existing one. The appearance of a rival league substantially reduces the monopsonistic power an existing league enjoyed as the only purchaser of players' services. This is particularly true if the existing league used a reserve clause and an amateur draft to suppress competition for players.

The consequences of competition between rival leagues include:

1. Escalating salaries for current players. New leagues commonly compete against existing leagues by bidding for talented players. The bidding war among the rivals inevitably escalates the amount of commitment each league has to make to keep or attract good players. The competition for players thus turns the labor market in the players' favor and changes it from a buyer's market into a seller's one. Players can use the threat that they will "jump to another league" as a pressure tactic to increase their salaries. Salaries are likely to increase the more effective the existing league has been at suppressing competition for players.

   A league's success at reducing competition for players reduces players' salaries, making teams more profitable. The profitability of existing teams is a reason for the formation of rival leagues. An existing league that suppresses players' salaries and does not expand the number of franchises is at risk of the formation of a rival league that will cause player salaries to increase, reducing the profitability of teams.

2. Increasing salaries for rookies. Bidding for rookies is also another focal point of competition among the rivals. For example, after signing a $36 million contract with CBS in 1964, the American Football League immediately started a bidding war with the NFL by making some large offers for exceptional college players. The United States Football League was another rival to the NFL in 1980s. This league adopted the idea of a star system and held its draft before the NFL's. By so doing, it was able to get some talented rookies. Rival leagues have to make reasonable offers that match the ability of the players in the market in order to receive their services.

The Nikki McCray case is a good example of the effect of a rival league on the players' labor market. A marquee player in the former ABL, McCray was instrumental in helping the Columbus Quest to win the Championship of the ABL in 1997. Immediately after winning the championship, she requested that the league renegotiate her contract, demanding a considerable increase in her salary and the right of first refusal on all major endorsement deals that the league would sign for its players. The league refused her demand. Rather than continuing to play in the ABL she signed a 3-year contract with the rival WNBA.

PLAYER UNIONS AND BILATERAL MONOPOLY

The labor markets for the four major professional sports leagues in North America (Major League Baseball, the National Football League, the National Hockey League, and the National Basketball Association) can best be described as bilateral monopolies. In each a monopsonistic buyer of labor, the league, faces a monopolistic seller of labor, the players' association. Together through negotiations, the league and players' association (union) determine matters regarding player compensation, including minimum pay, pensions, insurance, free agency, and methods for handling grievances.

The outcome of the process is influenced by the negotiation philosophy and strategy the parties use. Two negotiation models have been widely adopted in professional sport: (a) the adversary model and (b) the cooperative mode (Staudohar,

1989). Using the adversary framework, each side of the negotiations contends for a greater share of the revenues generated from the league's operations. The parties' strategies in negotiation lead to offensive tactics calculated to force the adversary to grant concessions and defensive tactics calculated to prevent the adversary from gaining concessions (Staudohar, 1989).

In contrast, the cooperative model is adopted in order to increase the mutual gains of the owners and the players, and the economic wealth of the league as a whole. The adoption of this model requires each party involved to abandon its adversary stance. "Instead of conducting negotiations in an atmosphere of crisis confrontation, the parties recognize and accept each other as partners in a cooperative venture" (Staudohar, 1989, p. 177). Mutual gain and survival are the goals of the negotiation. Embracing the cooperative model means that the two sides at the negotiation table may be willing to move their demands toward the middle and to find a wage rate that is satisfactory for both.

In the adversary model, the negotiators view the collective bargaining process as a zero sum game. If one side wins, the other side loses. In the cooperative model, the negotiators view the collective bargaining process as a variable sum game. In a variable sum game, one party's gain need not come at the expense of the other party. In a variable sum game, everyone can win, everyone can lose, or you may have a winner and a loser.

The adversarial model best describes most of the history of labor relations in professional sports leagues over the last forty years. The extent to which this is true varies across the leagues since labor relations in each league have exhibited cooperation and confrontation at times. In each of the leagues the collective bargaining process has resulted in settlements with and without work stoppages.

| **Free Agency in Professional Sports** | The key development in the modern era of labor relations in professional sports has been effective free agency. Under free agency, players can sell their services to different teams in a league, making the market for their services more competitive and less monopsonistic. Each of the four major sports leagues arrived at free agency in different ways. In each sport, the leagues have attempted to restrain the growth of salaries that has followed free agency. |

MAJOR LEAGUE BASEBALL

The modern era of labor relations in professional sports began with the hiring of Marvin Miller as the executive director of the Major League Baseball Players' Association (MLBPA) in 1966. Given his experience with the United Auto Workers and United Steel Workers Union, his hiring made the relationship between MLB and MLBPA more adversarial. Since 1972 there have been eight strikes or lockouts in Major League Baseball.

The owners locked out the players in 1973, delaying spring training. One of the features of the settlement was arbitration of salary disputes before an independent arbitrator. In 1975, a case involving two players, Andy Messersmith and Dave McNally, came to arbitration. They contended they were free agents because they had played the 1974 season without a new contract, thereby fulfilling the requirement under the reserve clause in their contracts. The arbitrator, Peter Seitz, agreed with the players. MLB appealed the decision in court and lost.

Free agency in MLB has resulted in significant increases in salary for players. Since 1975, a major issue between MLB and the MLBPA has been the effort of the owners to negotiate restrictions that will reduce player salaries. Negotiations centering on efforts to reduce player salaries have been acrimonious and have resulted in work stoppages. The mistrust between owners and players was heightened by collusion among the owners to not bid for free agent players in the mid to late 1980s. The collusion to refrain from signing free agents led to lower salary increases, but violated the collective bargaining agreement and led to successful grievances by the MLBPA.

The adversarial nature of the relationship between MLB and the MLBPA resulted in a strike in 1994, which canceled post-season play. In the next set of negotiations in 2002, the parties were able to arrive at a settlement without a work stoppage, the first time since 1970. Among the reasons for the settlement were (1) relative unity among the owners, (2) no attempt for radical change of the system of free agency, (3) the direct financial cost to players and owners of a strike or lockout, and (4) fear of the impact of a strike on the overall demand for baseball as entertainment (Staudohar, 2003). Concern over the continued health of the game may have led players and owners to a more cooperative view of negotiations.

NATIONAL FOOTBALL LEAGUE

Effective free agency developed in the National Football League (NFL) through the courts. In the NFL, free agency existed prior to MLB; however, the league rules governing free agency greatly limited the ability of players to earn higher salaries. Prior to 1970, players could become free agents, but when they signed

Photo courtesy of iStockphoto

with another team, the team signing the new player had to compensate the team that lost the player. The system continued in the 1970s with the form of compensation modified under an agreement between the NFL and the National Football League Players' Association (NFLPA). The compensation increased the cost of signing free agents to the point where very few players moved.

The NFLPA was unsuccessful at winning effective free agency through collective bargaining despite two work stoppages in the 1980s. In 1988, the NFLPA filed an antitrust suit against the NFL for anticompetitive practices in the labor market. While the NFLPA lost the lawsuit at the appellate level, the NFL did institute a new form of free agency. The new system was less restrictive than its predecessor, but still heavily constrained the movement of players through free agency.

The NFLPA lost on appeal because the judge had ruled the union could not use the antitrust laws to win what it had failed to win at the bargaining table. In order to use the antitrust laws to challenge the NFL's labor market practices, the NFLPA had to decertify itself as a union. In 1989, the NFLPA decertified as a union. In 1990, Freeman McNeil and several other NFL players filed an antitrust suit against the NFL. Victories by the players in court were followed by an out-of-court settlement. The settlement featured important gains for both parties. Players with four years in the league could sell their services to the highest bidder but the bidding was constrained by a salary cap tied to league revenue.

The presence of favorable outcomes for both sides reflected uncertainty over the outcome in court. While the players won the case in the lower court, the outcome at the appellate level was not guaranteed for either side. As a result, both sides had incentive to try to reach an acceptable out-of-court settlement. This helped foster a less adversarial approach and replace it with a more cooperative approach by both sides.

NATIONAL BASKETBALL ASSOCIATION

From 1967 to 1976, there were two major leagues in professional basketball, the National Basketball Association (NBA) and the American Basketball Association (ABA). The existence of rival leagues reduced the importance of free agency to players because it created some competition in the market for the services of players, increasing salaries. Competition between the leagues also reduced the profitability of teams and created pressure for a merger.

Before teams from the ABA could be absorbed into the NBA, a variety of lawsuits among players, teams, and player associations had to be settled. In 1976, an out-of-court settlement was reached, which resulted in free agency for players starting in 1980. Free agency resulted in higher player salaries and losses for teams. The escalating salaries in the NBA made the owners and players realize cooperation between them was necessary for the survival and prosperity of the league. In 1983, the players' union and the owners introduced the first salary cap in professional sport history, which guaranteed 53% of league revenues for players.

The cooperative approach of 1983 deteriorated over time. Between 1983 and 1998, negotiations became more adversarial. The National Basketball Players' Association (NBPA) filed an antitrust suit in 1994 alleging anticompetitive practices against the NBA. The NBPA lost, as the courts were not willing to interfere in the collective bargaining process. Following the loss in the courts, a group of players started the process to decertify the union so the antitrust laws could be used by the players. The possibility of decertification and an antitrust suit helped push the sides to a settlement but increased animosity between owners and players. That animosity helped lead to a lockout by the league in 1998.

After 3 years of implementing the 6-year 1995 collective bargaining agreement, the owners demanded a renegotiation of the agreement as allowed under the contract. The 1998 NBA lockout was triggered by an impasse in negotiations between the league and the union, because the union rejected the owners' demand for renegotiation of the collective bargaining agreement prior to its expiration. In particular, the owners sought to get rid of the so-called Bird Rule, which states that money individual teams use to re-sign their own free agents is not counted against their salary cap limit.

The abandonment of the Bird Rule and the subsequent imposition of a hard salary cap were among several major issues the owners wanted to renegotiate with the National Basketball Players' Association. Other issues included free agency, a rookie salary cap, and minimum salaries. Once their demand to renegotiate the agreement was rejected, the owner called a lockout (Staudohar, 1999). The eventual settlement did not include the end of the Bird Rule but did feature maximum salaries linked to years of service. In general, the contract contained provisions reducing the ability of players to negotiate higher salaries.

NATIONAL HOCKEY LEAGUE

In the 1970s, the National Hockey League, like the NBA, faced a rival league, the World Hockey Association, which reduced the monopsonistic power of owners in the NHL. When the two leagues merged in 1979, the collective bargaining agreement between the NHL and the National Hockey League Players' Association (NHLPA) allowed players to become free agents but required compensation. As in the NFL in the 1970s, the level of compensation was high enough to discourage teams from bidding on free agent players.

Following a strike in 1992 and a lockout in 1994, the collective bargaining agreement seemed to favor the owners (Staudohar, 2005). The contract featured a salary cap for rookies under 25 and free agency restricted to older players. Despite the restrictions, player salaries increased as owners were willing to sign older free agents and evade the rookie salary cap through the use of bonuses. Given the failure of these restrictions, and due to concerns over decreasing national television revenue, the owners looked for a salary cap in the 2004 negotiations. A salary cap was unacceptable to the NHLPA.

In the negotiations, neither side was willing to move on the issue of a salary cap until after the lockout had resulted in the cancellation of a significant portion of the season. Even when the two sides agreed to a salary cap, the difference in the amounts acceptable to the two sides was so great, a compromise could not be reached in time to save the season. The lockout in 2004–2005 resulted in the cancellation of the entire season.

When a contract was signed between the NHL and the NHLPA the owners largely succeeded in achieving their goals. While free agency was expanded under the agreement, the inclusion of a hard salary cap means salary gains for free agent players will be limited. The settlement also contained a provision cutting the salaries of players under contract by 24 percent (Staudohar, 2005).

INTEREST GROUPS IN BILATERAL MONOPOLIES

The bilateral monopolies in the labor markets in the four major league sports have negotiated varying degrees of free agency for players. The labor market for free agent baseball players is the least constrained, while the market for hockey players is the most constrained. The negotiations that have produced these results have mostly been adversarial in nature with brief flashes of cooperation.

One reason for the adversarial nature of the negotiations is the make-up of the two sides. It is difficult to cooperate with the other party when your own side is characterized by disagreements. The bilateral monopolies in professional league sports' labor markets feature many different interest groups within each of the two parties negotiating a contract. For example, the 1995 attempt to decertify the NBPA was led by dissident players unhappy with the progress in negotiations. Diverse elements also exist within team ownership. Typically there are some owners who, because of their market situations, prefer a hard line approach to labor negotiation, while others favor a more conciliatory approach. To present a united front, some leagues have fined owners for talking to the press during labor negotiations.

Despite the difference among owners and players and between the two groups, there are common interests. An example of a league rule that serves owners and current players is the amateur player draft used in professional sports. The system is a product of an agreement orchestrated by the two parties involved in a bilateral monopoly, the owners and the players' unions. As found in the research of Quirk and Fort (1992), the draft system helps redistribute the wealth between the veterans and rookies. This is logical because the players' union represents mainly the economic interests of the veteran players. The salaries not paid to those newly drafted players may be available for the teams to make larger offers to veteran players in the free agent market.

Factors Affecting Demand in Professional Sports

The demand for players in professional sports is determined by their marginal revenue product (MRP). A player might affect the revenue of a team in two direct ways. The most direct is the fame of a player. The higher the fan recognition of the player (e.g., Michael Jordan), the larger the impact the player may have on the team's revenues. A player may also affect the marginal revenue product indirectly by improving the win-loss record of a team. This increases the popularity of a team and thus its revenue (Quirk & Fort, 1992).

For teams concerned with profit, MRP is an essential criterion in making decisions about whether to sign a player. A team has to evaluate how much in gate receipts, merchandise and concession sales, parking revenue, etc. it may generate as a result of signing a prospective player. A team should offer a free agent player an amount less than or equal to the player's expected MRP with the team. The MRP of a player will depend on the team and on the market in which the team operates.

MRP is also a useful concept when evaluating trades. If a team perceives that a player on another team may help to improve its winning performance and therefore its revenue, the team may be willing to trade a player on its roster for that player. The MRP of the to-be-traded player is perceived by the team as less than or equal to the MRP of the acquired player.

MRP depends on the productivity of the player and the demand for the entertainment the player helps produce. The MRP of soccer players is higher in Europe then in the United States; as a result, the best players in the world tend to play in Europe, where they can earn more due to their higher MRP there. In general, the flow of hockey talent has been toward North America because players can generate more revenue for a team in the NHL than elsewhere in the world.

Determination of a Player's Marginal Revenue Product

The determination or estimation of a player's marginal revenue product has been one of the focuses of research by economists in that last few decades. The study conducted by Scully on Major League Baseball in 1974 led the inquiry in this matter. Scully's work is based on an assumption that "a team's revenues increase when the team wins more games, and the performance of players contributes to team revenue only by changing the team's winning percentage" (Boal & Ransom, 1997, p. 100). So a player's marginal revenue product is defined as "the ability or performance that he contributes to the team and the effect of that performance on gate receipts" (Scully, 1974, p. 916).

To estimate a player's marginal revenue product, Scully used a two-step model. First, a regression analysis was performed to identify the variables affecting a team's revenues. Examples of the factors used in the regression equation include team winning percentage, host population, and team's league affiliation. The study concluded that a team's revenues would increase $10,330 for each additional winning percentage point (Scully, 1974). Determining the contribution of individual players on the team to the winning percentage is the second step of the model. One of the assumptions of Scully's model is each player's contribution is independent of and distinct from those of his or her teammates. This assumption has been criticized given the joint nature of production in sports, where the production of one player is dependent on the production of other players. This criticism is particularly valid for studies estimating a player's marginal revenue product in sports that require collaboration and teamwork, such as football and basketball. Some studies have attempted to deal with the joint nature of production in sports (Scott, Long, & Somppi, 1991). One of the uses of estimating MRP has been to assess the degree to which free agency has resulted in athletes being paid their MRP.

Many professional athletes work as entrepreneurs in their sports. They are owners of their own services in the sport industry and may choose among alternative uses of their abilities. Just as teams consider MRP of players in making decisions, these athletes make decisions based on their own MRP. This is often the case in professional or elite individual sports, such as tennis, golf, track and field, and figure skating. As entrepreneurs, these athletes make capital and labor investment decisions to maximize their income. In many cases, the largest part of the cost of participating in an event is giving up the opportunity to participate in another event. For example, professional tennis players often have to decide the tournaments in which they want to compete.

Summary

This chapter provided an overview of the operation of labor markets in the sports industry with particular emphasis on professional sports. The demand for labor depends on the productivity of workers and the demand for the product labor produces. Education, training, and access to capital all tend to increase labor productivity. Labor supply is largely determined by the value of the alternative uses of a potential workers' time.

In competitive labor markets, firms compare the wage rate with the additional revenue from hiring another worker. The additional revenue from adding another worker is called the marginal revenue product of labor (MRP). As long as MRP exceeds the wage rate, the firm should hire another worker. In a competitive labor market, workers receive their MRP.

Where there is a single buyer of labor (called monopsony), workers are paid less than their MRP because of the lack of competition for their services. The labor markets for the major professional sport leagues are bilateral monopolies, where a monopsonistic buyer of labor (the league) faces a monopoly seller of labor (the players' association). In a bilateral monopoly, the wages and working conditions are determined by the collective bargaining agreement between the league and the players' association.

Over the last thirty years in professional sport leagues a major issue has been free agency—the ability of players to offer their services to competitive bidding. Leagues attempt to negotiate restrictions on the labor market, such as implementing salary caps, while player associations try to resist such constraints. Disagreements about restrictions on the labor market have led to work stoppages in all four major sports leagues.

Chapter Questions

1. Explain why some workers who work very hard have low productivity.
2. Explain why marginal revenue product determines the demand for labor.
3. What would an increase in opportunities outside of the labor market do to the supply of potential workers?
4. Evaluate the following statement:
   The existence of a rival league reduces the monopsonistic power of a sports league.
5. What is a bilateral monopoly?
6. Explain why free agency increases the desire of professional sports leagues to have a salary cap.
7. Compare and contrast the development of free agency across the four major sport leagues.

Chapter Ten

REGULATION OF SPORTS

Introduction

Government regulation of commercial activities of private firms has always been a topic of discussion in economics because it is believed that the breadth and depth of government involvement in those activities may have a profound impact on the decision-making process of the involved firms (Pappas & Hirschey, 1987). In addition, industry self-regulation is also a topic that receives attention from economists. Sport managers need to understand why and how government regulates, what constraints the firms in the sport industry may encounter due to government regulation, and how industry self-regulation works as a supplementary form of regulation. The chapter will examine issues related to both government and industry regulations.

Concept of Regulation

The term "regulation" can be defined in several different ways. Generally, it refers to "the intentional restriction of a subject's choice of activity, by an entity not directly party to or involved in that activity" (Mitnick, 1980, p. 5). Within the context of the sport industry, the subject is all the firms and organizations in the sport industry, and the party unrelated to the activity conducted by the sport firms and organizations is government. Through regulation, government establishes various requirements and restrictions for and constraints on the activities of the sport firms and organizations. Regulations include laws and subordinate rules issued by all levels of government, ranging from federal to local (Jacobs, 1997). For example, one way that state governments protect the wildlife and environment is to set restrictions on fishing activities. Such restrictions include the requirement of licenses and the limitation on fish type and where the anglers can fish.

The meaning of regulation can also be understood from a different perspective that pertains to the regulatory actions taken by a private industry or non-governmental, self-regulatory body. This is commonly known as "industry self-regulation." Industry self-regulation is defined as the process of influencing activity of members of an industry through the establishment of rules and procedures, which are adminis-

Regulation of Sports

The owner of the New Jersey Devils sold the team to a company affiliated to YankeeNets, the parent company of the New York Yankees and New Jersey Nets. The acquisition of the Devils by YankeeNets would make it possible for the three affiliated teams to bundle themselves together in promotion and marketing. This would no doubt give the Yankees a greater advantage over its counterpart, the New York Mets, in terms of market shares and penetration. Is the acquisition anti-competitive? What should government do to ensure that the Yankees do not have any unfair advantage over the Mets?

tered by a control-agent organization. Thus, while examining the issues related to regulation of sports, the regulatory mechanisms imposed by the government and the regulatory actions voluntarily taken by a specific sector of the sport industry must be discussed. For example, while considering a professional sport franchise as a regulatee, there are two types of regulators: the government and the league-wide regulatory authority. The regulations exerted by the government are at the level of inter-organizational regulation. Its purpose is to ensure fairness of competition and economic efficiency. Examples of government regulations include the antitrust laws and the National Labor Relations Act. The league-wide regulation is found at the intra-organizational level. Regulation at this level is designed to ensure the management efficiency of the league as a business firm and to achieve its goal of profit maximization.

Government Regulation

The involvement of government in a market economy has been a controversial topic for many years. Some argue that if an industry is left alone by the government, open competition will assure the market will operate efficiently over time. This side favors a laissez-faire approach in which the government intervenes as little as possible and allows mechanisms in the market to move it toward efficiency (Schiller, 1989). They also argue government regulations are often costly and, while the intent of the regulations may be good, the result is that the costs exceed the benefits, which will ultimately have a negative impact on the consumer (Hirschey & Pappas, 1995). Moreover, they believe government officials generally lack the industry expertise necessary to understand the impact of the regulations they impose, which results in regulations that often fail to meet their objectives (Hirschey & Pappas, 1995). These government failures may end up being worse than the market failures legislators were trying to correct (Schiller, 1989). The Reagan Administration in the United States is a recent example of a group that held these beliefs and pushed for a reduction in business-related regulations (i.e., deregulation).

However, there is another side that suggests government regulation is necessary for the market to operate at maximum efficiency. They argue that while the laissez-faire approach would work fine in a perfectly competitive industry, perfect competition rarely, if ever, exists (Schiller, 1989). In fact, they identify a number of imperfections in the market that prevent optimal outcomes from occurring without government regulations (Schiller, 1989). These imperfections are called market failure. In other words, market failure refers to the inability of an unregulated market to achieve allocative efficiency in all circumstances. The following are examples of how government regulations prevent market failure:

1. Externalities—As discussed in Chapter 6, externalities are indirect benefits or costs of an activity (Schiller, 1989) or the social costs and benefits not included in the price of the product or service (Richardson & McConomy, 1992). Within the context of regulation, it means the indirect benefits or cost as a result of an action taken by the regulatory body (i.e., to regulate or not to regulate). For example, a company producing a large number of baseball bats may face government regulations because it is killing too many trees, which is damaging the environment and decreasing the supply of wood available for other

products. The government may react by limiting the number of bats the company can produce or by taxing the company for each bat that is produced, so fewer bats will be made and the environment will not be negatively impacted. However, externalities may also be positive. For example, a youth sport program for disadvantaged youth is expected to provide a number of societal benefits. Since the financial benefits to a for-profit organization of such a program would be limited, the government may provide these programs or subsidize other organizations so they will be able to afford to provide the programs.

2. Public goods—Public goods are goods or services that cannot be consumed exclusively (Schiller, 1989). The government often provides public goods, such as national defense and roads, which forces all taxpayers to contribute. Otherwise, these necessary goods and services would not be produced by the market because there would be no way to make people pay to eliminate the free riders (i.e., those who use, but do not pay).

3. Market power—Whenever one or more producers have control over industry prices and/or output, it is likely that optimal outcomes will not be reached (Schiller, 1989). These firms will often produce less than the consumer-desired output and charge a higher price for that output (see Chapter 4 for discussions of monopolies, cartels, etc.). There are a number of government regulations, such as antitrust laws, which seek to control organizations with an excessive amount of market power.

4. Natural monopoly—In some cases, the concentration of market power in one firm may be most efficient (Schiller, 1989). It occurs when one firm can produce all of the output desired by consumers and can do it cheaper than could a number of firms working separately. The government may allow such monopolists to exist, but regulate the activities of such an organization to make sure they do not abuse their monopoly power.

5. Inequities—In some cases, the market may distribute income in an undesirable way (Schiller, 1989). Without government intervention, some people will have far more than they need, while others will lack the basic necessities (Schiller, 1989). Again, the government can correct some of these inequities through regulation. For example, the minimum wage laws in the United States are designed to prevent employees from being paid a wage that is so low that they could not afford the basic necessities.

Overall, it appears that in recent years, the side supporting government regulation of the market economy appears to be winning. Government regulation "has undergone a period of exponential growth during the past two decades" (Hirschey & Pappas, 1995, p. 668). A major goal of some of these regulations is to ensure a healthy level of competition in each industry. In order to ensure competition, a series of regulations, referred to as the antitrust laws, have been enacted. These regulations are designed to prevent firms from having too much market power. As discussed in Chapter 4, when a firm has considerable control over the market (e.g., a monopoly, a cartel), they tend to charge consumers higher prices (Shepherd, 1970) and to reduce production below an optimal level (Schiller, 1989). So, while the antitrust laws are often used by firms claiming that competitors are behaving unfairly, they are ultimately designed to protect consumers by assuring that the marketplace remains competitive and firms will not reduce production and charge higher prices. As we will discuss, these regulations have had an impact on the operations of sport organizations. Detailed discussion of the antitrust laws and their application in the sport industry can be found in Chapter 11.

REGULATORY SYSTEMS OF GOVERNMENT

The regulatory systems of government in the United States are mainly established at two levels: the federal regulatory system and the state regulatory system. The government and its three branches comprise the federal regulatory system. This system in general regulates the sport industry by passing various sports laws and laws that are applicable to the sport industry (by the Congress), monitoring the execution of the laws (by the judicial system), and imposing administrative regulations (by various governmental agencies under the executive branch). It is commonly acknowledged that most government regulation in the sport industry is found in the first two branches of the federal regulatory system, and the regulatory actions taken by these two branches, especially the judicial system, seem to link primarily to the antitrust laws and their applications. In the past, the judicial branch appeared to be unwilling to judge whether violations of the antitrust laws were being committed by a sport organization.

The legislative branch of the federal government plays a critical role in overseeing and regulating the sport industry. It passes various laws that may be applicable to the sport industry (e.g., the antitrust laws and Title IX), enacts sports-related legislation (e.g., The Sports Broadcasting Act), and conducts hearings to gather new information to assist in either developing a new law or amending an existing one. The numerous congressional hearings on whether or not the antitrust exemption granted to Major League Baseball should be revoked are examples that illustrate the last regulatory function of the legislative branch in the sport industry. The regulatory influence of the legislative branch of the federal government on the sport industry is also seen through the operations of various federal commissions. For example, the Federal Trade Commission enforces a variety of federal antitrust and consumer protection laws to ensure that the market is functional competitively, efficient, and free of undue restrictions. Application and interpretation of the law in the decision of real differences and in decision of cases and controversies are two main powers granted by the U.S. Constitution to the judicial branch.

The regulatory power executed by the judicial branch to the sport industry is reflected in the rulings of the U.S. Federal Courts on many cases that involve the interpretation of the antitrust laws and Title IX. The executive branch of the federal government executes its regulatory responsibility in several different ways. For example, the president can issue an executive order to temporarily terminate a work stoppage as a result of either a player strike or an owners' lockout. The department under each cabinet member, on the other hand, is responsible for the administration and enforcement of some of the federal statutes that may be applicable to the sport industry.

Many restrictions on the sport industry are also set by the state regulatory system, which is in place for the same reasons that fostered the federal system. However, the scope of state-imposed regulatory measures is much more limited and state specific. Most sport-related restrictions occur in such areas as sport agencies, fishing, hunting, and various forms of athletic competitions. For example, a large number of U.S. states have passed statutes to control the sport agency business. On the other hand, athletic commissions have also been created in many states to regulate athletic competitions, especially combative sports such as kickboxing. Rules and regulations are therefore adopted for the sake of protecting the athletes as well as the public.

ROLE OF GOVERNMENT

It has been long believed that the government should function as the manager of an economic system under managed capitalism (Elliott, 1985). The managerial functions of government are actualized in the following areas:

1. Through its "framework" activities, a government can establish rules, regulatory legislation, and policies as guidelines for firms. With the guidelines as boundaries of activities or conducts, firms may formulate their operational strategies that are deemed not only economically sound, but also legal and legitimate. An example of this type of government activity is the antitrust laws.

2. Through its preservative intervention and measures, a government can protect and support a particular industry. The Sports Broadcasting Act, passed by the U.S. Congress, to a certain extent, was drafted for the sake of protecting the best interest of professional sports. The legislation exempted the collective negotiation of TV contracts from the reach of the antitrust laws.

3. By passing various statutes and administrative regulations, a government can control private businesses. For example, the National Labor Relations Act of 1935 is used to control unfair labor practices by employers and labor unions. An independent federal agency, the National Labor Relations Board, was created to enforce the law. Players' unions in professional sports have frequently used this law to protect their members and gain advantages in collective bargaining.

TYPES/RATIONALES OF GOVERNMENT REGULATION

Through regulation, a government usually intends to achieve one or all of the following three basic objectives:

1. To ensure free competition among private firms and ultimately economic efficiency through the application of antitrust policy (Mueller, 1996).

2. To correct the serious flaws in the marketplace that lead to external costs (Weidenbaum, 1992).

3. To protect the public interest.

So, based on its intention, government regulation can be categorized into three basic types: economic regulation, political regulation, and social regulation (Jacobs, 1997; Pappas & Hirschey, 1987; Weidenbaum, 1992). Economic regulation refers to the intervention of the regulatory body for the sake of promoting competition and market entry or exit so as to enhance the economic efficiency of the market. In short, it is used by the government to prevent market failure and to ensure economic efficiency. An example of economic regulation in all industries, including the one we call the sport industry, is the antitrust law. It is used to limit the growth and size of large competitors (Pappas & Hirschey, 1987). To preserve the power and sovereignty of consumers in the competitive markets is another reason why government regulates. The restrictions exerted by government for this purpose is called "political regulation." In competitive markets, consumers' preferences play a very important role in influencing firms' decision in pricing and quantity. "Firms have substantial incentives to produce products consumers want, and to produce them in desired quantities" (Pappas & Hirschey, 1987, p. 460). Without government regulation and oversight, a firm in a certain product market could keep growing in size, eventually monopolizing that market. In that case, the firm becomes a price maker and has great discretion pertaining to pricing and output. Under these circumstances, consumers would suffer great losses of power and sovereignty. Social regulation is often used to achieve some non-economic goals, such as health, safety, environment, and social cohesion. The restrictions set by governments on fishing activities, as mentioned above, is a good example of social regulation, because the restrictions are intended to protect the environment and wildlife. This chapter mainly discusses the economic and political regulations imposed by the government.

APPROACHES OF GOVERNMENT REGULATION

Three approaches have been used by the government in dealing with matters in the large industries that require its involvement. The use of antitrust laws is one of them. With the provision of the laws, the government may ensure the fairness in competition among firms. As long as the spirit of the laws is not being violated, the government would not take a stance or action to handle the matter. The other two approaches are "laissez-faire" and "public supervision" (Mueller, 1996).

Laissez-faire Approach

The adoption of the laissez-faire approach by the government in a free market economy will ultimately lead to the creation of private monopolies (see Chapter 4 for basic economic theories about and characteristics of a monopoly). This approach has been proven to be problematic. Market failure is a major problem that has been identified to be associated with private monopolies (see also Chapter 4). Monopoly is less efficient than competition because it creates a deadweight loss by restricting output, resulting in reduction in consumer surplus (see Figures 10-1 and 10-2 for details). Consumer surplus refers to the difference between the value of a good and its price. It is shown as the shaded area in Figure 10-1. In a competitive market, consumers have to only pay the amount of money signified by the curve Pc for each unit bought (Parkin, 1993). However, in a monopoly, the monopolist usually sets its output at the point where marginal revenue equals marginal cost, in order to maximize its profit. As a result of the decrease in output, the monopolist turns consumer surplus into its monopoly gain and charges consumers higher prices without fear (monopoly pricing).

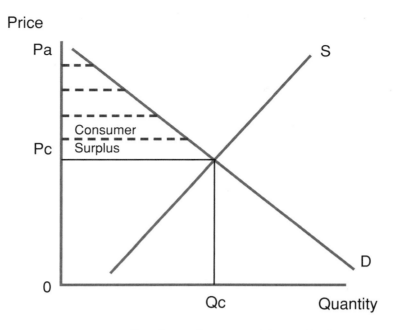

A Perfect Competitive Market

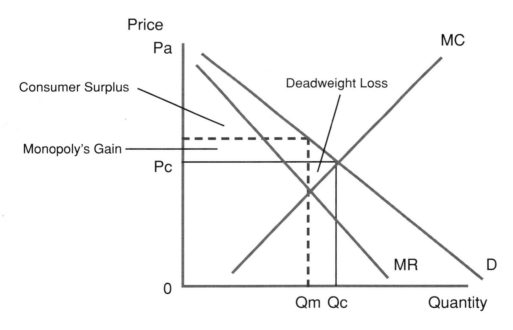

A Monopoly Market

Figures 10-1 and 10-2. Comparison of a Perfect Market and a Monopoly Market

The monopolist's restriction on output results not only in the loss in the consumer surplus, but also in the producer surplus. Producer surplus refers to the difference between a producer's revenue and the opportunity cost of production. It can be calculated by summing differences of the price and the marginal cost of producing each unit of output (Parkin, 1993). A deadweight loss measures the total loss of consumer surplus and producer surplus, and it indicates the allocative inefficiency caused by the monopolist's reduction of output below its efficient level (Parkin, 1993). A comparison of Figure 10-1 and Figure 10-2 reveals two important points:

1. The quantity of a product (i.e., the availability of the product to consumers) is reduced in a monopoly market due to the monopoly's restriction on output.

2. The price for the product will be higher in the monopoly market. The reduction in consumer surplus leads to the increase in difference between the value of the product and its sale price.

The inefficiency existing in a monopoly will in turn cause market failure. As Richardson and McConomy (1992) indicate, market failure could happen if the five conditions or criteria for perfect competition are not met. That is, if there are a limited number of sellers in the market; if the firm has power over consumers on pricing of the product; if the product is not standardized and homogenous; if there are barriers to entry into or exit from market; and if information about the product is not widely available to consumers, market failure is an inevitable consequence.

Market failure is commonly observed in the sport industry, especially in professional sports. It is true in most all cases that there is generally only one seller of each major professional sport in North America (e.g., National Football League in professional football, National Basketball Association in professional basketball, Major League Baseball in professional baseball). This sole seller often takes advantage of the situation to exercise its monopoly power by setting restrictions and barriers to entry. By so doing it violates the first and second conditions that prevent a market from failure. It is exceptionally hard, if not impossible for a new league to make inroads into a market that has been exclusively controlled by an existing league. The adjustments needed to be made by the new league are tremendous. For example, it needs to earn (1) respect from the public who has been exposed only to the product of its rivalry, so as to establish a solid fan base, and (2) support from sponsors and the media, which have been very friendly to the present league.

Photo by Jason Antony, courtesy of stock.xchng.iv

The costs involved in the forming of a new league are also considerable, especially when there is a heated competition with the established league for players. Due to the fact that Americans have long been exposed to the current traditional forms of various professional football, basketball, and baseball, it is extremely difficult for those who want to enter the market and to compete with the well-established, well-known, and well-recognized league in a given sport. Because of the several reasons mentioned above, the new entry will have difficulty competing unless it develops a new product to differentiate it from that of the existing league. If it decides to differentiate its product, the existing league would continue to hold on to its monopoly power and enjoy it to its fullest extent. Arena Football would be a good example.

Another violation of the conditions for perfect competition is found in the area of information asymmetries. Again, due to the familiarity of the products (e.g., team names and logos) of the existing league and its affiliated franchises, and the constant marketing bombardment of the league and teams through the media, the general public may not have the knowledge to differentiate the quality and price of the products of the two competing leagues. In other words, they tend to see the existing league and its teams as being of higher quality even if it is not.

Externalities also exist and are often high in professional leagues. The externality costs in professional sports include the use of taxpayers' money by state and municipal governments to subsidize a professional sports franchise in a certain locality, which may include sports facility renovation and construction, tax breaks and concessions, and nominal rental fees. To a certain extent, the more public consumption of the product and service of a professional sports league as a monopolist, the higher the externality costs will be.

Despite the violations of the conditions of perfect competition, the professional sports market is generally unrestricted by the government. In such an unregulated market, a particular league operates in a manner similar to that of a monopolist. It sets restrictions on the number of games to be played, and the number of franchises to be granted and/or expanded. The fewer the number of franchises in a league, the greater economic rent it can actualize. How large should a professional sports league be to achieve economies of scale, and to exhaust all of the efficiencies associated with its size? It seems to the owners and management of a specific professional sports league that the optimal size is "big," big enough to monopolize the market. However, the owners and management never want to expand the league to the optimal size.

Many monopolists that once dominated their industries have ultimately fallen victim to their own inefficiency, including high salaries for both management and labor (Mueller, 1996; Jones & Ergas, 1993). This is true in the case of professional sports. The players' salaries have been escalated to the point that many teams have to spend more than 60 percent of their revenues on them. Inefficiency is found in the management of individual franchises as well. It is believed that the key reason why so many professional sports teams, especially those in Major League Baseball, operate in the red, is the inefficiency of their management and the monopoly market structure.

Allocative efficiency will occur when marginal cost equals price, and it will be found only in a regulated industry. It is one of the reasons, as argued by sport fans, that government should attempt to restore and maximize total consumer surplus through the application of other regulatory policies in addition to the antitrust laws.

The economic theories in industrial resource allocation reveal that the development and utilization of modern technology have inevitably led to the creation of oligopoly in many product markets. The competitive firms in the oligopoly market tend to collude and conspire in some way to create a collusive oligopoly market (closely similar to a pure monopoly market), which is necessary not only to the maximization of profit, but also to the maximization of output. The oligopoly situation creates a functional conflict between size of production and efficiency. The history of professional sports in the United States has witnessed the development of several collusive oligopoly markets in professional sports and the problems that have resulted from the creation of such markets. The merging of the National League and American League into Major League Baseball and the association between the NFL and AFL are classic examples that illustrate the collusive oligopoly markets in professional sports. As indicated in Chapter 5, the economic characteristics of a collusive oligopoly market are similar to those of a monopoly market. Inefficiency is therefore often associated with this type of market as well.

Public Supervision

Public supervision is the third approach that government may adopt to regulate an industry. The approach calls for close government scrutiny to an industry. The basic assumption underlying this approach is the public interest theories. The public interest theories of regulation "assume that [government] regulation is established largely in response to public-interest-related objectives" (Mitnick, 1980, p. 91). The public interest theory of government regulatory behavior provides another theoretical foundation for government to take actions to achieve an efficient allocation of resources. For example, professional sports have been perceived as public goods. Public goods are defined as "goods and services which are available to other persons even while being consumed by one person" (Southwick, 1985, p. 721). However, such "public goods" have taken advantage of the support of the enthusiastic fans and "rip them off" with no mercy (Dell'Apa, 1993). The "rip-offs" are found in at least the following three areas:

1. Monopoly pricing. Due to the monopoly control of the availability of professional sport games, the owners of sport franchises force the public to pay an extravagant amount of money to use their services and products (Howard, 1999).

2. Control over franchise expansion. Professional sports take advantage being operated in a monopoly market and reluctantly adds new franchises. The scarcity of professional sports teams has fueled the competition among municipalities to fight against each other and "bribe" teams with considerable subsidies in order to lure a professional sports franchise.

3. Designated area for operations. By dividing the country into exclusive, designated territories for operations, local franchises are ensured that they can "shift television rights from over-the-air stations to cable networks without fear that a local broadcaster would compete by importing another team's games" (Dell'Apa, 1993, p. 6). Individual professional sports teams can therefore maximize their local television revenues though such territorial restrictions.

It is for the reasons mentioned above that advocates of public interests argue professional sports must be regulated much as government has regulated other public-oriented industries (e.g., utility, transportation). This regulation will ultimately eliminate the deadweight loss and inefficiency caused by monopolistic practices.

To ensure lower prices and higher quality that flow from effective competition, and to ensure fairness for business firms, the U.S. government passed the Sherman Act in 1890, and the Clayton and Federal Trade Commission Acts in 1914, to declare both monopolization and the restraint of trade to be unlawful. The antitrust laws were the legal foundation of government regulation. Chapter 11 will provide detailed discussion on all antitrust-related laws and regulations. Ever since the passing of the laws, the federal government has appeared to take a laissez-faire stand or a reactive approach to the problems in the sport industry, especially in the professional sports segment, even though some congressional inquiries and hearings were conducted into professional sports (Johnson & Frey, 1985). Historical cases in professional sports have demonstrated that it is unrealistic to expect a stable growing economy simply as a result of the existence of such regulatory legislation. With the intention of promoting fairness in competition and preventing monopolistic practices, the U.S. government passed and reinforced the antitrust laws. However, the Sports Broadcasting Act, which was passed in 1961, has allowed professional sports leagues to collectively pool television rights to all games of their member teams and to sell them to the national networks without violating the antitrust legislation. Such a contradiction in public policy creates numerous problems. The professional sports leagues see this as empowerment and encouragement from the government for their monopoly practices. The creation of this act again illustrates the ineffectiveness of government regulation in professional sports. The inability of government in providing regulatory supervision has been affirmed to be problematic.

Industry Self-Regulation

As mentioned previously, industry self-regulation refers to the process of influencing the activity of the associates through the establishment of rules and procedures, which are administered by a control-agent organization (Stern, 1981; Wotruba, 1997). The rules are basically drafted to serve as norms and/or standards of behavior for the affiliated members of the organization. In other words, they define the limits of acceptable behavior. Industry self-regulation can be implemented at two levels of business activity: company and industry. Most industry self-regulation activities take place at the industry level. Often a control-agent organization develops and administers policies to which all the members agree. These policies are believed to be in the best economic interest of the industry as a whole.

Many regulatory mechanisms (e.g., rules, policies, procedures) found in the sport industry are deliberately developed by individual sports control-agent organizations to regulate the affiliated members (e.g., franchises, institutions) for the sake of economic stability and growth. In professional sports, these regulatory mechanisms include, but are not limited to, revenue sharing, national TV contracts, amateur drafts and leagues' control over logos and trademarks. In collegiate athletics, various rules set by national governing bodies in player recruitment are also examples of self-regulatory practices. In other segments of the sport industry, industry self-regulation is also widely used. For example, the Automobile Competition Committee for the United States (ACCUS) is recognized by the Federation Internationale de l'Automobile (FIA) as the National Sporting Authority (ASN) for the United States. Championship Auto Racing Teams (CART), Indy Racing

League (IRL), National Association for Stock Car Auto Racing (NASCAR), and Professional Sports Car Racing (SPORTS CAR) are some of the member clubs of the ACCUS. Affiliated teams and individuals must comply with all the rules and regulations set by those clubs in such areas as license, equipment, and conduct.

The consumers of sport products and services also play a role in the regulatory process. They can provide feedback to both regulators (the government and the control-agent organization) regarding whether their rights have been violated by an individual firm from which they have purchased products or services. If the complaint is legitimate and a substantial number of consumers are affected, the government may step in to address the issue and put pressure on the firm involved (e.g., an injunction was issued by the court to stop the baseball strike in 1995). The control-agent organization may also react to the consumers' feedback by adopting corresponding regulatory policies to deal with the perceived problem. Figure 10-3 shows the regulatory model in the sport industry.

RATIONALE FOR INDUSTRY SELF-REGULATION

According to some economists, the problems found in the sport industry, especially in professional sports, could be solved eventually by the market's and the industry's self-regulatory mechanisms. Government should leave the sport industry alone and any attempted interventions are deemed unnecessary. Is industry self-regulation a miraculous cure to all the problems in the sport industry? According to Wotruba (1997), the basic motive for an industry to embrace and develop self-regulation mechanisms and policies is that self-regulation will benefit members as a whole economically. The industry self-regulation would achieve one or all of the following five basic goals:

1. To promote equity in competition among members. To maintain a relative balance in financial and athletic ability among affiliated members has been one of the important tasks for the control-agent organizations in many segments of the sport industry, especially those involved in athletic performance and competition.

2. To enhance members' competitive positions in the market. The collective negotiation of all professional sports leagues in the United States with the national television networks is an excellent example to illustrate this intention. By con-

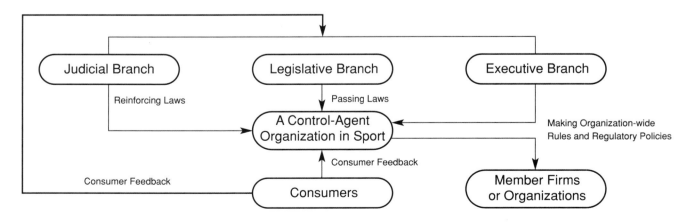

Figure 10-3. A Regulatory Model in the Sport Industry

trolling the right to negotiate, a professional sports league, like the NFL, has great economic advantage at the negotiation table over any national television network that wants to telecast its games and make the market into a seller's one.

3. To promote and maintain outcome uncertainty. Outcome uncertainty is the most essential element of sport competition, regardless of whether it is in professional sport or in amateur athletics. Therefore, all the control-agent organizations have rules and regulations to ensure the integrity of competition.

4. To maximize its profit as a business entity. While recognizing profit maximization as a common goal of all business firms, many control-agent organizations in the sport industry also have specific rules and regulatory policies to ensure that profit maximization for the involved firms as a whole is the ultimate goal.

5. To ensure the safety of participants and spectators. For those industry segments (e.g., car racing) that involve great physical risks to participants and spectators, their control-agent organizations have to develop rules and regulations specifically for that purpose. For example, all promoters or organizers of all SPORTS-CAR-sanctioned car-racing events must provide proper liability and participant accident insurance with certain minimum limits.

In some cases, industry self-regulation is also intended to discourage competition among members, ultimately reducing their costs related to competition. Without rules and regulations, individual members may try whatever they can to gain advantage in competition. Often, such competition away from the competition site is very costly. For example, if the NCAA did not have any restrictions on campus visits by prospective student athletes, what would happen?

FORMS AND ISSUES OF SELF-REGULATION IN PROFESSIONAL SPORTS

Self-regulation in professional sports takes two major forms. The first one is exerted through the establishment of various regulatory policies within each league. Examples of league-wide regulatory policies include (1) the luxury tax and revenue sharing, (2) the salary cap, (3) the amateur draft, (4) the collective negotiation of national television contracts, and (5) league-wide sponsorship agreements. The use of a syndicated ownership (or single entity ownership) structure is the second form of industry self-regulation observed in professional sport.

League-Wide Regulatory Policies

In general, the league-wide regulatory policies are intended and established for the following five reasons:

1. To more evenly distribute the wealth. The recent establishment of a luxury tax and increased revenue sharing by the owners in Major League Baseball exemplifies such an intention. By so doing, they hope to reduce the disparity among affiliated teams in terms of their economic wealth.

2. To control player salaries through the implementation of a salary cap. A salary cap is actually used to serve two purposes. It not only helps the owners by slowing and eventually stopping the escalating salaries, but also narrows the gap of

spending on players between the wealthier franchises from big markets and the poorer ones from small markets.

3. To more evenly distribute player talent. For example, the worst franchises are given better positions in the amateur draft. By doing this, the league hopes to equalize the opportunities (for success) by individual franchises. In theory, the amateur draft, together with other league-wide regulatory policies, may prevent a highly successful franchise from dominating and a franchise that is currently unsuccessful from staying at the bottom forever.

4. To negotiate more lucrative national television contracts. By negotiating national TV contracts this way, a professional sports league can achieve a major economic goal. It precludes the big market franchises from obtaining all of the television exposure and all of the television revenues. Strictly from a commercial perspective, the national television networks will be much more likely to televise the games played by big market teams to maximize advertising revenues because of the considerable television exposure in those markets. The league's control over the right for negotiating national TV contracts guarantees the small market teams the opportunity to be exposed to the national television audience and, more important, to receive an equal share of the television revenues, which is vital to the survival of some franchises.

5. To maximize and evenly distribute licensing revenues through the use of league-wide licensing agreements. The league-wide agreements ensure that the small market teams or the teams with the worst records will receive equal shares of the revenues obtained from the sales of licensed merchandises. These revenues are desperately needed for these organizations to be financially capable of signing big-name players to stay competitive.

A professional sports league confronts many regulatory issues if its franchises are independently owned and a league functions as a control-agent organization. Franchise relocation is one issue that has become a focal point of discussion lately. From a pure economic standpoint, a professional sports league will use its regulatory power to regulate the relocation of its member franchises only if the action is in the best economic interest of the league (Vrooman, 1997). In other words, a professional sports league may hesitate to prevent its members from relocating if the league will prosper economically with members who do not move obtaining a share from the franchise's stadium extortion and keeping the value of the expansion opportunity untouched. This scenario happens when the franchise moves from a city that has higher expansion value than the proposed new location. It will be in the best economic interest of the league to take a tough stand to oppose any relocation proposal if the direction of the move is reversed, that is, the franchise will relocate to a city that has a greater expansion value.

However, the self-regulatory power of the league has not prevented franchise movement. In 1996 alone, four NFL teams, five MLB franchises, and at least one team in both the NBA and the NHL moved or threatened to move to another city. By threatening to relocate, these professional sports franchises forced the host cities and communities to commit more resources to the teams. Historically, the federal government, especially its judicial branch, has held the position that franchise relocation was a matter for the professional sports league and the league had the authority to prevent its franchises from relocating. However, the exercise of such authority was often challenged by the franchise intending to move. These franchises claimed that the league's actions were a violation of the antitrust laws, and such an allegation was upheld by the court in the case of the *Los Angeles Memorial Coliseum Commission v. the National Football League* (1984). As a result, individual professional sports franchises, except in Major League Baseball, were able to take advantage and counter against any restrictive efforts exercised by the league that prohibits them from relocating to other cities. It is believed that the application of the antitrust laws has inevitably weakened the authority of individual professional sports leagues to use their regulatory power to deal with the franchise relocation issue. Some suggest that the current situation calls for further government intervention and a strong role in handling this matter.

Syndicated Ownership (or Single Entity Ownership) Structure

Discussion related to this type of industry self-regulation can also be seen in Chapter 6. The syndicated ownership structures have been utilized in several professional sports leagues, such as the American Basketball League (folded in 1999) and Major League Soccer. Discussion of the syndicated ownership structure may provide the student with insight into how and why it is considered a new way of self-regulation in the professional sport industry and how it works. In general, all syndicated professional sports leagues have the following common characteristics:

1. The league owns all players' contracts, the most valuable assets of a league, and can move players from team to team based on the best economic interest of the league;

2. Players' salaries are determined by the league based on such criteria as performance and seniority; and

3. There are two types of ownerships of individual affiliated teams: licensees and investors. As a licensee, an owner has to (1) pay a fee to the league for the exclusive right to market and operate a team in a particular area, (2) pay an annual membership fee, and (3) underwrite the costs of marketing his or her team locally. As an investor of the league, an owner has an exclusive right to operate a franchise in a geographic location.

The adoption of such a syndicated structure in a professional sports league may solve most of the regulatory issues that are associated with the traditional non-syndicated structure (e.g., the antitrust challenge brought by players, competitive imbalance, etc.). There are several obvious regulatory benefits. A professional sports league that adopts the syndicated ownership structure will virtually operate as a single business entity. The league can legitimately implement a variety of regulatory policies and practices and is free from many antitrust attacks. In other words, no claims can be made by players on the ground of unreasonable restraints of trade. Operating as a single entity will also enable the league to avoid franchise relocation-related issues and, thus, avoid the associated antitrust scrutiny. Regardless of the form chosen, industry self-regulation is utilized to counter the market forces in a free competitive market. In addition, it is also considered an effective survival strategy for individual leagues in monopolistic competition against their rivals.

FORMS AND ISSUES OF SELF-REGULATION IN COLLEGIATE ATHLETICS

To a certain extent, all the intercollegiate athletic associations (i.e., NCAA, NAIA, and NJCAA) regulate their members through similar regulatory rules and policies. This chapter mainly discusses the forms and practices of self-regulation in the case of the National Collegiate Athletic Association, or the NCAA, the biggest national governing body in intercollegiate athletics. As a private, non-governmental regulatory body, the NCAA is responsible for overseeing the athletic programs at more than 900 institutions. To obtain its goals, the NCAA has formulated many regulatory policies. It hopes through the implementation of these policies, the affiliated member institutions will benefit economically as a whole. The regulatory practices of the NCAA include, but are not limited to, the following:

1. Setting up restrictions on recruitment of student-athletes, specifically on the number of contacts and campus visits. A national letter of intent is introduced as another regulatory measure to serve the same purpose.

2. Controlling the rights for contract negotiation with television networks for all sports except football.

3. Setting up limits on size of coaching staff and their salaries.

4. Setting up limits on number of athletic scholarships that can be awarded to student-athletes in all sports.

5. Regulating the duration and intensity of student-athlete participation (i.e., setting up limits on length of season and schedules of practice).

6. Establishing a system to detect and penalize the member institutions that have violated set policies (DeSchriver & Stotlar, 1996; Koch, 1984; Stern, 1981).

When the NCAA was formed by the member institutions in 1910, its primary function was to develop rules of play and set up eligibility codes for its member institutions. As intercollegiate athletics has evolved, it has gradually become a control-agent organization, whose main function is to oversee the implementation of its regulatory rules and policies. Due to its role in the development and enforcement of regulations, the NCAA has thus been perceived as an economic cartel in many ways (DeSchriver & Stotlar, 1996; Koch, 1984). Chapter 5 has a detailed description on an economic cartel in terms of its characteristics and functions. To be economically effective as a cartel, the NCAA has to implement various rules and policies to regulate and control collectively the behavior of the affiliated member institutions. The main goal for doing this is threefold:

1. To minimize the unwanted competition among the members (e.g., the NCAA places restrictions on recruiting and on number of scholarships allowed based on levels of competition),

2. To enhance the competitive position of the organization as a whole in the market, ultimately strengthening the mutual gains of the members. The NCAA

collectively negotiates a television package for the championship tournament in all sponsored sports, except in football.

3. To level the playing field and attempt to ensure a competitive balance among its member institutions so as to strive for joint revenue maximization on the part of membership (Stern, 1981). It is believed that the survival of the NCAA is dependent upon its ability (1) to limit the financial clout of its big-time football and men's basketball members, and (2) to redistribute big-time men's basketball income to its general membership.

The implementation of its regulatory rules and policies is not problem-free. Many problems are caused by the friction between its organizational structure and cartel policies, and between the intentional opportunism of individual member institutions and the mission of the NCAA as a control-agent organization. The following are three significant problems that the NCAA has faced for decades, which will continue to be irritants for the NCAA in years to come.

1. The NCAA has too many member institutions (approximately 1,000 schools) to oversee. It is extremely difficult, if not impossible, to keep track of the activities and transactions of all these institutions. It is believed that the NCAA has not yet developed effective methods to detect and punish the member institutions that violate its cartel rules (DeSchriver, 1997). The strategies the NCAA has used in dealing with problems stemming from the large membership include (a) dividing the membership into divisions and levels of competition (e.g., Division I-A, and I-AA) based on certain criteria and allowing each division to have its own governance structure to make rules that are applicable to institutions in that particular division, and (b) setting membership requirements (e.g., Division I-A) as barriers to entry to ensure the homogeneity of institutions affiliated with a certain division. By so doing, the NCAA tries to ensure that member institutions in the same division will have similar interests and financial capabilities.

2. The number of points of initiative is exceedingly large, which could be one of the reasons why there are so many membership violations. One strategy that the NCAA has used is to keep restructuring its membership to produce more homogeneity among the membership of its various divisions. Restructuring is aimed at reducing the number of points of initiative and increasing its cartel effectiveness.

3. Legal challenges from member institutions for violation of their property rights as a result of price-fixing practices. (See the next chapter for more discussion on this matter.)

RISK OF SELF-REGULATION

The implementation of various regulatory policies in a specific segment of the sport industry (e.g., professional sport) has helped (to a certain degree) to homogenize the membership to improve its financial and athletic competitive ability. However, it is not problem-free. It is commonly recognized by economists that an antitrust violation is one of several potential problems or risks while implementing the self-regulation program or policy. The judicial branch of the government often examines all the circumstances to determine whether the activities and policies implemented by an industry for a self-regulation purpose are anticompetitive

(Jacobs & Portman, 1997). Any self-regulation programs, policies, and activities that are anticompetitive and discriminatory, or implemented without fair procedures, are very likely subject to antitrust challenges.

This is certainly true in the case of professional sports. The owners and the league management have frequently been accused of collusion and conspiracy by players. Individual owners also sometimes contend that the league-wide regulatory policies violate the antitrust laws (e.g., Dallas Cowboys owner Jerry Jones' antitrust lawsuits against the NFL for the latter's control over all franchise logos, trademarks, and licensing products). The contention against the regulatory policies has resulted in ceaseless labor turmoil and work stoppages, and has intensified the internal friction among owners, ultimately undermining the economic stability of a professional sports league. Moreover, courts have frequently ruled in favor of players and owners who have accused the league of violating antitrust laws. The challenges of the legitimacy of league-wide regulatory policies and the problems that have occurred accordingly raise the issue of what regulatory role the government should play.

INDUSTRY SELF-REGULATION AND COMPETITIVE BALANCE

In a free competitive market, the market force tends to promote a virtuous circle for winning teams (Gratton & Taylor, 1985). The teams with better winning records may generate more and more revenues due to higher attendance. With more money in their hands, owners can then sign more lucrative contracts with marquee players to retain dominance and success (Gratton & Taylor, 1985). Furthermore, the sizes of markets in which affiliated franchises operate vary in terms of population, average household income, and the size of TV markets. The differences existing in these areas create disparity among franchises pertaining to the revenues they can possibly generate locally. As part of the entertainment industry, which relies heavily on gate receipts, the financial wealth and ability of individual franchises are, to a great extent, affected and determined by the financial backing that they may receive from the local community. One good example that illustrates such disparity in local support (gate receipts, local media contracts, and other revenues from the stadium) exists in Major League Baseball. The annual revenues received by New York Yankees in 1996 were about $93.9 million, whereas the Milwaukee Brewers' revenues were only $29.5 million in the same year. Evidently, the former franchise will be much more financially capable of acquiring marquee players than the latter in a free competitive market environment. Hypothetically, if the league does not use any regulatory policies in player signing and players can freely change teams at will, the economic condition of the league would suffer because the wealthier franchises from bigger markets would be able to obtain all of the talented players and dominate the player market. "Empirical evidence of the historical distribution of the win percent among clubs [in professional baseball] shows a lack of competitive balance" (Scully, 1995, p. 83).

To maintain the stability of the league, the strategy of revenue sharing is used to take wealth from the rich franchises and give it to the poor franchises for the sake of breaking the so-called virtuous circle for the winning franchise (Gratton & Taylor, 1985). Evidently, if a league operates under a complete free competitive market environment, it would be extremely difficult for franchises with less financial capability and local support to survive. Under this circumstance, league-wide policies must be employed to level the "playing field" among franchises. Theoretically, the economic efficiency of the operation of a professional sports league will be obtained only if competitive balance between individual franchises and stability of operation is ensured.

DILEMMA OF INDUSTRY SELF-REGULATION AND ROLES OF GOVERNMENT

It is believed that the best outcome of regulation comes from the use of a regulatory system that incorporates the mechanisms of both government regulation and self-regulation (Wotruba, 1997). Nevertheless, the mixture in use of these two types of regulatory mechanisms in professional sports seems to render some unintended and unwanted consequences. As mentioned earlier, the government regulates professional sport mainly through its legislative and judicial branches, while the executive branch does not get involved much in the regulation of the sport industry as it has in other industries. The antitrust laws were some of the few pieces of legislation that have a great regulatory effect on the sport industry. Compliance with these laws has been monitored and reinforced by the judicial branch of the government. Although the intention of the laws was to promote free competition and economic efficiency, the use of the laws has weakened the power of a professional sports league in its self-regulatory efforts.

Future Models in Sport Regulation

Many chaotic situations that have occurred in the sport industry, especially in professional sports in the U.S., have prompted the public to rethink the role of government and to readjust its theoretical positions about the issue of whether the government should play a stronger and more specific role to regulate professional sports. It is believed that the weakness of or lack of governmental regulatory mechanisms has indirectly provoked these negative situations.

A longstanding controversy in professional sports management has been whether the government should regulate professional sports like it does other segments of the business world. Advocates of regulation strongly urge that some sort of governmental involvement and regulation be installed in professional sports to stabilize the economy in that particular segment of the sport industry, and to respond to the "public-interest-related objectives" (Mitnick, 1980, p. 91). Without the intervention of government, like in other industries, economic efficiency will be difficult to achieve, and professional sports leagues will continue to monopolize resources and dominate the demand and supply relationship, eventually fixing the price and controlling the public goods. According to Dell'Apa (1993), professional sports have been able to conduct the business side of their operations largely outside of governmental control and public scrutiny. The government's passive stand has continued to cause considerable trouble for professional sports and the general public. However, the opponents contend that the government intervention and "public policies commonly are followed by unintended consequences" (Frey & Johnson, 1985, p. 264). They contend that the problems occurring in professional sports are caused by the imperfection of the free market system. These problems will be solved eventually by the market's as well as the industry's self-regulatory mechanisms. The government interventions are unnecessary. So, should the government be involved? If so, how does it ensure the public interest will not be unfairly hampered? These questions do not have clear-and-cut answers.

Summary

This chapter presented economic theories related to both government and industry self-regulation. The government regulates industries for both economic and social reasons. This chapter mainly discusses why and how government regulates the industries from an economic perspective. Allocative inefficiency and market failure are considered two primary reasons why industries need to be regulated by the government. Problems found in professional sports are attributed to the lack of government involvement in the sport industry.

Industry self-regulation is another form of regulation that has been addressed in the chapter. This discussion focuses on why an industry regulates itself and how it can do it effectively. Examples of self-regulation in professional sport and collegiate athletics are provided. Issues related to self-regulation in both professional sport and collegiate athletics are also discussed.

Chapter Questions

1. Using an example in the sport industry, explain the concept of government regulation.
2. Elaborate on the three basic types of managerial and economic functions of government.
3. Explain why the government would need to regulate an industry.
4. Using the concepts "deadweight loss" and "market failure," discuss why monopoly is less efficient than competition.
5. Define the concept "industry self-regulation" and explain why industries want to impose regulations onto their members.
6. Discuss how a professional sports league regulates the affiliated franchises.
7. What are the forms of self-regulation in collegiate sports?
8. Discuss the relationship between industry self-regulation and competitive balance.
9. What are the regulatory policies and practices of the NCAA as a control-agent organization?
10. What are the problems the NCAA faces as a control-agent organization, and what are the coping strategies it has used to provide solutions to those problems?

Learning Activities

1. Return to the beginning of the chapter and reread the scenario. After reading this chapter, what are your answers to the two questions raised?
2. Compare and contrast government regulation and industry self-regulation in the sport industry with one of the other industries (e.g., telecommunication, automobile, airline).
3. Organize a class debate on the advantages and disadvantages of government regulation as well as industry self-regulation.

Chapter Eleven

ANTITRUST ISSUES IN SPORT

Introduction

The purpose of this chapter is to explain the impact of antitrust laws on the sport industry. Broadly speaking, the purpose of the antitrust laws is to promote competition in markets. An understanding of antitrust is important to decision makers in the sport industry because the laws have helped shape and continue to shape the sport industry. Antitrust laws limit the actions of firms in the industry.

In the United States, the judiciary is the final arbitrator of what laws mean. Court interpretations have played a significant role in determining how the antitrust laws are enforced. Economic analysis has influenced the evolution of court interpretation of the antitrust laws. Disagreements among economists about the extent and nature of competition in markets help generate uncertainty about the interpretation of antitrust laws by the courts.

Statutes

At the federal level, the first antitrust law was the Sherman Act passed in 1890. There are two relevant sections to the Sherman Act. Section 1 makes contracts, combinations, or conspiracies in restraint of trade illegal. Section 2 makes illegal monopolizing or attempting to monopolize any part of trade or commerce. The Sherman Act applies to interstate commerce. Activities solely within a single state are not subject to the Sherman Act.

Since its passage in 1890, the courts have struggled to interpret the Sherman Act. Two court cases illustrate the courts' early struggle with the Sherman Act. In *United States v. E. C. Knight Co.* (1895), the Supreme Court ruled that a series of mergers resulting in a firm with 98% of sugar refining capacity legal because it involved manufacturing and not commerce (Sullivan, 1977, pp. 579–581). In *Northern Securities Co. v. United States* (1904), the Supreme Court stated that the Sherman Act "is not limited to restraints of interstate . . . trade or commerce that are unreasonable in their nature but embraces all direct restraints imposed by any combination . . ." (Sullivan, 1977, p. 582).

In both cases the Supreme Court interpreted the Sherman Act literally, and in both cases the results were disquieting. Mergers that result in a single firm having 98% of the market clearly result in a manufacturing monopoly, which can result in harm to society. Making all restraints of trade illegal would harm society because some actions that restrain trade help firms achieve goals which benefit society. A professional sports league restrains trade if it bans a player who has bet on games in which she participated. Society would not benefit by making that restraint of trade illegal since the restraint helps the league maintain the integrity of its product. The Supreme Court has backed away from the literal approach adopted in the E. C. Knight Sugar and Northern Securities cases.

Due in part to dissatisfaction with the Court's interpretation of the Sherman Act, Congress passed the Clayton Act in 1914. The Clayton Act lists three activities that are unlawful if they lessen competition: (1) price discrimination, (2) exclusive and tying contracts, and (3) the acquisition of the stock of a competing corporation. The Clayton Act also exempted some activities of labor unions from antitrust prosecution.

Table 11-1. U.S. ANTITRUST LAWS

• Sherman Antitrust Act (1890)

Section 1: Makes contracts, combinations, or conspiracies in restraint of trade illegal.
Section 2: Makes it illegal to monopolize or attempt to monopolize.

• Clayton Act (1914)

Section 2: Makes price discrimination illegal.
Section 3: Makes exclusive and tying contracts illegal.
Section 7: Prohibits the acquisition of the stock of a competing corporation.

} when the effect is to substantially lessen competition of another company.

Section 6: Exempts labor unions from the antitrust laws.

• Federal Trade Commission Act (1914)

Established the FTC to police unfair and deceptive business practices.

• Robinson-Patman Act (1936)

Amendment to the Clayton Act
Revises prohibition against price discrimination.
Prohibits predatory pricing.

• Wheeler-Lea Act (1938)

Amendment to the FTC Act
Makes unfair or deceptive trade practices illegal.

• Celler-Kefauver Antimerger Act (1950)

Amendment to the Clayton Act
Makes it illegal to purchase the assets of another company if it will substantially lessen competition.
Expands scope of the Clayton Act to cover vertical and conglomerate mergers.

• Hart-Scott-Rodino Antitrust Improvement Act (1976)

Amendment to the FTC Act
Requires the FTC and Justice Department be notified prior to mergers or acquisitions.

In the Clayton Act, Congress provided the courts with guidance as to which practices it believed could have anticompetitive effects. Congress did not provide the courts with a precise standard. While it listed practices that could be illegal, it did not make the practices illegal unless they lessened competition.

Price discrimination—the act of selling a product for different prices not justified by differences in the cost of production—was made illegal only if it lessened competition. An exclusive contract to purchase or sell a product only to/from another firm was made illegal only if it lessened competition. Acquiring the stock of a competing corporation was also made illegal for the same circumstances. Congress placed the courts in the position of deciding when these actions lessen competition.

Price discrimination, exclusive contracts, and mergers occur in the sports industry. The Hagerstown Suns, a minor league baseball team, offers lower admission prices at selected games to individuals who bring a "church bulletin" to the ballpark. Different consumers pay different prices not based on differences in the cost of production. Ticketmaster has an exclusive contract with the New York Yankees to sell tickets to games. Foot Action, a retailer of athletic shoes, was acquired by competitor Foot Locker. These activities are legal under the Clayton Act if they do not lessen competition in the judgment of the courts.

In addition to passing the Clayton Act in 1914, Congress also established the Federal Trade Commission (FTC) with the Federal Trade Commission Act. The FTC, an independent government agency, was charged with enforcing the Clayton Act as well as Section 5 of the Federal Trade Commission Act. Section 5 made unfair methods of competition illegal. The courts ruled Section 5 applied to unfair methods which injured competition.

The Clayton Act was amended in 1936 by the Robinson-Patman Act and in 1950 by the Celler-Kefauver Act. The Robinson-Patman Act revised the treatment of price discrimination and prohibited predatory pricing, which is pricing below average variable cost to force competitors out of business. The Celler-Kefauver Act made it illegal to purchase the assets of another company when it substantially lessened competition. Asset acquisition of a competitor was not covered by the Clayton Act since it prohibited the acquisition of the stock of a competing corporation. The Celler-Kefauver Act expanded the scope of the Clayton Act beyond the acquisition of competitors to cover the acquisition of any firm that lessens competition.

The Wheeler-Lea Act (1938) expanded Section 5 of the Federal Trade Commission Act to prohibit unfair methods of competition that injures consumers. The Hart-Scott-Rodino Antitrust Improvement Act (1976) required the FTC and Justice Department be notified prior to mergers or acquisitions above a specified size.

EXEMPTIONS

Congress has exempted some activities from antitrust examination. In addition to the statutory exemptions written by Congress, the courts have established non-statutory exemptions to the antitrust laws through court precedents. Statutory and non-statutory antitrust exemptions have had significant effects on the sports industry.

With the Sports Broadcasting Act of 1961, Congress explicitly gave professional sports teams the ability to legally negotiate league-wide contracts, as opposed to team-by-team deals. The law significantly increased the bargaining power of professional sport leagues in television negotiations and helped them to negotiate higher television rights fees. The law gave leagues the ability to restrict the output of televised games to increase league profits. The Sports Broadcasting Act of 1961 did not apply to the NCAA. The antitrust laws were used in the 1980s to allow individual colleges and universities to sell television rights to their games. This will be explained later in this chapter.

Under the Clayton Act, certain activities (e.g., boycotts, pickets) of labor unions that may restrain trade are not subject to prosecution under the Sherman Act. The statutory exemption is complemented by a non-statutory exemption. The non-statutory exemption has developed through rulings in the courts. The non-statutory exemption makes legal restraints of trade within the context of collective bargaining.

In *Brown v. Pro Football* (1996), the Supreme Court ruled that a unilateral decision by the National Football League to pay non-roster players a salary of $1000 a week was not an antitrust violation because of the collective bargaining arrangement between the National Football League and the National Football League Players' Association (NFLPA). Even though the NFLPA had not agreed to restrain salary competition for non-roster players, the Supreme Court ruled the restraint legal because the issue had been subject to the collective bargaining process. In 2004, Maurice Clarett, a former college football player, challenged a National Football League rule preventing him from selling his services as a player to teams in the NFL. The Second Circuit cited the non-statutory exemption in deciding the National Football League rule legal.

Perhaps the most famous exemption from antitrust is the one enjoyed by Major League Baseball (MLB). MLB's exemption rests on the 1922 Supreme Court decision in *Federal Baseball Club of Baltimore, Inc. v. National League of Professional Baseball Clubs, et al.* The Court concluded that the antitrust laws did not apply to MLB because it was intrastate, not interstate commerce. The Court stated in later decisions (*Flood v. Kuhn*, 1972; *Toolson v. New York Yankees*, 1953) that after the Court's initial ruling, it became the responsibility of Congress to pass legislation to revoke baseball's antitrust exemption, and since Congress had not passed legislation, this was an indication that it did not believe the federal baseball decision should be overturned.

In 1998, Congress passed the Curt Flood Act, which revoked baseball's antitrust exemption only as it applies to player employment issues. If the Major League Baseball Players' Association (MLBPA) were to decertify itself as a union, it could file suit under the antitrust laws alleging that the actions of Major League Baseball are restraints of trade in the market for labor. Decertification is necessary because as long as the MLBPA is the exclusive bargaining agent for the players in the collective bargaining process, the non-statutory labor exemption holds.

In *Radovich v. National Football League* (1957), the Supreme Court made clear that Major League Baseball's antitrust exemption does not extend to other professional sport leagues.

ENFORCEMENT

Antitrust proceedings may be initiated by the Antitrust Division of the Department of Justice, the Federal Trade Commission, or by private parties (individuals or groups). While the Antitrust Division may institute criminal cases, the FTC only files civil cases. The government tends to focus on cases where the violation is clear or where the outcome has significance for society (e.g., the prosecution of Microsoft for antitrust violations). The vast majority of antitrust cases are filed by private parties who believe they have been injured by violation(s) of the antitrust laws by other parties. Antitrust activity in the sports industry is consistent with the overall pattern of private party suits rather than government action.

If the court decides an antitrust violation has occurred, it may fine individuals up to $100,000 and imprison them for up to 3 years in criminal cases. Organizations may be fined up to $1 million for violating antitrust laws. Private parties damaged by antitrust violations are awarded triple damages in civil cases. There is no limit on damage awards. The potential for large damage awards is part of the reason for the large number of private suits relative to government action.

The Antitrust Division and the FTC depend on individuals injured by antitrust violations filing suit. People injured by antitrust violations have an incentive to file suit because of the possibility receiving damage awards. To some extent, private suits are substitutes for government enforcement actions. Damage awards also provide a disincentive to violate the antitrust laws.

In cases involving the government, potential damage awards provide an incentive for the defendants to agree to consent decrees. Under a consent decree, the defendant promises to change behavior while not admitting guilt. A consent decree unlike a guilty verdict or plea is not conclusive evidence of guilt in possible subsequent private party lawsuits. With a consent decree, the government and the defendant can avoid the cost and uncertainty of a court trial.

Private party suits may also end with a settlement rather than a verdict in court. For example, a 2002 suit by Texas Motor Speedway against NASCAR for failing to sanction a second race at the track resulted in a negotiated settlement between the parties. The suit included allegations of antitrust violations and a breach of promise by NASCAR to sanction a second race at Texas Motor Speedway. Under the settlement, Texas Motor Speedway was allowed to purchase a racetrack in North Carolina and transfer a NASCAR event from the North Carolina track to the track in Texas. As part of the settlement, Texas Motor Speedway withdrew its suit against NASCAR.

BASIS FOR COURT DECISIONS

The Supreme Court uses two basic approaches to antitrust cases. Under the per se approach, the prosecution needs only to prove the activity in question has occurred. The court has adopted a per se approach to price fixing under Section 1 of the Sherman Act. If the prosecution in an antitrust case proves the defendants have fixed (or attempted to fix) prices, the court will convict. The court is unconcerned with the reasonableness of the prices or any justification for the price fixing. If the courts are convinced the action has occurred, the defendants are guilty.

The Ladies Professional Golf Association (LPGA) was found guilty of a per se violation of the antitrust laws in 1973 when it suspended Jane Blalock for cheating. Since the decision to suspend Ms. Blalock was made by other players on the LPGA Tour, the court ruled the suspension was a group boycott of a competitor. A group boycott of a competitor (like price fixing) is a per se violation of the antitrust laws. The court was uninterested in the reasonableness (or unreasonableness) of suspending a player for cheating.

Under the rule of reason approach, the prosecution must prove the alleged action has occurred and that society would be better off if the action was not permitted. The genesis of the rule of reason approach is that an action may have both anticompetitive and socially beneficial effects. The courts may adopt a rule of reason approach to an action that restrains trade but increases efficiency.

In a rule of reason case, the court considers the purpose of the action. Is it intended to help achieve a legitimate business purpose (such as increase efficiency) or is its primary purpose to restrain trade? Having a legitimate purpose is not enough. Under the rule of reason, the court examines the restrictiveness of the restraint of trade: Is it the least restrictive means possible to achieve this purpose (Drowatzky, 1997)?

While a group boycott of a competitor is a per se violation of the antitrust laws, a decision by a group to not deal with an individual (or firm) is subject to the rule of reason. In 1954, Jack Molinas was suspended by the National Basketball Association (NBA) for betting on games. His antitrust suit against the NBA was dismissed by the courts in 1961. The court ruled that the NBA's decision to suspend a player for gambling on games was a restraint of trade that was legal, because it was in the best interest of the league to prevent players from gambling on NBA games.

Which actions merit a rule of reason rather than a per se approach has developed in the courts over time in antitrust cases. The actions subject to per se treatment can and have changed. The antitrust treatment of tying contracts, a requirement that a consumer purchase good A in order to purchase good B, may be changing (Ahlborn, Evans, & Padilla, 2004). In the past, the court has treated a requirement to purchase good A as a condition of purchasing good B as a per se violation if the seller dominated the market for good B. Given recent decisions, the courts may be moving in the direction of considering efficiency gains from tying contracts as socially beneficial and therefore moving toward a rule of reason approach to tying contracts.

The evolving treatment of tying contract in antitrust cases is consistent with the alternative views of barriers to entry explained in Chapter 4. Those who view advertising, product differentiation product bundling, and economies of scale as barriers to entry are likely to be unhappy with the movement toward the rule of reason approach in tying contract cases. Those who view advertising, product differentiation product bundling, and economies of scale as forms of efficiency will welcome the movement toward a rule of reason approach.

MERGERS

Since mergers may affect the level of competition in industries, they are subject to review under the antitrust laws. There are three types of mergers. Horizontal mergers occur between two or more competing firms; one example would be if two athletic footwear companies, such as Adidas and Nike, were to merge. Vertical mergers involve firms in a buyer-seller relationship. A merger between Adidas (a sports apparel and shoe company) and Foot Locker retail stores would be an example of a vertical merger. A conglomerate merger occurs when the companies involved are not competitors and have no significant buyer-seller relationship.

Conglomerate mergers include mergers between companies producing the same product in different geographic markets (i.e., geographic market extension mergers), mergers between companies producing related products (i.e., product extension mergers), and mergers between firms that are basically unrelated in any meaningful way (i.e., pure conglomerate mergers). As examples, a merger between a chain of fitness clubs in Kentucky and a chain in Illinois would be a geographic market extension merger, a merger between a racquet ball club and golf course would be a products extension merger (both are in the fitness industry), and a merger between Rawlings Sporting Goods and Ernest & Julio Gallo wines would be a pure conglomerate merger (the companies are in unrelated industries).

The legality of mergers depends on their effect upon competition. Mergers often have legitimate purposes and may increase competition through increasing efficiency and reducing costs. If a merger improves the efficiency of a firm, it puts competitive pressure on other firms to improve their efficiency, which benefits consumers. A horizontal merger may make a firm more efficient in production, a vertical merger may improve efficiency in the distribution of products, and a conglomerate merger may increase efficiency in obtaining financing by reducing the firm's risk through diversification.

In antitrust enforcement, the procompetitive effects of mergers are weighed against their anticompetitive effects. The type of merger that receives the most antitrust

Photo by Alek von Felkerzam, courtesy of stock.xchng iv

scrutiny is horizontal mergers because they are more likely than other types of mergers to have anticompetitive effects. In the extreme, horizontal mergers can create monopoly by combining all firms in a market. The closer the market is to monopoly after a proposed merger, the more likely an antitrust challenge to a merger.

The decision by antitrust authorities in the United States not to challenge the proposed merger between Reebok and Adidas in 2005 provides insight into the current state of antitrust enforcement toward horizontal mergers. Even though the market for athletic footwear is concentrated, with the top four firms having approximately 75% of the market, a merger between the second and third largest firms was not challenged. The merger between Adidas and Reebok is viewed as procompetitive because the combined firm may be able to more effectively compete against the industry leader, Nike. Given its market share, a merger between Nike and any significant firm in the market is likely to be challenged. While other firms in a concentrated market may grow through merger to challenge the dominant firm, growth through merger by the dominant firm is unlikely to be acceptable under the antitrust laws.

In today's legal environment, vertical and conglomerate mergers are unlikely to be challenged. Vertical and conglomerate mergers are seen as having few if any anticompetitive effects. Instead, they are defended as a source of efficiency, potentially increasing competition in a market.

MONOPOLIZATION

The Sherman Act makes monopolizing or attempting to monopolize trade or commerce illegal. One of the difficulties in enforcing the Sherman Act's prohibition of monopolization is the problem of superior business practices and products. A firm with superior business practices or products can monopolize a market through eliminating competitors by offering consumers more satisfaction for their money. Punishing a firm that has achieved monopoly (or near monopoly) by being more efficient then its competitors harms consumers.

For example, punishing Wal-Mart for driving local mom and pop sporting goods stores out of business is likely to harm consumers. Wal-Mart can charge lower prices because of discounts from buying in large quantities from suppliers and other efficiencies in their operation. Given the relatively low barriers to entry into the local retail sporting goods market, if Wal-Mart were to raise prices to a monopoly level following the exit of existing stores, new stores would open, reducing Wal-Mart's profit. Wal-Mart's lower prices are likely to benefit customers long into the future.

Economists in general do not believe predatory pricing (pricing below costs to drive competitors out of business) is a significant source of monopoly. For prices to be predatory and violate the antitrust laws prices must be below cost. Pricing below costs causes losses for the firm. To compensate for those losses, the firm must raise prices once other firms have left the market. If a firm raises prices to the monopoly level, new firms will enter, making it impossible to sustain higher than competitive prices. Earning losses to drive competitors out of business does not make sense if a firm cannot recoup those losses with higher prices. When chain stores are able to charge lower prices than mom and pop sporting good stores, it is not predatory pricing but competitive pricing given lower costs due to greater efficiency.

One of the issues courts decide in a monopolization case is the definition of the relevant market. The relevant market is used by the court to assess whether or not a firm has monopolized or attempted to monopolize a market. In general, defendants in monopolization cases argue for a broad definition of the market while the prosecution argues for a narrow definition. A broad definition of the market typically leaves the defendant with a smaller market share and less likely to be convicted of violating Section 2 of the Sherman Act. If accused of monopolizing the market for professional football, the NFL might argue it competes in the much broader entertainment industry, an industry where it clearly does not have a monopoly.

PRICE FIXING

The Sherman Act makes price fixing illegal. Colluding with competitors to fix prices violates the antitrust laws. It does not matter if the firms involved are large or small, if the prices charged are reasonable or unreasonable, colluding with competitors is illegal. According to the United States Justice Department, price fixing includes cooperation by competitors to "establish or adhere to uniform price discounts; eliminate discounts; adopt a standard formula for the computation of selling prices; notify others prior to reducing prices; fix credit terms; maintain predetermined price differentials between different quantities, types, or sizes of products; and maintain floor prices" (United States Department of Justice, 2003, p. 6).

The Justice Department treats bid rigging and market allocation by competitors the same as price fixing. In both bid rigging and market allocation, firms conspire so as to avoid competing with one another for customers. In bid rigging, competitors decide which firms will win contracts to supply customers when the contracts are awarded through a bidding process. Market allocation is when competitors divide customers amongst themselves so as to avoid competition.

An agreement by competitors to fix prices, rig bids, or allocate markets does not have to be in writing to violate the law. If the plaintiffs (either government agency or private party) convince the courts that firms have agreed to fix prices, rig bids, or allocate markets, the firms will be convicted even without evidence of a formal agreement. The courts treat price fixing, bid rigging, and market allocation agreements as per se illegal.

Not only are agreements to fix prices, rig bids, or allocate markets illegal, but they are also difficult to successfully implement. To increase price, industry output must be reduced. While firms promise to cut production, each firm is tempted to produce more to take advantage of the higher price caused by the decrease in output of other firms. If firms give in to the temptation, industry output is not decreased and price does not increase. In a bid rigging scheme, firms are tempted to undercut their rivals to win contracts they have not been assigned. In a market allocation agreement, firms may choose to compete for customers not assigned to them.

If the major producers of athletic shoes were to decide which firms would enter into contracts with which universities to provide shoes for their athletic programs, it would violate the Sherman Act. Not only would this market allocation agreement be illegal, it would also be difficult to maintain. It is easy to imagine shoe companies entering into negotiations with colleges and universities not assigned to them to further raise their profile.

THE DUAL NATURE OF PROFESSIONAL SPORTS LEAGUES AND ANTITRUST

The nature of professional sports leagues makes enforcement of the antitrust laws problematic. Professional sports leagues are simultaneously a single entity and a collection of competing firms. The dual nature of leagues is evident in the distribution of revenue across teams. While some revenue streams are shared evenly across all teams in a league, other streams are retained by the individual teams. The dual nature is important to antitrust considerations because actions which may be legal as a single firm may be illegal as an agreement of competing firms.

A firm may decide where to locate production facilities without worry of prosecution under the antitrust laws. In 1980, the NFL denied the request of the Oakland Raiders to move to Los Angeles to play in the Coliseum. In 1982, the Raiders and the Coliseum successfully challenged the NFL's decision based on the antitrust laws, and the Raiders moved to Los Angeles without the NFL's approval. The courts have adopted a rule of reason approach to restraints imposed by a league because the courts recognize some cooperation among teams in a league is necessary for the league to operate efficiently.

Exemptions to the antitrust laws are important to professional sports leagues. In the Sports Broadcasting Act of 1961, Congress gave professional sports leagues the right to sell their television rights as a single firm rather than as competing firms. The statutory and non-statutory labor exemptions have enabled professional sports leagues to negotiate restrictions as part of collective bargaining agreements which otherwise would be subject to scrutiny under the antitrust laws.

The maximum salary limitations (per team and per player) in the NBA are unlikely to be successfully challenged using the antitrust laws because it is the result of an arms-length (i.e., fairly negotiated) agreement between the owners and the players' union.

The statutory and non-statutory labor exemptions are important even to Major League Baseball due to the passage of the Curt Flood Act in 1998. While Major League Baseball is exempt from the antitrust laws due to judicial precedent, Congress has limited the exemption in the area of labor relations. In the absence of a collective bargaining agreement, restrictions by Major League Baseball on players could be challenged under the antitrust laws.

The ability of leagues to negotiate restrictions on competition as part of collective bargaining agreements has enabled them to act together to establish rules regarding player movement, allocation, and salaries without concern about the antitrust laws. In the absence of those agreements, league rules on player movement, allocation, and salaries would be subject to antitrust consideration and evaluated on a rule of reason basis. Avoiding antitrust lawsuits is desirable in part because of the uncertainty involved in antitrust cases.

The uncertainty of the outcomes of antitrust cases is illustrated by the 1982 decision to allow the Oakland Raiders to move to Los Angeles despite the NFL's disapproval. In a similar antitrust lawsuit in 1974, the California Seals were forced to abide by the NHL's decision to not allow them to play in Vancouver. Both antitrust suits involved teams wanting to relocate without the approval of the other teams in the league. In one case the team won, in the other the team lost.

Under the rule of reason approach used to decide antitrust cases involving restrictions on competition by a league, the court considers the intention and extent of the restriction. One of the incentives created by the uncertainty over the courts interpretation of the intent and restrictiveness of league rules is for antitrust suits to be settled out of court through negotiations. The uncertainty of the outcome of an antitrust case is one of the reasons Dallas Cowboys owner Jerry Jones and the NFL reached a negotiated settlement in a dispute over marketing rights in 1996.

Jones believed his team would be better off if they handled their own marketing and licensing rather than sharing in the revenue generated by agreements negotiated by the NFL as a whole. Having the league act for the teams reduces competition among NFL teams to obtain marketing and licensing agreements and could be considered a restraint of trade if the league is viewed as a collection of competing firms. A league-wide approach to marketing and licensing reduces revenue disparities among teams, which may improve competitive balance and in turn enhance the quality of the league's product. Uncertainty over how the courts would interpret the intent and extent of the restriction gave both parties an incentive to come to an agreement rather than risking losing in court.

ANTITRUST ACTIONS BY COMPETING PROFESSIONAL SPORTS LEAGUES

Antitrust lawsuits can be part of the strategy of a newly formed sports league to gain parity with an existing sports league, or it can be the result of the failure of a new league. Litigation in this area has been related to a variety of issues. First, established leagues have been accused of attempting to control geographic markets (Berry & Wong, 1986). For example, in *American Football League v. National Football League* (1963), the American Football League (AFL) accused the NFL of trying to monopolize the best markets. Shortly before the creation of the AFL, the NFL added franchises in Minnesota and Dallas, two prime sites the AFL was targeting. The court ruled the NFL had as much right as the new league to those geographic markets and was under no obligation to cede those areas to the AFL (Champion, 1993). Both leagues could put teams in those locations and compete for fans.

Second, established leagues have been accused of trying to control the player market (Berry & Wong, 1986). For example, the World Hockey League (WHL) successfully argued in *Philadelphia World Hockey, Inc. v. Philadelphia Hockey Club, Inc.* (1972) that the NHL's reserve clause made it impossible for players to leave their NHL team for a WHL team (Masteralexis, 1997). The NHL was monopolizing the player market and preventing the WHL from signing the marquee players the league needed to be successful.

Third, established leagues have been sued for their attempts to control stadium usage (Berry & Wong, 1986). Because a given area may have only one suitable facility, if a team from the established league owns the stadium or signs an exclusive use agreement with the facility, a new league may not be able to place a franchise in that area. The cost of a new facility would be a significant barrier to entry that may be impossible to overcome. The decision in *Hecht v. Pro Football Inc.* (1977) clearly indicates the courts believe that actions by teams to maintain exclusive control over a facility are limited by the antitrust laws (Berry & Wong, 1986).

Fourth, the leagues have been accused of trying to control television markets in order to eliminate competition (Berry & Wong, 1986). Because television revenues are a significant percentage of total team revenue, over 50% in some leagues (Howard & Crompton, 1995), if the established league can keep the new league from obtaining a lucrative national television rights agreement, they can keep the new league from successfully competing. The most famous case involving control over the television market was the *United States Football League v. National Football League* (1986). Although the jury agreed the NFL had monopolized the television market, it did not believe the harm done to the USFL by the NFL's actions was significant and awarded the USFL only $1, automatically tripled to $3 (Maurice & Smithson, 1988). The jury believed the USFL's trouble with obtaining a good television contract was more related to the weakness of the league than to any NFL actions.

Finally, existing leagues have been accused of trying to control access to corporate sponsors (Cavanaugh, 1999). Following the demise of the American Basketball League (ABL), a professional basketball league for women, the state attorney general of Connecticut investigated the actions of the Women's National Basketball League (WNBA) for antitrust violations. Among the areas of his investigation was concern over the WNBA's actions in the markets of sponsorships and television contracts.

ANTITRUST AND THE NATIONAL COLLEGIATE ATHLETIC ASSOCIATION

The National Collegiate Athletic Association (NCAA) resembles a professional sports league. The NCAA can be seen as a single entity or a group of competitors working together. Since the NCAA dominates the market for intercollegiate athletics, it is not surprising the NCAA has been subject to antitrust litigation. Wins and losses by the NCAA in antitrust cases have had significant effects on intercollegiate athletics.

A crucial antitrust victory for the NCAA occurred in 1983 when the courts ruled against the Association for Intercollegiate Athletics for Women (AIAW). The AIAW governed intercollegiate athletics for women beginning in 1971. In the early 1980s, as the NCAA began to offer championships for women athletes in a variety of sports, universities and colleges left the AIAW for the NCAA. The AIAW responded to the defections with an antitrust lawsuit against the NCAA for attempting to monopolize the market for women's intercollegiate athletics. A federal district court ruled for the NCAA and the decision was not appealed. Two important antitrust defeats for the NCAA followed its victory in the AIAW case. The first case involved the sale of broadcast rights to intercollegiate football games, the second the earnings of college coaches.

Prior to the mid 1980s, the NCAA negotiated a national television contract for college football on behalf of its member institutions (*National Collegiate Athletic Association v. Board of Regents of the University of Oklahoma and University of Georgia Athletic Assn.*, 1984). This arrangement resembled the current practice of the NFL. The association-wide negotiations allowed the NCAA to limit the output (i.e., number of games televised) to increase the price charged (i.e., the television rights fees paid by the stations to broadcast games). The agreement limited the output per organization (i.e., number of games on television for each school) and attempted to spread the revenue more evenly among the members.

Some of the more powerful members of the NCAA believed they could do better without the agreement. They could sell more output (i.e., televise more games) and increase the total revenue they would receive (i.e., individual share of the television rights fees). Many of the major football powers formed the College Football Association (CFA) to negotiate a contract that would increase revenue and the number of games televised (Drowatzky, 1997). This second contract resulted in litigation between the NCAA and the CFA member schools led by the Universities of Oklahoma and Georgia (*National Collegiate Athletic Association v. Board of Regents of the University of Oklahoma and University of Georgia Athletic Assn.*, 1984).

The Supreme Court agreed with the schools that the NCAA's association-wide television agreement was anticompetitive and led to an increase in prices and a decrease in output (Horowitz, 1984). This restraint of trade was a violation of the antitrust laws under the rule of reason because the Court believed the restraint's primary purpose was to inhibit competition and not to increase efficiency. The case was judged under the rule of reason rather than as a per se price fixing case because cooperation among the competitors is necessary to produce the product, intercollegiate football games. The impact of the case has been similar to the demise of a price fixing agreement. Output (the number of games on television) increased significantly, price (the rights fees on a per game basis) decreased, and the total revenue earned by the NCAA has declined relative to what it would have been with a single seller of television rights.

The second important antitrust defeat for the NCAA involved efforts to control the earnings of some basketball coaches at member institutions. To reduce cost of its members, the NCAA in 1991 passed a bylaw establishing a maximum salary for a type of basketball coaching position at Division I institutions (Hamilton, 2003). The affected coaches began a class action suit against the NCAA claiming the rule was anticompetitive and a violation of the antitrust laws. In *Law v. National Collegiate Athletic Association* (1995), the court agreed with the coaches. Using the rule of reason, the court found that the restraint was not justified by a legitimate purpose. Damages were found by the court to be over $22 million, which under the antitrust laws was trebled to approximately $67 million (Hamilton, 2003). The NCAA finally settled the case for $55.5 million.

The NCAA is likely to continue to face antitrust lawsuits because of its dominance of intercollegiate athletics and the cooperation among competitors required to produce the product. Given the nature of production, restraints imposed by the NCAA are likely to be judged under the rule of reason. If the NCAA can justify the restraints to the courts as serving legitimate purposes, the NCAA will win; if they cannot convince the courts of the restraint's reasonableness, they will lose.

The uncertainty of outcomes of antitrust cases involving the NCAA is illustrated by two recent antitrust cases. Both cases involved NCAA rules limiting participation in outside of regular season intercollegiate basketball tournaments. The NCAA won an antitrust case (*Worldwide Basketball and Sports Tours, Inc v. NCAA*, 2004) filed by preseason basketball tournament promoters when the Supreme Court refused to hear an appeal of an appellate court's decision in favor of the NCAA. The NCAA purchased the National Invitation Tournament (NIT) to settle an ongoing antitrust lawsuit (*MIBA v. NCAA*, 2004) filed by the NIT.

In the cases "two courts reached very different conclusions with respect to relevant market on fundamentally the same allegations" (Antitrust Update, 2005, p. 6). In one case, the court did not see anticompetitive harm because of the lack of a distinct market in which the damage occurred and therefore dismissed the complaint of the preseason basketball tournament promoters. In the second, the court ruled the NIT's suit could continue because of the possibility of anticompetitive harm in a distinct market. Both cases involved similar NCAA restrictions, yet in one case the court dismissed the suit and in the other allowed it to continue.

There is significant risk for the NCAA from possible antitrust lawsuits. The NCAA could face antitrust litigation by student athletes, particularly those in the revenue-producing sports. NCAA rules restrict competition for players, which reduces the compensation players receive. NCAA rules also limit the income athletes can earn from other sources. For example, athletes cannot endorse athletic footwear; instead schools endorse this product in return for revenue that could go directly to athletes had the rule not existed.

The NCAA argues its athlete compensation rules are not anticompetitive but are designed to protect the athlete and to maintain the integrity of amateur athletics. This benign view of the NCAA's rules is not shared by all. Robert Barro has described the NCAA as "the clear choice for best monopoly in America" because of its ability to suppress completion for athletes (Barro, 2002, para. 6). According to Barro, NCAA rules are comparable to the actions of a cartel. They are designed to keep revenue for the member institutions at the expense of student athletes.

Under the rule of reason approach used in antitrust cases, the courts decide which view of NCAA rules restricting competition for student athletes is appropriate. Given the possibility of alternative interpretations of NCAA restrictions on athletes and institutions, there are varying degrees of uncertainty about how the courts will rule in any one case. The NCAA must consider the antitrust implications of restrictions it places on student athletes and on institutions given the potential for antitrust suits.

Summary

The purpose of this chapter was to explain the antitrust laws and their importance in the sport industry. In the United States, the courts interpret the laws Congress writes. The antitrust laws and their interpretation have changed over time. Exemptions to the antitrust laws that have significance in the sport industry have been created by Congress and the courts. Major League Baseball's exemption, the labor exemption, and the Sports Broadcasting Act of 1961 are examples.

While some actions are per se illegal, such as price fixing, others are subject to the rule of reason. Under the rule of reason, the courts compare the harm done to competition by an action with the benefits of the action from increased efficiency. Since restrains of trade by a league may reduce competition among its members but may also increase the efficiency of the league, making it more competitive, antitrust challenges to league rules are often decided on a rule of reason basis. This is true for both professional and amateur sports.

Chapter Questions

1. Briefly explain the major federal antitrust laws.
2. Evaluate the following statement: Only Congress can create exemptions to the antitrust laws.
3. Why are the actions of sport leagues that restrain trade evaluated on a rule of reason basis?
4. List three possible horizontal mergers in the sport industry that you believe should not be allowed. Explain why you believe these mergers should not be allowed.
5. Why do defendants in a monopolization case prefer a broad definition of the relevant market?
6. Briefly explain three antitrust issues that arise between rival professional sport leagues.
7. Evaluate the following statement: If some large schools belonged to the National Association of Intercollegiate Athletics, the National Collegiate Athletics Association would face fewer antitrust issues.
8. Why is there uncertainty about the outcome of antitrust cases involving the rules of professional sports leagues?

Chapter Twelve

INTERNATIONAL ISSUES

Introduction

Sport management professionals today face many issues that have never been dealt with before. Some of those issues have an intentional connotation, such as globalization. Globalization has made the world economy more interdependent, more open and transparent, and more competitive. The globalization of sport has paralleled and been influenced by this trend. Today, sport is widely viewed as a cultural universal or global phenomenon. The increased internationalization of sport business activities and the demand from the sport industry for managers who are educated and trained to be capable of handling various international business matters have grown considerably. The globalization of sport calls for sport management professionals to devote more of their attention to international issues. This chapter is intended to provide sport management students with information that may help them understand those issues. Specifically, the chapter will address the following: Why does an economic system affect the sport governance in a certain nation? What is the theoretical foundation in economics for globalization of sport? How can sport organizations expand internationally? What are the organizational patterns of sports clubs in the world?

International Issues

Susie Ford, a student who graduated from one of the NASPE/NASSM-approved graduate sport management programs, was recently hired as an assistant to the chief operating officer of NGS International, a sporting goods company. Due to the heavy competition in the domestic sporting goods market as well as the relative saturation in the kind of sporting goods that the company produces, its management wants to open up a new market in South America. So Susie's first assignment is to develop a plan for the company to expand into the market in South America. What kind of information should Susie collect to complete this project? What will the expansion plan look like?

Types of Economic Systems and Sport Governance

INTRODUCTION TO ECONOMIC SYSTEMS

An economic system is "a set of relations among decision-makers and between decision-makers and economic variables. It consists of the sum of ideas, goals, methods, and institutions used in society to resolve these economic issues in some more or less organized or 'systematic way'" (Elliott, 1985, p. 3). The economic systems embraced and adopted by various countries are distinguishable in three major areas (Elliott, 1985; Parkin, 1993):

1. The structure of an economic system. The "structure [of economics systems] refers to salient features that characterize an economic system and distinguish it from others" (Elliott, 1985, p. 5), which may include, but are not limited to,

ownership, control of the means of production, locus and organization of economic power, and social processes for economic coordination. For example, the economic system in the People's Republic of China before the 1980s approximates *centralized socialism*, in which the government owns and controls all enterprises. Economic power is unilaterally possessed by the government because it decides what to produce, how to produce it, and how much to produce. As a result of economic reform starting in the 1980s, some decentralization has occurred in the Chinese system, and private ownerships have been permitted to join the state enterprises in production since then.

2. Various aspects of economizing behaviors of an economic system. Using various incentive arrangements, a specific economic system has its own methods of allocating resources, distributing income, and maintaining economic stability. These methods are referred to as the economic behaviors of the system. Scarcity of resources forces an economic system to choose a method, which can satisfy to the greatest extent the needs of society, to allocate and use the scarce resources and to distribute income among different economic classes so as to maintain ultimately the economic stability of the system. Generally, the economic behavior of the economy in the United States can be best interpreted by the term *managed capitalism*. The federal government often uses various monetary and fiscal policies (adjustments made to the interest) to promote economic stability.

3. The performance of an economic system. How efficiently and equally the resources are distributed is one main criterion used to evaluate the performance of an economic system. The other areas related to the performance of an economic system are employment, price stability, and growth.

In general, socialism, welfare state capitalism, and capitalism are the three most represented and endorsed economic systems (Parkin, 1993). Socialism represents the type of economic system that is based on state ownership of capital, means of production, and land; and resources are allocated based on a central economic plan (Parkin, 1993). Two main versions of socialism are derived from the classic socialist theories: (a) centrally planned socialism and (b) decentralized socialism. Prior to the economic reforms in the 1980s, as mentioned previously, the economy of the People's Republic of China was in principle typical, centrally planned socialism. Considerable changes have taken place in this system in recent decades. More and more privately owned enterprises are joining the public counterparts in production. To a certain extent, the current form of the economic system in the People's Republic of China would probably be better labeled as decentralized socialism, another version of socialism. In the decentralized system, private elements are included in the ownership and control of the means of production. The public sector, however, still maintains its control over the economy. Decentralized socialism shares some traits with both centrally planned socialism and capitalism.

Capitalism, on the other hand, is "an economic system in which the means of production and distribution are privately owned by individuals or corporations who receive the income earned thereon" (Shim & Siegel, 1995, p. 53). The evolution and alterations of the classic theories on capitalism have created several versions of capitalism. Managed capitalism is one version of capitalism that warrants some further discussion. Managed capitalism is a particular condition that can be used to denote the type of economic system found in the United States. The government controls the economic activities of the private sector by regulation, subsidy, support, and mediation.

Welfare state capitalism, also referred to as "the social democracy system," is an economic system that stands in between the capitalist and socialist systems. This system has been adopted in the United Kingdom and in several Scandinavian countries, such as Norway, Denmark, and Sweden. The social democracy system is still a capitalistic-based system. A certain level of social ownership (or state government) in the industry and its control over the private sector are maintained for the sake of reducing social inequality in society and promoting societal cooperation and stability. Representations of social ownership are typically found in such industries as public utilities, basic industries, and financial enterprises. Industries in these areas are usually nationalized to prevent exploitation of consumers. Economic decisions are based on four basic social processes—price system, democracy, bureaucracy, and bargaining—and the government has consciously regulated the market to ensure competition and economic efficiency (Elliott, 1985). Table 12-1 compares the characteristics of managed capitalism and centralized socialism.

Table 12-1. Comparison of the Characteristics of Managed Capitalism and Centralized Socialism

Dimensions	Economic Systems and Characteristics	
	Managed Capitalism	Centralized Socialism
Level of economics development	Highly developed	Underdeveloped, but developing
Resource base	Highly capitalistic	In the process of transformation into capitalistic
Ownership-control of instrument of production	Predominantly private-capitalist and corporate; separation of ownership and control	Dominantly government ownership-control
Locus of economic power	Dispersed, yet concentrated in large-scale private and public organizations	Government, central planning board (CPB)
Organization of economic power	Mixture of centralization and decentralization	Dominantly centralized
Social processes for making and coordinating economic decisions	Mixture of competitive/monopolistic price system, democracy, bureaucracy, and bargaining	Dominantly government hierarchy
Motivational system	Individual economic gain	Government promotion of social goal

Source: The table is modified from Elliott (1985), *Comparative Economic Systems*, Table 9-1, page 165.

SPORT GOVERNANCE UNDER VARIOUS ECONOMIC SYSTEMS

The sport governance system in a nation is a function of the structure and behavior of its own economic system. Based on this assumption, three major types of sport governance systems have been identified accordingly as corresponding to the economic systems discussed above: (a) the centralized sport governance system, (b) the decentralized sport governance system, and (c) a combination of the other two types of governance systems.

The centralized sport governance system, commonly adopted by the economies that embrace socialism, refers to the sport managing system in a nation in which a specific government unit at every level of government is responsible for overseeing sport-related affairs and operations. In general, the sport governance system in the People's Republic of China is an example of the centralized sport governance system. The General Administration of Sport (formerly the State Sports Commission) is empowered by the Chinese government to handle all matters in the sport industry in the nation. Its responsibilities include, but are not limited to, (a) establishing sport policies and overseeing their implementation, (b) developing strategic plans for sports development, (c) preparing and coordinating competitions for all high-performance sports, and (d) setting up specific policies for the sport industry and promoting the development of a sport market.

The decentralized sport governance system refers to the sport managing system in a nation in which government has no or very limited involvement in managing sport, and no government units at both the federal/national and state/provincial levels are specifically established for sport. The government utilizes the same legislation passed for the business community to regulate the sport industry. Various non-government entities, such as individual national sports-governing bodies and administrative associations, split the power and assume the responsibility of regulating a specific segment of the sport industry. The sport governance system in the United States illustrates precisely the decentralized sport governance system. For example, collegiate sports are regulated and controlled respectively by three different national associations (i.e., NCAA, NAIA, and NJCAA). There is no specific entity in either federal or state government functionally set up for managing sport at all. There are no or limited policies developed by the government to handle sport-related matters. There are no or limited financial subsidies provided by the government to sport development in the country.

The sport governing systems in many nations can be characterized as a combination of the two previously mentioned types of sport governance systems. The sport governance systems in both Canada and Australia exemplify this type of combination system. Governments in these countries have a great deal of involvement in developing sport policies for the public sector, but they exercise very limited supervision over the sport operations controlled by the private sector. In other words, their governments do not regulate and police the private sport sector as much as they do the public sport sector. For example, as a government entity at the federal level, the Australian Sports Commission is responsible for the delivery of funding and development of Australian sport through the implementation of the government's sport policy and the support of a wide range of programs designed to de-

Table 12-2. Characteristics of the Three Basic Types of Sport Governance Systems in the World

	Centralized System	Decentralized System	Combination
National Policies	There are policies outlined by government for sport development in all sectors of the sport industry	No specific policies are made by government for sport development	National policies are drawn specifically for mass sport development and for national pride
Funding	Government provides funding to sports organizations at all levels	No government subsidies are provided to sport organizations	Funding is provided by government to national sports organizations
Organization/Structure	There are government units at all levels of government responsible for overseeing sport development	No government units are set up specifically for sport development; sport development is the main responsibility of various national sport organizations	Similar to the centralized system, but the government units are set up mainly for promoting sport and fitness among its citizenry
Control/Regulation	Government regulates sport organizations in both the public and private sectors	Government regulates the sport industry as it does other industries	Government regulates the public sector of the sport industry

velop sporting excellence and increase participation and achievement by all Australians (Australian Sports Commission, 2006). Similar circumstances can be found in Canada. Sport Canada is an agency within the government's fitness and amateur sport directorate. Its major responsibilities include (a) strengthening sport leadership, (b) providing strategic support for high performance programming, (c) promoting technically sound sport development, (d) enhancing opportunities for sport participation, (e) maximizing the benefits of hosting, (f) promoting linguistic duality in the Canadian sport system, (g) strengthening the ethical foundation of sport, (h) expanding the body of knowledge about sport, (i) strengthening Sport Canada program and policy evaluation, and (j) harmonizing the Canadian sport system (Sport Canada, 2005). Table 12-2 summarizes the characteristics of the three main sport governance systems in the world.

Government Involvement in Sport and Controversies

Government involvement in sport varies from country to country. The involvement is either though the implementation of sport policies and legislation or through the investment of pubic funds for sport development. According to Coakley (2001), governments at various levels in a particular nation are generally motivated to get involved in sport for a number of obligatory reasons (Coakley, 2001). The most common or conventional reasons are to maintain fitness and physical abilities among citizens (International Working Group on Women and Sport, 2002; Robertson, 2003); to promote the prestige and power of a group, community, or nation; to promote a sense of identity, belonging, and unity among citizens; and to promote economic development in the community or society (Coakley, 2001).

How a government should involve itself in the promotion of sport development in a nation has long been a controversial subject. Should the government spend limited financial resources on promoting opportunities for its citizens to participate in sport, ultimately improving their levels of physical fitness? Or should the government invest its fortune to promote economic development in the community (Coakley, 2001) through sponsoring initiatives that aim at promoting spectatorship of sport-related games and entertainment? Or should the government adopt an approach that will address both? The spirit of this approach was well reflected in the *Game Plan*, a recent government report published jointly by the Prime Minister's Strategy Unit and the Department for Culture, Media and Sport in Great Britain. The plan called for developing a 20-year strategic plan government involvement in attracting "mega" sport events, such as Olympic Games, football's World Cup and the world athletic championships, for increasing the levels of mass participation in sport and fitness activities, and for developing world-class athletes through increasing grassroots participation in sport and elite sporting excellence (Robertson, 2003).

Increasing government involvement in bidding for international sport events may require hundreds of millions of public funds to be spent on improving the conditions of existing facilities or building more facilities. According to those who advocate the use of taxpayers' money for sport facility development and for bringing mega sport events, the spending is justified by the economic impact generated from those events. Spectators attending those events will inject new wealth to the host community and nation. For example, it was estimated that the Georgia Department of Revenue collected approximately more than $176 million net revenue from the 1996 Atlanta Summer Olympic Games.

Nevertheless, such an approach of investing millions in sport event bidding and development has been heavily criticized by proponents who urge more government attention and funding in community-related sport and physical activity (Christie, 2003). They insist that it be a government's basic responsibility to encourage community-based health promotion, physical fitness, and participation in sport, and to stress that a national policy must be developed for this purpose. It has been a common phenomenon observed worldwide that the increased spending on bringing mega sport events often leads to the decline of governmental funding in supporting the grassroots and community sport. As the British government proposed to spend more resources to bid for the 2012 Olympic Games, it was estimated that more than 70,000 community sports clubs have or will be forced out of business due to lack of funding and government support (Guardian Newspapers, 2003).

In many countries around the world, governments have become increasingly involved in elite sport development for the sake of promoting the prestige and power of their nations (Coakley, 2001). While affirming the continuous commitment to encouraging sport participation among their citizens, those governments constantly adjust their strategies for international sport competition.

Because of the continuing development of new technology, the last decade of the 20th century saw tremendous global interactions and international competitions in

Globalization of Sport

many areas. No exception was found in the sport industry. The intensified races and competitions among nations in such events as the Olympic Games and the world championships sponsored by various international sport federations and among teams within a professional sports league that crosses national borders have been noticed everywhere (Thoma & Chalip, 1996; Wilcox, 1994). To accomplish the objective of winning international competitions, many nations and sport enterprises in those nations have taken advantage of the globalization of sport. For example, the international sports channel, ESPN, broadcasts to over 165 countries in Asia, Europe, and Latin America. Due to the labor-intensive nature of manufacturing sporting goods, many American firms, such as Nike, have shifted much of their production to East Asia, where wage rates are generally lower and thus allow the company to achieve the greatest efficiencies in production.

THEORETICAL FOUNDATION OF THE GLOBALIZATION OF SPORT

Globalization is a process of political, economic, and cultural penetrations among nations. In the context of sport, globalization refers to the increased interactions and integration among sport organizations and enterprises around the world. The law of comparative advantage, also known as the law of comparative costs, is an economic doctrine that provides a theoretical explanation of the process of globalization in sport (Yeh & Li, 1998).

The theoretical crux of this law is summarized in the following two points:

1. Whether or not one of two regions is absolutely more efficient in the production of every commodity that is in order, if each specializes in the products in which it has a comparative advantage (greater relative efficiency), trade will be mutually profitable.

2. An ill-designed prohibitive tariff, far from helping the protected factor of production, will reduce the real wage by making imports expensive and by making the whole world less productive through eliminating the sufficiency inherent in the best pattern of specialization and division of labor.

Table 12-3. Production and Demand for Regions A and B (Before Trade)

Region	Cost	Demand	Total Cost
A	@X = $1	X = 40	$40
	@Y = $3	Y = 20	$60
			$100
B	@X = $3	X = 20	$60
	@Y = $1	Y = 40	$40
			$100
A + B			$200

Table 12-4. Production and Demand for Regions A and B (After Trade)

Region	Cost	Produce	Total Cost
A...........	@X = $1.........	X = 60............	$60
	@Y = $3	Y = 0	$0
			$60
B..........	@X = $3	X = 0	$0
	@Y = $1	Y = 60	$60
			$60
A + B			$120

Therefore, these two regions can share benefits because the total number of products manufactured by these two regions increases and the total costs of producing the products decrease (Samuelson, 1970). This law can be further explained with an example. A and B are two different regions. Both regions need products X and Y. Table 12-3 illustrates their initial production and demand before trading with each other.

As Table 12-3 shows, both A and B have their production strengths (X for A and Y for B); however, A and B also have their weaknesses (Y for region A and X for region B). If there are no trade barriers between these regions, and their production factors (e.g., wages or transportation fees) are the same, each region can identify its own advantages and disadvantages and produce only one product, which will cost it less (X for region A, and Y for region B), then trade its surplus products to the other region. Table 12-4 indicates their situation after trade.

Region A produces X, and region B produces Y. Both regions produce more units than their domestic demands require; then their total costs reduce to $60. They can exchange the extra 20 units and satisfy their mutual demands.

OUTCOMES OF GLOBALIZATION

From the perspective of the law of comparative advantage, globalization may have three possible outcomes:

1. Specialization. When nations and firms are aggressively pursuing profit maximization, specialization is an inevitable outcome. Without specialization, opportunity costs will be increased, which may lead to inefficiency in resource allocation.

2. Increasing output. The production factors (e.g., labor) that are saved as a result of specialization may then be reused in the production process to generate greater output.

3. Increasing the gap between the rich and the poor. There are always suggestions for how to share increased wealth. According to the law of comparative advantage, nations and firms will concentrate on the production of a particular product and trade it to each other due to the effect of specialization. However, each

nation or firm involved in the trade may not receive the same share of the profit. Those nations and firms that are wealthier have advanced technologies that allow them to create economies of scale in their production, have better marketing abilities, and usually generate greater profit. Consequently, if this trend continues, the gap between the rich and the poor will be gradually widened.

While the first two outcomes mentioned above are highly desirable, the third should be prevented. Economists, especially those from the less developed nations, are constantly seeking ways to increase the level of productivity or output without increasing the gap between rich and poor nations.

APPLICATIONS OF THE LAW OF COMPARATIVE ADVANTAGE

Having been refined by various economists, the law of comparative advantage has become one of the important principles observed closely in international trade for almost 200 years. Its application in globalizing the world economy is fourfold. First, in order to save costs on materials and on transportation, many business conglomerates tend to establish overseas divisions to produce parts for their products or directly sell them locally.

Many enterprises tend to set up their overseas markets to product- or sale-specific products directly, which may save the costs of materials and transportation.

Trade alliances, agreements, and contracts are set among nations for their mutual benefits.

Many nations set up duty or tariff barriers to prevent their domestic resources, either natural materials or human resources, from being exported massively or to prevent "dumping" from other countries that may be harmful to their domestic industries. As a result, competition and cooperation coexist among international business interactions and while international trade drives globalization.

Many nations join alliances to save their trade costs, such as the European Community (EC) and the General Agreement on Tariffs and Trade (GATT). Under the framework of those alliances, and as a result of cooperation, such as setting up similar tariffs or production prices among various nations, their members have many equal economic opportunities. People in the membership countries can also mobilize from one nation to another easily for business reasons, which may assist in improving the economic situation of the whole economy (Nicolaides, 1989).

GLOBALIZATION OF SPORT IN ELITE SPORTS

From the perspective of sport economics, sport events and games are viewed as intangible products. The production of those events and games involves several unique elements, such as human resources (e.g., athletes, umpires, coaches, and officials), facilities and equipment, and money. Professional sports and other highly competitive "nonprofessional" sports included in the sport programming of such events as the Olympic Games, the Pan America Games, the Asian Games, the Commonwealth Games, and in the tournaments sponsored by various international sport federations are two major forms of elite sports.

There are three ways that the law of comparative advantage can be used to interpret and explain various phenomena associated with the globalization of sport. First, the law can help a nation select its ideal sports for implementation. Strategically, in order to win medals in international competitions, such as the Olympics, it is important for the sport leadership of a country to compare its resources with those of its counterparts in such areas as number of talented athletes, levels of talent, budgets, and facilities. The comparison could lead to the proper selection of specific sports that are compatible biologically with its athletes and economically with the country's financial capability, ultimately enhancing the possibility for its athletes to win in international competitions. This strategy is extremely critical for those nations that have limited financial resources and athletic population. Clumpner (1994) indicated that some more populous nations, such as China, Germany, and the United States, may have advantages in drawing more talented athletes from their own population than might other less populated countries. However, the size of population may not automatically guarantee success in those sports that require specific physical attributes. Due to special environmental and traditional living styles and body compositions, people from certain areas of the world have the advantage in certain sports events such as long-distance running for African athletes, table tennis, gymnastics, and diving for

Asian athletes, and winter sporting events for the athletes from the countries in the Frigid Zone (Miller & Redhead, 1994). The geographical and anthropological advantages may increase the possibility for athletes from these regions to win international competitions.

The law can also be used to explain the global movement of labor in the sport industry, such as talented athletes, experienced coaches, and other sports-related personnel. Importing human resources can help a nation or a sports organization save costs and enhance its competitive advantage. As mentioned previously, from the perspective of international economics, human resources are an important production element that can be mobilized internationally in the modern era. This also holds true in the world of elite sports. To reduce the costs of player development, franchises in Major League Baseball and Major League Soccer (MLS) often recruit a relatively large number of players from Central and South America. Similarly, the National Hockey League (NHL) has recruited players from Russia and Canada. Canadian ice-hockey players are also exported to Europe, Australia, and Asia (Genest, 1994). The franchises in the National Basketball Assocation (NBA), in recent years, have also drafted many exceptional players from other nations, such as Yao Ming from China, Manu Ginobili from Argentina, and Tony Parker from France. In the 2004–2005 season, there were 80 foreign players on the rosters of 30 NBA teams (Lombardo, 2003). The importation of foreign players can help a league not only reduce its costs on personnel development, but also alter its lineup of foreign players and assist its effort to expand internationally.

Similar applications can be seen in amateur elite sports. Through international exchange agreements, talented athletes can train in the nation with advanced training facilities and technology. For example, colleges and universities in the United States each year recruit many elite athletes from other countries. In the 2003–2004 season, among the top 100 men's single players in the Intercollegiate Tennis Association's national ranking, 63 of them were foreign nationals. In the women side, 47 of the top 100 came from other nations (Glier, 2003). The number of foreign players playing NCAA Division I basketball nearly tripled from 1993–2003. There were 392 during the 2002–2003 season (Pointer, 2005). This practice has been considered a win-win strategy for both the host institution and the student-athlete. The institution can use the athlete's athletic talent to serve its interest. The athlete can enjoy the high-quality training facilities provided by the institution and the opportunity to compete and improve his or her athletic competitiveness.

The final application of the law is found in the area of international expansion. Professional sports leagues and/or sports franchises are always looking for opportunities and alternatives to increase sources of revenue. One commonly adopted approach is to extend their markets into other countries and regions. For example, the Indy Racing League (IRL) is considering the possibility of expanding into Canada and Mexico in the 2006 season (Warfield, 2004). According to the law of comparative advantages, it is often more efficient and profitable to extend a market overseas than to keep it domestically because of the maturity of the domestic market and lower labor costs. The increased extension of NBA's influence in the world is another excellent that illustrates how a professional sports league in United States takes advantage of its popularity to expand into the global markets (the NBA's efforts in international expansion will be discussed in detail in the following section on International Expansion).

Eitzen and Sage (1997) anticipate that the future of the international market for the professional sport industry is optimistic due to the improvements in economy and technology in many region. Thus, it will be considerably expanded. Results of the professional sports leagues' efforts in international expansion demonstrate the validity of such a prediction.

ISSUES IN GLOBALIZATION OF SPORT

Some issues must be dealt with in the future to facilitate the process of globalization of sport. Monopoly and dumping are two of those issues that warrant a further discussion. The existence of monopolies in the world of elite sports has created many controversies. For example, a Japanese baseball pitcher named Hideki Irabu was traded to the San Diego Padres as the result of an agreement between the Lottes, a professional baseball team in Japan, and the Padres. Irabu has long desired to play for the New York Yankees. So he demanded to be traded to the Yankees. Nevertheless, according to MLB's policies, the only team that he can play for is the Padres unless the Padres agree to release or trade him, or if he retires from the Lottes. In other words, Irabu did not have the opportunities to pitch for any other MLB team at will due to the monopolistic agreement between the Japanese professional baseball team and the San Diego Padres. A similar situation occurred in Europe. Since the 1970s, free movement of players from team to team within the European Professional Football (soccer) League has been broadly discussed among the representatives of players, owners, the European Community, and the European Free Trade Association. The use of a quota system to determine the number of foreign players that a team could recruit, and the method of compensation (transfer fees) made to the team that loses a player from the team that receives that player are two main issues of the discussion (Miller & Redhead, 1994). Although the rules on player transferring have been challenged for the purpose of creating a free labor market in the sport industry within the European Community since 1974, during these 20 years the situation did not improve until the recent ruling of the European Court of Justice, which declared the transfer rules illegal.

It is commonly acknowledged that athletes from certain regions or nations are usually more athletically skilled in some sports than those from other parts of the world. Some advantage is also found in coaches from those regions or nations. In other words, they seem to have a better understanding of those sports, such as table tennis in China, tae kun do in South Korea, and basketball in the United States. Since the early 1980s, many Chinese table tennis players have immigrated to other nations and represented those nations in various international competitions. Accordingly, a large majority of players competing in some international championships and tournaments in table tennis are Chinese. Although in many cases the athletes did not violate the rules set by the international sport governing body, their achievements in the competition had little or no impact on the development of table tennis in those countries. The immigration of athletes from a country to other nations in the world due to their athletic superiority in that sport is called dumping.

The dumping phenomenon is also found in basketball. Many American basketball players are recruited by professional basketball teams in many other countries and regions, such as Taiwan, Japan, and the Philippines. The dumping and importation of foreign players has raised some concerns in those nations because of the effect on the welfare of native players. Young native players may get fewer opportunities to play at the professional level. To protect their native players, governing bodies in basketball in some nations (e.g., the Chinese Basketball League in Taiwan) have developed policies to limit the number of foreign players allowed to play on each team. From the perspective of international economics, the implementation of such protectionist policies, however, is not problem-free. First, these policies are deemed to restrict an enterprise, such as a professional sport franchise, from looking for better resources (i.e., outstanding overseas players). Second, these policies erect barriers to prohibit international free trade (Yeh & Li, 1998).

Besides monopoly and dumping, extortion is another issue that is confronted by professional sports leagues. Specifically in professional basketball, foreign teams have tried to lock their young players into long-term contracts, hoping to maximize the buyout fees when the players are drafted by NBA teams. For example, Hemofarm, the Yugoslavian team with which Milicic was affiliated before playing for the Pistons, signed Milicic to a ten-year deal when he was just fifteen years old. Using legal maneuvers, Hemofarm successfully forced the Pistons and Milicic to buyout negotiations three years later when Milicic was about to be drafted by the Pistons. The negotiations led to Milicic agreeing to pay off the remaining seven years of his contract. A similar situation occurred to the case of Yao Ming. It took two years of negotiations and millions of dollars to bring him to the NBA (Lombardo, 2004).

International Expansion

RATIONALE FOR INTERNATIONAL EXPANSION

International expansion refers to the expansion of a firm or organization into targeted foreign nations for economic growth. Fighting for market shares and growth has been considered one of the major reasons for firms and organizations in sport wanting to get involved in international expansion. According to Allen (1993), there are more opportunities to grow and gain market shares in a new and low-competition market that is still growing than in a saturated and fully mature market, as the latter is usually much more competitive. In addition, the increasing prosperity and demand for new sports in many regions overseas are two more reasons for international expansion (Maynard, 1995). The increased interest in sport and the subsequent growth in sport population have added numbers to the bandwagon of globalization in sport. The growth in the population of sport participation, in turn, will create tremendous opportunities in international expansion for firms in the sport industry. International expansion is no longer simply an option for many businesses, but a vital means for survival. It is believed that the benefits of international expansion are enormous. These benefits include, but are not limited to

1. additional growth opportunities;

2. added revenues or profits and financial gain;

3. increased market penetration and shares; and

4. greater international identity and more name recognition (Go & Christensen, 1989).

Additional Growth Opportunities

The development of a subsidiary league in a foreign region and the expansion of a franchise to a new foreign market are two commonly observed applications for firms in the sport industry to expand internationally. For example, the development and operation of the NFL Europe (former the World League in Europe) serves two basic strategic purposes for the National Football League in the United States: (a) exportation and promotion of American football in Europe and (b) international expansion and growth. The World League or the later NFL Europe is an introductory version of the NFL. Through this subsidiary's presence and presentation in Europe, NFL management intends to educate Europeans about American football and hopes to cultivate fans, ultimately forming a favorable fan base in that market. Further expansion efforts (e.g., adding new franchises in various European cities) will be made once the situation warrants. Seeking additional growth opportunities globally will not just occur in professional sports leagues. *ESPN The Magazine* launched the preview issue of its Chinese-language edition in October 2004 and started to publish monthly in mainland China and Hong Kong in December 2004 (Adams, 2004). The Chinese edition was the magazine's first effort to expand internationally for growth opportunities and for increasing its brand equity because of the 1.3 billion people in China.

Added Revenues or Profits

The increase in growth opportunities will inevitably boost the sales of television rights and licensed merchandise of the firms (e.g., professional sports leagues) that expand internationally. During the 2003–2004 season, 750 million people in 212 countries and regions in the world were able to watch NBA games and programming, thanks to the 151 global television partnerships the NBA established (Lombardo, 2003). Sports apparel giants, such as Nike and Reebok, have also become strategically involved in global expansion to capture more profits from their overseas operations. For example, Nike has recently invested about $10 million in Melbourne, Australia, to develop the first superstore outside of North America ("Nike to Open," 1997). On the other hand, Reebok has acquired the NBA's exclusive apparel licensee in Asia, which gave it the right to develop and market apparel and accessories in Asia (Lombardo, 2003), and planed to have 600 outlets in China selling officially licensed NBA merchandise (Lombardo, 2004).

More Market Penetration and More Market Shares

To obtain more market penetration and more global market shares is another perceived and acclaimed benefit of international expansion. The NBA and its properties group have set up offices in Hong Kong, Melbourne, Tokyo, Barcelona, Geneva, and, most recently, Beijing to penetrate unsaturated markets in Asia and Europe for the sake of increasing sales in NBA merchandise. The acquisition of the Washington-based Advantage International and the London-based API Group by the global advertising giant Interpublic (IPG) in 1997 also exemplifies the trend of international expansion in this particular regard (Jensen, 1997). The growth and development of cable and satellite television systems have given professional sports all over the world an increased international presence. Many firms in the sport industry have taken advantage of technological development to promote their names and products in the hope of becoming global brands, eventually hiking their global market shares. The management of Manchester United, one of the top English soccer clubs, has realized the massive popularity of the club in Asia and accordingly taken a proactive approach to promote itself in that region. Some of the strategies include participating in exhibition games and staging a sales office in Hong Kong (Bawden, 1999).

Monopolistic Market Control

To gain monopolistic market control in a particular segment of the sport industry is another reason that some firms develop plans to expand internationally. The World Golf Championship by the PGA Tour starting in 1999 is a good example of this rationale. Greg Norman and a private promoter wanted to start a world tour of eight annual events. Fearful of losing its control over the market and its players, the PGA Tour immediately launched the event called World Golf Championship (*Sport Business*, 1997).

EXAMPLE OF THE NBA'S EFFORTS IN INTERNATIONAL EXPANSION

As the NBA brand matures domestically and in North America, international expansion becomes a logical choice for its next move. To ensure the successfulness of its global efforts, the NBA has been involved in a variety of well-calculated endeavors to execute its plan for international expansion since the 1980s (Lombardo, 2003).

1. Tapping into the foreign player markets.

2. Sponsoring clinics in Africa and China.

3. Playing preseason games in foreign countries. The Houston Rockets and the Sacramento Kings played their first preseason games in Beijing and Shanghai in the 2004–2005 season. The China trip not only brought live NBA basketball games to Chinese audiences, but it also gave some of the league's sponsors, such as McDonald's, Coca-Cola, Anheuser-Busch, Reebok, Eastman Kodak, etc. the opportunity to leverage their investment in the lucrative Chinese market.

4. Opening new offices in Beijing in addition to the existing ones in Europe, Australia, Hong Kong, and Taiwan. The NBA will also open offices in Brazil and Argentina in the near future.

5. Granting the exclusive rights to foreign markets to its sponsors, and providing NBA-licensed products in more than 100 countries (about 20% of its $3 billion in merchandise sales comes from outside the United States).

6. Using NBA.com to further its global branding (about 42% of Internet traffic

on NBA.com was international in 2003). The NBA currently has nine foreign-language web sites.

7. Pursuing a joint venture with the Chinese Basketball Association that would grant the NBA partnership status in arena development throughout China or marketing rights for the Chinese national men's basketball team

8. Increasing the number of broadcasted NBA games and programming on foreign soil. Among all of the NBA's efforts in growing its international business, television programming is the most advanced (Lombardo, 2004).

In early 2001, NBA Commissioner David Stern announced that the league was considering either adding a team overseas or creating an international league as part of its international expansion plan. The plan was put on hold due to concerns over lack of fan support and the event on 9/11.

FORMS OF INTERNATIONAL EXPANSION

Experts in international law have pointed out that when thinking of expansion internationally, a company should consider three strategic factors: rationale for expansion, urgency, and format for expansion (Graham, Ruggieri, Clements, & Cody, 1994). The format for expansion refers to the various forms of international expansion that sport enterprises may adopt in their efforts to develop globally. The following are some of the common forms utilized by the sport enterprise in international expansion.

Overseas Subsidiary Operations

Establishing overseas operations (e.g., subsidiary leagues or divisions) has been proven to be an effective, self-generated way to grow for sport enterprises. After its establishment, the subsidiary can then expand in the region by further granting franchise rights to local firms and providing direct services to these affiliates. As mentioned previously, the NFL Europe sponsored by the National Football League in Europe has helped promote American football outside of North America. The league currently has franchises in London, Amsterdam, Scotland, Barcelona, Dusseldorf, and Frankfurt. Using overseas divisions to increase market penetration and share is a popular practice among sport enterprises.

Acquisitions or Mergers

The takeover of or merging with a company in a foreign territory is another common form of international expansion in the sport industry. Through acquiring a foreign company, the sport enterprise will either increase its market share or gain competitive edge in the world monopolistic competition for control of a certain product. The merger with a sport business firm in the targeted region or nation to form an alliance represents another aspect of this expansion approach.

Franchising or Licensing

Franchising is the third form employed by the sport enterprises, especially by the sporting goods firms, to expand into the global market. For example, Chicago-based Sportmart has 12 franchised stores in Japan. The sport enterprise using this type of expansion acts as a franchisor, granting a license to a company or individual as a "licensee" who pays fees or royalties to the licensor (i.e., the franchisor) to operate an outlet that uses the franchisor's name and logo and sells the franchisor's designated products.

To expand into other countries and regions, many sport enterprises use one or more of the following three franchising approaches: joint venture, master licensing, and direct licensing. The strategy in joint venture calls for joining forces with local investors, local governments, or even local competitors in the targeted nation or region to gain market entry. The sport enterprise establishes a joint venture agreement or partnership with a company or individual in a foreign market, and the partner will be in charge of the on-site operation. The Golf Channel and International Management Group worked together to expand the network in Southeast Asia in 1996. Specifically, Japan, Taiwan, and Australia are three nations or regions affected by the expansion effort. A joint venture was set up in Japan to distribute the signal. In using master licensing as a strategy, a license is granted to a company or individual in the intended market for expansion by the franchisor. The licensee can then operate the franchise under its ownership. In addition to granting a license for operation to a company and individual in the intended market, the franchisor will also provide the franchisee with financial backup and support of personnel. This type of strategy is called direct licensing (Go & Christensen, 1989).

Direct Expert

This approach calls for the sport enterprise to create dedicated export sales representative positions or to employ traveling export sales representatives in a foreign city to coordinate direct foreign sales in a designated region. An alternative to this is to hire a local distributor or agents in that region to represent the company.

ISSUES OF INTERNATIONAL EXPANSION

The sport enterprise that intends to expand internationally may find that its expansion efforts could be blocked by the differences existing in many areas between its home country and the intended market or nation for expansion. An understanding of these differences and the issues that arise as a result of the differences would help the sport enterprise become better prepared and develop a strategic plan to deal with those issues prior to their expansion entry into the market or nation. Of many issues that could be faced by the expanding sport enterprises, the ones in finance and legality are of greatest importance and are worth further discussion. In addition, the logistic aspect of international expansion is also an issue that must be dealt with.

Financial Issues

Exchange risks and different taxation systems and banking laws are some of the issues that sport enterprises need to consider when developing their expansion plans. Exchange risks are the first issue that needs careful attention. An exchange risk refers to the risk that adheres to fluctuations in exchange rates, eventually affecting the performance of a company involved in international expansion. In other words, "an asset denominated in or valued in terms of foreign currency cash flows will change in value if that foreign currency changes in value over time" (Folks & Aggarwal, 1988, p. 89). Companies are exposed to three types of risk: translation exposure, transaction exposure, and economic exposure (Folks & Aggarwal, 1988).

1. Translation exposure refers to the effect on the balance sheet of the company as a result of the adverse, substantial changes occurring in the exchange rate between the company's home currency and the one of the targeted foreign market.

2. Transaction exposure is experienced by the company because of the fluctuation in the translated amount of the foreign currency between the invoice date and the payment date. This type of exposure usually happens to a firm involved in an importing or exporting business.

3. Economic exposure reflects the degree of decline in the overall economic value of a company that is involved in the international business due to the changes in exchange rates. Speaking in the terms of international expansion in sporting goods, the extent of the risk exposed by a sporting goods company in exchange rate changes depends on how competitive the markets of its major inputs (e.g., where it purchases its raw materials) are with those of its major outputs (where it sells its products).

The second issue that an expanding sport enterprise must face is tax levy and collection. As previously noted, one of the two essential goals for international expansion is to make a profit from the overseas operations and repatriate it back to the home country. The actualization of this goal, nevertheless, requires the involved sport enterprise to have a clear understanding of the tax system and structures and of the government regulations and policies of the targeted nation on repatriation. In particular, attention needs to be paid to the exchange control and taxation policies.

The government of the nation that the sport enterprise has expanded to may have certain regulations and policies to prevent funds from entering or leaving its country. The rationale for the policy set to restrict fund inflows is to prevent devaluation of the host nation's currency. On the other hand, the prevention of fund outflows is used when the host government is short of foreign exchange or has heavily borrowed from external sources. By prohibiting fund outflows, the government can ensure that a certain amount of foreign hard currency will be available when needed.

The tax regulations and policies play an important role in the process of fund transfers (e.g., repatriation). The dividends, interest payments, or royalties that a sport enterprise earns from its operations in a foreign nation may be subject to a so-called "withholding tax" by the host government.

Business structures may affect the amount of tax liability that a company owes to the government of the targeted nation. (The four major forms of business structures that may be used by the sport enterprise in international expansion have been discussed previously.) First, in addition to various levels of government income taxes, the subsidiary of a sport enterprise is also subject to a withholding tax if aftertax cash will be repatriated. The withholding tax rate for a foreign subsidiary in the United States is 30%, which may be reduced from 5 to 10% by treaties. According to the Canadian tax laws, a so-called "branch tax" has been imposed on the Canadian branch operation or a Canadian subsidiary of a foreign company although the latter repatriates its profits to the parent company. In other words, should the subsidiary decide not to reinvest the aftertax earnings in its Canadian operation, it will be required to pay a branch tax, which was 25% in 1997. Tax treaties between the Canadian government and other nations may reduce this tax from 25% to anywhere between 10% and 15%. Second, the sport enterprise that enters the targeted foreign market as a corporation or partnership will be subject to the same tax conditions as those of a foreign subsidiary. Third, in general, the income earned by a sport enterprise that uses the direct expert approach (i.e., using an independent distributor to conduct business for it as its representative or agent in the targeted market) will not be subject to the host country's taxation.

Legal Issues

One legal issue that sport managers may face involves the different ways of applying and interpreting the antitrust policies. Sport firms that are considering international expansion must be aware that the target region or nation may have its own version of laws that are mainly adopted to promote free and fair competition. The application, implementation, interpretation, and reinforcement of these laws may vary from country to country. Although the primary goal of antitrust legislation is the same in many countries, that is, to prohibit anticompetitive agreements that set restraints to deliberately hamper competition, the definition of restraints differ (Hawk, 1988). It is imperative that people involved in international expansion understand the differences between the antitrust laws of their countries and those of the host nation.

The competition policy adopted by the European Union (EU) deserves special mention. All member states of the EU form a single market, and a competition policy was enacted in 1993 to ensure that the competition among companies from all EU nations would be free from restraints. The antitrust laws adopted by member states themselves are deemed supplemental to the unified antitrust policies. A comparison of the competition law of the European Union and the antitrust laws of the United States is given below. Through the comparison, concerned professionals in the sport industry can gain an understanding of the antitrust legislation in these two regions.

1. Both the European Union's and the United States' antitrust laws recognize the promotion of competition as a principle. Nevertheless, the antitrust law of the former has been developed primarily for the promotion of integration of separate economics of Member States in the European Union, whereas the antitrust law of the latter was drafted mainly to promote true competition.

2. Although the EU's antitrust law emphasizes the political and social values of competition (e.g., fairness), U.S. antitrust law highlights the economics value of competition (e.g., allocative efficiency).

3. The European Commission is the sole enforcer of the antitrust law implementation in the European Union. In the United States, multiple enforcers of the

antitrust law coexist, including the Justice Department (hard-core cartel behavior and large horizontal mergers), the Federal Trade Commission (large horizontal mergers and anticompetitive practices), the enforcement arms of individual states, and private enforcement and actions (outside the merger area).

The differences in existing government policies and regulations may create barriers for a sports enterprise to expand internationally. For example, according to the North American Free Trade Agreement (NAFTA), each nation involved in the agreement should not discriminate against companies from other NAFTA nations to keep them from gaining access to and using telecommunications transport networks and services in their territory. In fact, Canada and Mexico expressed reservations about implementing the agreement. The Mexican government today still controls satellite communications and mandates that radio broadcasting and radio and television services be reserved for Mexican nationals (Rogers & Arriola, 1997). The same kind of protectionism is also noticed in Canada. The Canadian government specifically sets Content Rules to limit the distribution of U.S. media products like ESPN in Canada. According to the Content Rules, 50% of any distributed broadcast signals in Canada must be Canadian related (MaCarthy & Wilcox, 1997).

Facility Issues

Other than financial and legal issues, firms and businesses that desire to expand internationally also will face such issues as costs of living. For example, the NBA's strategic plan for international expansion called for bringing more NBA games to China and establishing an NBA franchise in Europe, or even developing an international NBA league. The quality of facilities in foreign nations, however, often does not meet the NBA's standards (Lambardo, 2004).

STEPS AND STRATEGIES FOR INTERNATIONAL EXPANSION

According to experts in international economics and trade, a plan for publicity must be developed prior to the commencement of any expansion action (Hayes, 1993). Having exhibition games played abroad is a common practice of American professional sports leagues intending to expand internationally. An example of this would be the game played by two NFL franchises each year in Mexico. Selection of an expansion market has been perceived as a critical concern for sports firms that are considering international expansion. When sports enterprises consider a market or nation for expansion, its potential must be examined in the following areas (Love, 1995):

1. The size of the population and the population's financial situation.

2. The population's knowledge and appreciation of the industry to be expanded.

3. The favorable disposition of the host country's culture toward the industry to be expanded.

4. The favorable nature of government regulations toward and restriction on the industry to be expanded.

5. The competition from the domestic segment of the same industry.

6. The growth potential of the market.

7. The political and economic stability of the host country.

8. The availability and cost of human resources.

Summary

In this chapter, international issues in sport economics were discussed. Specifically, several types of economic systems (e.g., capitalism, welfare state capitalism, market socialism, and socialism) and their respective sport governance systems were examined so as to provide information about how individual economic systems dictate the selection and use of various sport governance systems. Globalization of sport, as an important economic issue, has also been discussed in this chapter. Specifically, the law of comparative advantage, the theoretical foundation for sport businesses to expand globally, was reviewed. Two basic applications of this law involved international monopoly and dumping. International expansion was another major issue in sport economics addressed in this chapter. Fighting for market share, growth, and profit supplies several reasons for a sport enterprise's wishing to expand internationally. The benefits of international expansion are enormous. Additional growth opportunities, added revenues or profits and financial gain, more market penetration and share, international identity and more name recognition, just to name a few, are commonly recognized benefits of international expansion. Overseas subsidiary operations, acquisition and merger, franchising and licensing, and direct export are the four basic types of international expansion utilized commonly by sport enterprises in their efforts to develop globally.

Several important issues related to international expansion were also reviewed. Exchange rate risks and differences in taxation systems and regulations, labor laws, and antitrust applications were examined. To expand into the international market successfully, a model for expansion was recommended.

Chapter Questions

1. Explain and distinguish between various economic systems.
2. What are the three common types of sport governance systems and their basic economic characteristics?
3. Explain the reasons for international expansion. List its four main benefits.
4. Using an example, discuss each of the four major forms of expansion that the sport enterprise may adopt in its endeavor to grow internationally.
5. What are the common financial issues confronted by the sport enterprises that want to expand their market globally?
6. What are the common legal issues facing sport enterprises that want to extend their market globally?
7. Elaborate on the strategies that could be incorporated by a sport enterprise into its expansion plan to penetrate a foreign market.
8. Compare and contrast the three common types of sport club systems.
9. Compare and contrast the three models of professional sport club operations.
10. Compare and contrast the three versions of professional sport club operations under Model 1.

Chapter Thirteen

FUTURE DIRECTION OF THE SPORT INDUSTRY: AN ECONOMIC PERSPECTIVE

Introduction

If someone from 30 years ago were to look into a crystal ball and observe the sport industry in the 21st century, it would be difficult for that person to fathom the changes that have occurred. If someone from today were to look into another crystal ball to observe the sport industry of 30 years in the future, just how much change, and of what kind, will have occurred? People of 30 years ago would have been unlikely to predict what was to happen, just as today we are unlikely to be able to predict exactly what the future holds. The previous chapters have demonstrated how an economic perspective can be used to analyze the sport industry as it currently exists. It is also important to look beyond the current environment to the future, to explore what it holds for the sport industry.

Sport management professionals should be concerned about the future. Some business firms develop plans for 20 to 30 years into the future. The sport industry has generally not looked that far out. For many sport organizations, 5 years forward represents long-term planning. However, those who want to start firms or those who want to ensure that their current firms will survive need to understand the nature of current trends, their meaning for the future, and the ways in which they will impact sport organizations. Managers of firms, both general and sport, are becoming more concerned about the time dimension of economic decisions. Firms must think not about short-term revenue maximization but about how today's decisions will contribute to long-term survival. For example, if professional baseball or the tennis industry is to survive, it must continue to attract fans. Where are those fans going to come from, and how can baseball and tennis develop the next generation of fans?

> ### Future Direction of the Sport Industry: An Economic Perspective
>
> *It's 2006 and Lee John, CEO of johnssports.com, is considering the future. His two-year-old company develops sports-themed software for computer games and has grown each year. Software is a rapidly-changing industry, and John wants to ensure that his business survives. The company focuses on mainstream sports with a customer base largely composed of males in their teens to mid-twenties. John wants to stay in the sports area but is thinking about whether he needs to expand into other sports or audiences. In his attempt to determine where future demand will be, what might he consider?*

Economic concepts will not change. In 30 years, economists analyzing the sport industry will still talk about market structures, supply and demand, and labor market inputs. However, the specific issues under analysis may very well change. The sport industry is part of the larger world, and the changes of the world thus impact the sport industry. Many industries are trying to look into the crystal ball. Manufacturing, health care, and education are all industries struggling with decisions about what the future holds. Mark R. Daniels, president of a Canadian insurance association, suggests several trends in the financial services sector (Daniels, 1999):

1. global structural change, marked by decreased government expenditures and tight fiscal management;

2. intense competition, from domestic and international firms and from nontraditional sources;

3. rapidly changing technology; and

4. changing demographics and changing markets.

These trends for financial services are similar to those the sport industry will encounter. In this chapter, we will first look at population changes as a foundation for discussing other changes. Then we will consider suppliers of sport, technology, and competition as three areas of importance for sport organizations and the industry.

A caveat is that change is unpredictable. Trying to describe what our society and the sport industry will be like in 10 . . . 20 . . . 30 years is difficult. There is no crystal ball and no way to be certain what will happen. We will make one assumption for the following discussion, that the basic institutional structures in our society will remain the same. We do not anticipate radical change in our political, economic, or family structures. Given that assumption, we will make some predictions for the sport industry (see Table 13-1).

Table 13-1. The Future of the Sport Industry

Changing demographics

- Slower population growth
- Aging population, with different demand pattern
- More diverse population, with different demand pattern
- Changed family structure, with different needs and time resources

Less government-supplied sport; more community-based and private enterprise supplied

- Self-regulation of sport as opposed to government regulation

Increased competition

- Niche marketing
- Consolidation of producers, through mergers and acquisitions
- Continued escalation of professional salaries and franchise valuations, although at a slower rate

Slowing down of the explosive growth of the sport industry

Increasing technology, including extensive use of the Internet

Future Trends and Their Impacts on the Sport Industry

A number of trends for the future are already clear and will impact virtually every industry in the economy, which include, but are not limited to, the demographic trends, the science and technology trends, and the economic globalization trends. These trends provide a foundation for any predictions about the future of the sport industry. These trends are interrelated. In addition to these four common trends, there are also some specific trends that are sport specific, such as supply of sport and competition. In the following section, all these trends and the impact they have on the sport industry will be discussed in detail.

DEMOGRAPHIC TRENDS

The term demographic refers to the physical characteristics of a population, such as age, race, sex, marital status, family size, education, geographic location, and occupation. These characteristics are keys in shaping the United States' economic life. Among them, age, race, and sex play a critical role in influencing the future of the sport industry.

If we analyze demographic trends, we will come to the conclusion that the U.S. will experience slower population growth. The U.S. population grew 102% over the previous 50 years; the projected increase for the next 50 years is 57% (U.S. Census Bureau, 1999). This feature implies that there will be fewer consumers in general, including sports fans and participants, in our society in the future. The impact will be on total consumption of goods and services. The sport industry may experience reduced demand for its goods and services. There will also be a tremendous amount of growth in the Hispanic and Asian populations in the United States, which will become increasingly diverse in ethnicity. In addition, the population is getting older. Such changes are causing the positions of power to change.

Age Distribution

In the United States, it is estimated that 16% of the population will be over 65 years of age by the year 2020, compared to 12.4% in 2004 (see Table 13-2). It is predicted that the number of Americans age 55 and older will almost double between now and 2030—from 60 million today (21% of the total U.S. population) to 107.6 million (31% of the population). During that same time period, the number of Americans over 65 will more than double, from 34.8 million in 2000 (12% of the population) to 70.3 million in 2030 (20% of the total population). Part of the growth is attributable to increases in life expectancy and part to the large mass of baby boomers growing older.

What do these changes mean for the general economy? Dowd, Monaco, and Janoska (1998) suggest three main effects on an economy of an aging population:

1. The labor force growth slows as older citizens keep their jobs and younger workers have difficulty entering the work force. This reduces the economy's potential to both produce and consume.

2. Government spending is impacted as much of government budgets are dedicated to entitlement programs, many of which are directed at older citizens.

3. Spending shifts with changing demand. Especially noticeable is a shift from consumption of goods to consumption of services (especially health care).

This aging of America will present many opportunities for the sport industry. According the Sporting Goods Manufacturers Association International (2003), the mature market, ages 55 and older, will grow by nearly 40% between 2000 and 2010. Over the last two decades, the sport industry has experienced explosive growth. To a large extent, this growth was created to match the demand created by the baby boom generation (i.e., Americans who were born between 1949 and 1964) as it moves through its consumer lifecycle. In 2005, there were about 77 million baby boomers. They are a prime market for health club memberships and home exercise equipment as they are actively seeking ways to remain healthy. Accordingly, new products, new services, and new retail concepts will have to be introduced to capitalize on this growth. This is one of the main reasons why the market for fitness-related products has been expanding in recent years (Sporting Goods Manufacturers Association International, 2005).

The change in age distribution pattern will affect the sport industry as the demand and consumption patterns differ among different age groups. Different age groups have different values and look for different experiences from their consumption. Younger people are developing interests in new sports, finding many of the ones the older generations enjoyed "boring." According to National Sporting Goods Association studies (Agoglia, 1999), the fastest growing sports in the United States in the 1990s were nontraditional ones such as roller hockey (+110%) and inline skating (+644%). Sporting goods manufacturers are producing new products for these audiences, ski resorts have targeted snowboarders, the International Olympic Committee added wind surfing and aerials as sports, and television programming now includes the X-Games. In 2005, the fastest growth segment of the sport industry was snowboarding (Estano, 2005).

As people become older, they change their consumption patterns (Gerontologist, 1999; Kelly & Godbey, 1992). Instead of playing hockey, they turn to golf; instead of watching football on television, they watch news programs related more to a healthy lifestyle; instead of taking ski vacations, they go on cruises. The traditional sport audience is moving into an age where it will not consume in the way sport

Table 13-2. U.S. Population Projections, by Age (%)

Age	2004	2020
18+	74.3	76.3
55+	21.0	29.5
65+	12.4	16.5

Source: U.S. Census Bureau (2004). *Fact Sheet.*
Web: *http://factfinder.census.gov/servlet/SAFFFacts?_sse=on*

Table 13-3. U.S. Population Estimates and Projections, by Race/Ethnicity (%)

	1900	1950	1980	2004	2020
White	87.9	89.5	80.9	75.6	63.8
Black	11.6	10.0	11.8	12.2	12.8
Hispanic	NA	NA	6.4	14.2	17.0

Source: U.S. Census Bureau (2004). *Fact Sheet.*
Web: *http://factfinder.census.gov/servlet/SAFFFacts?_sse=on*
NA = not recorded separately

organizations have been accustomed to them consuming (Hofacre & Burman, 1992). Although the sport industry as a whole may not suffer considerably, specific segments may be greatly impacted.

Ethnic/Racial Distribution

Demand also changes with changes in ethnic/racial group population patterns. A second trend is increasing diversity (U.S. Census Bureau, 2005). The U.S. Hispanic population became the largest minority in the United States in 2002. As Table 13-3 demonstrates, this particular minority group is the fastest growing ethnic/racial group in the United States, projected to increase from 14.2% of the population in 2004 to 17% in 2020. The African American population will increase from 12.2% to 13%. Other ethnic groups will also experience growth, such as Asian Americans. Overall, the traditional majority white population is projected to decline from 75.6% to 64% of the U.S. population in the next 15 years.

The changes in ethnic/racial distribution in the United States provide sport businesses many new opportunities to increase sales and profit, and to attract many new customers. Producers of sport, whether involved with sporting goods or activities, should recognize the potential impact of the change. Some organizations have already begun. The USTA and USGA have created programs to appeal to minority groups (Taylor, 1999), Major League Soccer and Major League Baseball are developing promotions and advertising to create demand in metropolitan areas where there are large Hispanic populations, and NASCAR has launched an urban marketing campaign in some American cities to raise awareness about their sport with minority groups (King & Warfield, 2005).

Other Patterns

Generation Y, a term describing those Americans who were born between 1979 and 1994, is the largest consumer group in the history of the U.S. and represents a dominant future market. As of 1999, this new generation sized 60 million. The traditional marketing approaches and messages have a tough time appealing to this group, since members of Generation Y seem to be attracted to brands that understand them and speak their language. Their medium of choice is the Internet. It drives diversity and the ability to know what's new in an instant. Companies unable to relate to this group will obviously miss out on a huge potential opportunity. These three demographic trends provide specific target markets for small retail niche opportunities in which some retailers can find a home.

The increasing rate of participation in sport by girls and women represents another pattern of changes in the demand and supply of sport in the United States. In the past decade, opportunities for females have greatly expanded. Women now participate in college athletics in record numbers, young girls play soccer and t-ball in record numbers, over 90,000 fans fill a stadium to watch the U.S. Women's Soccer team win the World Cup, female athletes are in demand as product endorsers, and sporting goods manufacturers create products designed specifically for women. A major contributor to these opportunities has been Title IX as well as the increased role of women in a number of areas of the economy.

Family patterns have changed from the two-parent, stay-at-home-mother family with children (61% in 1950 and 53% in 1999; U.S. Census Bureau, 1999). A growing number of single-parent families and families where both parents work outside the home affect demand for sport goods and services. On the one hand, parents are looking for places to send children for supervision. A University of Michigan study showed that children 12 and under have 75% of their weekdays programmed for them (Agoglia, 1999). Such programming might include sport camps, club teams, and after-school recreation programs provided by government, community organizations, and/or private enterprise. On the other hand, the opportunity costs to support voluntary sport organizations, as coaches, organizers, and fund-raisers, may be high.

In any society, income is not distributed equally (Kelly, 1985). There is concern in the United States that not everyone shared in the economic boom of the 1990s. What will the future hold? What groups will have resources (e.g., financial, time) to be able participate in various segments of the sport industry? Within the spectator segment of the industry, there is concern that many individual fans are being priced out of the ability to go to games and events, whereas corporations, with their ability to afford (and get tax deductions for) tickets, corporate boxes, advertising, sponsorships, and fund-raising, will dominate the audience.

SCIENCE AND TECHNOLOGY TRENDS

Technology changes rapidly. At the minimum, it changes some of our decisions; that is, taking an airplane to a destination ski resort for a weekend instead of going by car for 2 weeks or going to a local resort; or it may make old skills, traditional organizations, and stable markets obsolete. Today, the personal digitized assistant (PDA) allows consumers to access email and the Internet from anywhere they travel. According to Daggett (2005), Smart Personal Object Technology (SPOT) will become the newest fad in the very near future. SPOT will be integrated in our watches, and essentially function as a PC. With this technology a user would project the image of both a screen and keyboard from the SPOT unit onto a tabletop or piece of paper and work as if using a regular PC and keyboard. As technology continues to get smaller, it becomes more and more an extension of our being (Daggett, 2005, p. 4).

When we thought about technology in the sport industry 30 years ago, we thought about instant replay cameras, aluminum tennis racquets, Astroturf, and waffle soles on running shoes. Today, when we think about the same topic, things like minute-to-minute Internet updates of sporting events, satellite distribution of worldwide sporting events, and golf clubs that add 40 yards length off the tee may come to mind. The development of science and technology creates many new products (e.g., titanium bats), new services (e.g., virtual reality golf courses), new channels of distribution (e.g., the Internet), and new alliances (e.g., CBS and SportsLine). Arguably the greatest technology issue facing the sport industry is the Internet.

According James Canton, chairman and CEO of the Institute for Global Futures (2005), there are important Internet trends that will shape American society in the 21st century. Some of them will also impact the sport industry greatly, such as:

1. The Net will become the first global knowledge network connecting billions of people with an unlimited number of channels.

2. The convergence of the Net, digital TV, and wireless phones will support interactive multimedia features that will transform business and society.

3. Direct real-time voice and video communications will greatly boost the Net's value as a tactical tool for business.

4. Net usage will accelerate, as low-cost, high-speed bandwidth becomes readily available over Fat Pipes of streaming multimedia.

5. Telepresence—the ability to feel and sense 3-D virtual places, things, and people—will drive universal adoption of the Net.

6. Access to information on any subject will be available anywhere over the Net and delivered by a variety of media appliances.

7. The Net will change lifestyles by providing many more choices for living and virtually tele-collaborating with anyone, anywhere.

8. Education, entertainment, health, and lifestyle pursuits will be reshaped by the Net as billions of people communicate and share information.

In 1999, the National Sporting Goods Association annual management conference held a one-hour panel discussion on the Internet and the sporting goods industry. In 1998, an estimated $78 million worth of sporting goods was sold over the Internet; some industry estimates anticipate that $3 billion will be sold within 5 years (McEvoy, 1999a). Companies such as Nike, Dick's Sporting Goods, and regional retail chains are setting up Web sites themselves or outsourcing site construction. The benefit to the firm is the ease of reaching consumers. A concern is that manufacturers may elect to sell directly to consumers, bypassing conventional retailers and shortening the chain of production. Google, Inc., provider of the most popular Internet search engine, Google, would make available downloadable videos of every NBA game after competition in the 2005–2006 season through its new Google Video Store (Fisher, 2006), while ESPN and ABC allowed their viewers to download video clips and games using the video iPod (Fisher, 2006).

Sport firms are using the Internet to provide information about their organizations, to sell directly to consumers, to create promotions, and to create sponsorships. The CEO of the Salt Lake Organizing Committee for the Olympic Games says that "the Olympics needs to become the e-Olympics" (Horovitz, 1999, p. B3). For the Salt Lake City Games, the Internet could be used for online ticket sales, ticket auctions, merchandise purchases, donations, obtaining volunteers, and sponsorship tie-ins. Internet firms are supporting the sport industry with advertising and sponsorship dollars. PSINet signed a naming right deal with the NFL Baltimore Ravens worth $105.5 million over 20 years, whereas Yahoo sponsors the America's Cup team and the U.S. Postal Service Cycling Team (*Street & Smith's SportsBusiness Journal*, 2000). According to *Street & Smith's SportsBusiness Journal* (2005), there were over 127 million sport-related Internet sites and 338.5 million unique visitors. All the professional sports leagues have established an office specially dealing with Internet marketing and sales. The prevalence of new technologies reflects changes in demand. For example, at the 1999 Extreme Games, of the 168 credentialed media, 70 were Internet sites (Ruibal, 1999). For the younger generation, the Internet is as relevant as sports magazines or television are to an earlier generation.

Many sport organizations have learned that they must keep up with technology and adapt new Internet and other computer technologies to stay competitive. At a metropolitan YMCA, members have their handprints scanned before they can enter the building. They begin their weight-cycle workout by checking a computer kiosk that tells them what their past workouts have been and what they need to do for the current workout. As they move to the stair climber, where they watch television programs off satellites, their heart rate is automatically monitored by sensors. At each stop in the facility, information is entered into a database that records what activities they participated in and for how long.

Although technological advancement presents many opportunities for firms, both to use and to produce new technologies, it also presents problems for sport organizations. Disputes arise over the proper role of technology. The NCAA, for example, banned the newest titanium baseball bats as being too dangerous for fielders. For the NCAA, the costs of using the bats (injuries) are higher than the benefits (more offense; McEvoy, 1999b). Bat manufacturers sued, alleging restraint of trade. In other cases, the issue is that technology is not regulated by any outside agency. The number of offshore Internet sports betting sites has exploded, worrying sport officials who see increased potential for contest-related problems due to the betting amounts. In the future, government must address the issue of whether it is appropriate to have government regulation or whether the technology industry and its various elements will self-regulate.

The development of other technology, such as the convergence of the Internet with TVs, telephones, kiosks, and wireless devices, will also create many tremendous opportunities for the sport industry. In a panel discussion entitled "Network Sports Presidents Roundtable: The Challenging Future Sports on TV" at the 2003 *SportsBusiness Journal*/Octagon World Congress of Sport, the panelists collectively believed that high definition television would represent the greatest impact of technology on the business of sports on TV (Adams, 2003).

ECONOMIC GLOBALIZATION TRENDS

As it escalates, globalization will be more extensive than it was before the 21st century, and will be a greater factor influencing the economy of the country. The new era of globalization, fueled by the innovations and evolution of Internet technology, will connect people around the world to the Internet and bring them together.

Sport enterprises will continue their existing globalization efforts through expansion, mergers, acquisitions, and other means, as globalization is an effective means in market development. The "globalize or perish" slogan, which implies the urgency for American firms to strategically explore beyond the border for survival, is also applicable to many segments of the sport industry, such as sporting goods manufacturing, professional sports, sport networks, etc. While lost labor costs is the main motive for sporting goods manufacturing firms to continue their globalization efforts, the global endeavors of professional sport leagues in the United States are driven by the aspiration of making their sport the global language and, accordingly, ensuring their financial viability in the long run. For example, globalization has been and will continue to be the core strategy of the NBA.

Globalization in sport will continue to encounter many of the same political, cultural, and sociological obstacles as discussed in Chapter 12. Prudent sport executives should develop a keen appreciation of issues related to globalization so as to take advantage of the economies of scale as the markets of their products expand internationally.

OTHER TRENDS

Provision of Sport

One issue an economy needs to consider is the balance between "human investment" and production. The question is, how many resources (wealth) should go directly to "taking care of people"—as in government-supplied education, social, and sport/recreation services—and how much should be directed to production so that goods and services can be supplied to citizens? When economic times are good (as was true for much of the 1990s), these decisions may be easier in that there are more resources available. However, when economic times are tough (as was true in the 1980s), these decisions are more difficult. Thus, economists attempt to forecast economic cycles to assist in making decisions about the future. However, as discussed in Chapter 3, forecasting is difficult. How a society supplies its citizens with goods and services is an issue.

In previous chapters, we have talked about the reasons that government, nonprofit community-based organizations, and private firms all provide recreation programs and sports facilities. In spite of the attention paid to recent government support for sport facilities, the future appears to hold less government involvement in sport in that area. That is, governments at the county and/or municipal levels are becoming reluctant to subsidize the construction of sports facilities used by professional sports franchises (Fish, 2005).

Changing population patterns will affect political decision-making. It is likely that government officials and legislatures will become both older and more ethnically diverse (Jones, 1999), corresponding to the general population shift. This sets the stage for more disagreement: older versus younger, traditional white majority versus minority. Historically, government has provided much support for recreation and sport, either directly or indirectly. That traditional support may change. Older citizens are more likely to vote than are younger citizens. For the elected official who wants to continue in office and has to weigh interests of competing groups, self-interest dictates listening to those who vote. At the minimum, we will see more political coalitions formed, with the resulting negotiation and compromise.

While it appears that politicians in general are reluctant to make any serious change in the way the sport industry operates and to increase governmental regulation of sport, they have periodically made inquiries into issues in the sport industry and stepped up their level of oversight. An example was the recently proposed legislature Clean Sports Act that aims to require standardized drug testing and stiff punishments for athletes who test positive for banned substances. Will the federal government intensify its involvement in sport in the future? The issue of whether or not it would be better off to have the government step in to regulate the sport industry or to leave regulation to the governing bodies of individual sport leagues through their own self-imposed rules (i.e., self regulation) remains a topic of debate. The history of government regulation indicates even when the federal government has been active, as with Title IX and the Civil Rights Restoration Act, it took a great deal of time to enforce the law. For all the discussion about Congress's reexamining baseball's antitrust exemption, the only modification to the exemption, in 1998, occurred because it was supported by Major League Baseball. The wisdom in the area of government regulation tends to suggest that the best role of government in the future may be to provide a threat under which leagues, conferences, and associations enact self-regulation.

If government does not supply sport, it will fall to community organizations and private enterprise to do so. Evidence for this already exists for community organizations such as Little League and Pop Warner Football, which have seen a consistent 8 to 10% growth rate in the 1990s (Agoglia, 1999). The future will see more sport provided through these mechanisms.

Competition

Competition is an element of sport participation. It is also an element in the provision of competitive sport. Professional sport teams and leagues compete, YMCAs

Photo courtesy Media Focus LLC

and private athletic clubs compete, sporting goods manufacturers compete, and television sports channels compete. As discussed in Chapters 6 and 11, one role of government is to ensure that competition exists through its antitrust laws.

With a slowing population growth rate, competition will become more intense within the sport industry. With fewer, and a changing mix of, consumers, many sport organizations will not survive the competition. Those that do will have to find a strategy that enables them to continue to operate. Some may do this by finding a niche market. For example, Major League Soccer will have difficulty rising to the level of the other four major professional sports in North America. However, it may do very well with a more limited role in the professional sport scene. Another means of survival will come through mergers and acquisitions. As discussed, the rationale for such activity is that mergers and acquisitions provide more efficiencies and synergy for the firms involved. It was predicted that the number of mergers between teams, leagues, and organizations will continue to rise in the future (Mahony & Howard, 2001). Although government will continue to oversee such behavior for monopoly considerations, the future will see a consolidation of firms involved in supplying sport. Formation of strategic alliances will also be a popular option for firms in the sport industry to adopt in the future. As mentioned in Chapter 5, a strategic alliance will provide the involved sport firms with a competitive advantage as resources, human or financial, will be pooled by the strategic partners to create synergy and cut costs.

Undoubtedly, the most public attention in the United States is given to the issue of competition within professional sports leagues. Although only a small part of the general issue of competition within the sport industry, competition within leagues receives disproportionate media coverage. Small market teams versus large market teams, revenue sharing, and salary caps are the common themes of discussion among those involved in professional sports. Professional sports leagues continue to talk about future expansion, thus diluting an already limited supply of very good players. Competition will continue to increase for that limited supply, resulting in higher salaries and larger gaps between those teams that can afford the salaries and those that cannot. Government will not regulate professional sport, so it is up to owners to self-regulate, via revenue sharing and/or salary caps. The mixed history of owners' being willing to engage in self-regulation does not promise much for the future.

Views of Leaders in the Sport Industry	In 1999, in an interview in *Street & Smith's SportsBusiness Journal*, several sport industry leaders gave their view of the future of the sport industry (Schoenfeld, 1999). The panelists included Todd Leiweke (Staples Center), Bob Whitsitt (Seahawks and TrailBlazers' CEO), and Kay Yew (University of Maryland Athletic Director). Although these leaders came from the spectator sport segment of the industry, some of their perspective relates to the entire industry. Their predictions follow.

1. Dollars will continue to increase throughout the sport industry, including valuations of professional franchises; gross gate receipts; and remuneration for players, coaches, and executives. Each time it seems as though the numbers cannot

go any higher, a franchise sells for a record amount or a player sets a new high for yearly salary. As discussed with demand and supply, excess demand for limited supply, whether of franchises or very good players, drives up prices.

2. Corporations will become increasingly involved at every level of sport. Corporate involvement will increase in several areas. One is ownership, which is already occurring, from media companies' purchasing sports teams to corporations' accumulating health clubs and golf courses. In major sports, ownership as ego gratification will fall by the wayside, in large part because of the dollars required. Individuals looking for that involvement may gravitate to minor leagues, which could see expansion. Sport firms will be diversified. As Whitsitt says, "Sports teams are in the arena business, the t-shirt business, the shopping mall business, the hotel business" (Schoenfeld, 1999, p. 38). Another involvement is in sponsorship, not only at the professional, commercial level, but down to high schools and recreational activities. Firms see their participation as a good economic decision, where benefits exceed costs.

3. The massive growth spurt of the 1980s and 1990s will be slowing down. That period of time saw tremendous expansion in leagues and teams, in television coverage, and in dollars spent. However, a maximum point is being reached. For example, the amount of time Americans spend watching television is near saturation. Television can provide more options but not more viewing time in a day. Although the panel did not talk about population changes, the slowing population growth and shift from the traditional 18- to 49-year-old white male sport fan will impact sport. The panel did see markets in which sport can grow; however, they view the growth as more restrained. Although other countries provide growth opportunities, international expansion for U.S. sports will come "indirectly, through promotions, targeted marketing, new media, and special events" (Schoenfeld, 1999, p. 34). Growth in technology will continue.

4. The television system will continue to fragment, but major sport properties will maintain their values. Cable television has allowed many sport activities (e.g., aerobics, extreme sports, beach volleyball) to receive exposure with a wider audience than would have been possible relying on in-person viewers. However, these are niche sports, and they are all competing for limited time and dollars. Over-the-air television will remain a stronghold for major sports events.

5. Revenue discrepancies between small and large markets in professional sports will be addressed with more income-sharing. The panel is perhaps more optimistic than are the authors of this text.

6. Technology advances will allow the sport industry to "operate more efficiently, but also will augment the total sports experience, both live and through a variety of media" (Schoenfeld, 1999, p. 34). Technology is changing the way in which people view and buy sports. Although the panel correctly sees technology impacting demand and supply, the costs and benefits will need to be addressed.

Summary

The sport industry in the United States and North America faces many challenges as it enters the 21st century. The explosive industry growth experienced in the last two decades of the 20th century is unlikely to continue. Population changes and resulting changes in demand will create a different environment for firms and organizations. Economic issues will include the nature of sport suppliers, the impact of competition, and changing technology. A requirement for managers of sport organizations is that they must anticipate and plan if they are to make effective decisions for the future.

Chapter Questions

1. How are sport organizations already beginning to adjust to the changing environment?
2. How have changes in sport industry technology impacted your sport experience?

Learning Activities

1. Create a time capsule for the year 2020. Make predictions about what you think the sport industry will look like. What will the most popular sports be, from both a spectator and participant perspective? Who will be the most powerful people (titles rather than names)? How much will tickets to the NCAA Final Four cost? What will the role of the Internet be?
2. Choose a sport organization. Write a memo to the CEO of the organization outlining how changing demographic trends are going to impact that organization.

References

A tighter rein on privatization. (1998, January 4). *Los Angeles Times*, p. 4.

Adams, R. (2003, March 17). Rights structure, shift to cable paint uncertain picture for nets. *Street & Smith's SportsBusiness Journal*, 29.

Adams, R. (2004, October 18). ESPN's magazine sets its sights on China. *Street & Smith's Sports-Business Journal*, 7.

Agoglia, J. (1999, June 21). The lost generation? *Sports Goods Business*, 34–35.

Ahlborn, C., Evans, D., & Padilla, J. (2004). The antitrust economics of tying: A farewell to per se illegality. *Antitrust Bulletin, 49*, 1, 287–341.

Allen, R. L. (1993). The why and how of global retailing. *Business Quarterly, 57*(4), 117–122.

American Recreation Coalition. (1998, July). Insights into trends, developments and other curiosities in the world of recreation. Washington, DC.

American Sports Data, Inc. (2003). *The superstudy of sports participation* (Vol. III). Hartsdale, NY: Outdoors Activities.

Antitrust Update. (2005). NCAA rule limiting participation in early-season college basketball tournaments survives antitrust challenge. Weil, Gotshal& Manges LLP. Winter 2004–2005. Retrieved February 28, 2006, from http://www.weil.com/wgm/cwgmhomep.nsf/Files/AUwtr05/$file/AUwtr05.pdf

Antonen, M. (2002, April 17). Teams tie ticket prices to demand. *USA Today*, p. 6c.

Armstrong, J., & Collopy, F. (1996). Competitor orientation: Effects of objectives and information on managerial decisions and profitability. *Journal of Marketing Research, 33*(2), 188–199.

Aubrey, J. (1999, August 2). Bad sign for Canadian clubs. *Ottawa Citizen Online* (p. 2). Retrieved March 28, 2000, from http://www.ottawacitizen.com/sports.html

Auerbach, A., & Kotlikoff, L. (1995). *Macroeconomics: An integrated approach*. Cincinnati, OH: South-Western College Publishing.

Auger, D. A. (1999). Privatization, contracting, and the states: Lessons from state government. *Public Productivity & Management Review, 22*(4), 435–454.

Australia Sports Commission. (2006). Funding. Retrieved February 2, 2006, from http://www.au sport.gov.au/

Barro, R. (2002). The best little monopoly in America. *Business Week Online*. December 9, 2002. Retrieved February 28, 2006, from http://www.businessweek.com/magazine/content/02_49/b3811038.htm

Bawden, T. (1999, May 6). Man Utd aims brand at Asian goal. *Marketing Week, 22*(14), 6.

Baye, M. (2003). *Managerial economics and business strategy* (4th ed.). New York: McGraw-Hill.

Behavior Research Center, Inc. (1993). *Cactus League attender survey: Executive summary*. Phoenix, AZ: Author.

Berger, J. T. (2001). Collaborate or evaporate: Firms partner up for success. *Journal of Property Management, 66*(3), 56–60.

Bernstein, A. (2002). Bout time: HBO pumped for boxing. *Street & Smith's SportsBusiness Journal*, 4, 8.

Bernstein, M. F. (1998). Sports stadium boondoggle. *Public Interest, 132*, 45–57.

Bernthal, M. J., & Regan, T. H. (2004). The economic impact of a NASCAR racetrack on a rural community and region. *Sport Marketing Quarterly, 13*(1), 26–34.

Berry, R., & Wong, G. (1986). *Law and business of the sport industries*: Vol. I. Dover, MA: Auburn House Publishing Company.

Blake, B. (2004, March 14). Analysis: Where do we go from here? *Speedwire*. Retrieved February 28, 2006, from http://www.speedtv.com/articles/auto/nascar/10219/

Boal, W., & Ransom, M. (1997). Monopsony in the labor market. *Journal of Economic Literature, 35*, 86–112.

Bork, R. (1978). *The antitrust paradox: A policy at war with itself*. New York: Basic Books.

Boyne, G. A. (1998). Bureaucratic theory meets reality: Public choice and service contracting in U.S. local government. *Public Administration Review, 58*(6), 474–484.

Brickley, J. A., Smith, Jr., C. W., & Zimmerman, J. L. (1997). *Managerial economics and organizational architecture*. Chicago, IL: Irwin.

Brooks, A. (2003). Challenges and opportunities facing nonprofit organizations. *Public Administration Review, 63*(4), 503.

Broughton, D., Lee, J., & Nethery, R. (1999). The question: How big is the U.S. sports industry? *Street & Smith's SportsBusiness Journal, 2*(35), 23–29.

Bureau of Economic Analysis. (1997). *Regional multipliers: A user handbook for the Regional Input-Output Modeling System (RIMS II)* (3rd ed.). Retrieved March 23, 1999, from http://www.bea.doc.gov/bea/regional/articles.htm

Burgi, M. (1997, March 10). A garden of cable delight. *Mediaweek, 7*(10), 5.

Burton, R., Quester, P. G., & Farrelly, F. J. (1998). Organizational power games. *Marketing Management, 7*(1), 27–36.

Business Wire. (2004, April 7). Athletic footwear market share report announced for first quarter of 2000; Nike holds commanding percentage of footwear market after first quarter. Retrieved February 28, 2006, from http://www.findarticles.com/cf_dls/m0EIN/2000_April_7/61368089/p1/article.jhtml

Buyers, C. (2004). Callaway Golf Company: Chipping it in from the rough. *RCB Capital Markets.* Retrieved February 28, 2006, from http://www.rbccmresearch.com/drw1.0.4/pdf/0%2C%2C30212%2C00.pdf

Cabrera, G. (2005). Legislative Analyst Report: Sports Commissions in Other Jurisdictions. City of San Francisco.

Cady, E. H. (1978). *The big game: College sports and American life*. Knoxville, TN: The University of Tennessee Press.

Cairns, J., Jennett, N., & Sloane, P. J. (1986). The economics of professional team sports: A survey of theory and evidence. *Journal of Economic Studies, 13*(1), 3–80.

Callaway Golf Company. (2005). Media Center. Retrieved December 19, 2005, from http://www.callawaygolf.com/en.cg.MediaCenter.PressRelease.article-13642.html

Cavanaugh, J. (1999, January 25–31). ABL action more likely in court than on it. *Street & Smith's SportBusiness Journal*, 43.

CBS SportLine. (1999). Home. Retrieved March 20, 2006, from http://www.sportsline.com

Champion, W. (1993). *Sports law: In a nutshell*. St. Paul, MN: West Publishing.

Christie, J. (2003). Breaking sports news. *The Globe and Mail.* Retrieved February 2, 2006, from http://Globeandmail.com

Clifford, F. (1993, October 2). Curry Co. turns over Yosemite concessions. *Los Angeles Times*, p. A18.

Clumpner, R. A. (1994). 21st century success in international competition. In R. Wilcox (Ed.), *Sport in the Global Village* (pp. 353–363). Morgantown, WV: Fitness Information Technology.

Coakley, J. J. (2001). *Sport in society: Issues and controversies* (7th ed.). New York: McGraw-Hill.

Coakley, J. J. (1994). *Sport in society: Issues and controversies*. St. Louis, MO: Mosby.

Coase, R. (1960). The problem of social cost. *Journal of Law and Economics, 3*, 1–44.

Colander, D. (1998). *Economics* (3rd ed.). Boston, MA: McGraw-Hill.

Coughlin, C., & Erekson, O. (1985). Contributions to intercollegiate athletic programs: Further evidence. *Social Science Quarterly, 66*, 194–202.

Crawford, D. (1997). Rival women's basketball leagues slug it out for supremacy on and off court. Columbus Business First, October 31, 1997. Retrieved February 28, 2006, from http://www.bizjournals.com/columbus/stories/1997/11/03/story4.html

Crompton, J. L. (1995). Economic impact analysis of sports facilities and events: Eleven sources of misapplication. *Journal of Sport Management, 9*(1), 14–35.

Crowe, S. (1999, March 13). Heavy intrigue: Holyfield-Lewis bout a big draw. *Los Angeles Daily News*, p. S1.

Daggett, W. (2005). International Center for Leadership in Education. Retrieved January 20, 2006, from http://www.leadered.com

Daniels, M. R. (1999, April 1). The future of the Canadian financial services sector. *Vital Speeches of the Day*, 364–369.

Datapol, Inc. (1988). *Economic impact of Major League Baseball spring training on the Greater Mesa, Arizona area*. Mesa, AZ: Author.

Dell'Apa, F. (1993, May/June). Do pro sports take advantage of their fans? *Public Citizen*. 10+.

Delpy, L., & Li, M. (1998). The art and science of conducting economic impact studies. *Journal of Vacation Marketing, 4*(3), 230–254.

Demmert, H. G. (1973). *The economics of professional team sports.* Lexington, MA: Lexington Books.

DeSchriver, T. D., & Stotlar, D. K. (1996). An economic analysis of cartel behavior within the NCAA. *Journal of Sport Management, 10,* 388–400.

Division of Research. (1990). *The economic impact of the MCI Heritage Classic on the economy of Hilton Head Island, South Carolina.* College of Business Administration, the University of South Carolina, Columbia, SC

Dowd, T. A., Monaco, R. M., & Janoska, J. J. (1998, September). Effects of future demographic changes on the U.S. economy: Evidence from a long-term simulation model. *Economic Systems Research,* 239–262.

Drowatzky, J. (1997). Antitrust law and amateur sports. *Sport law for sport managers.* Ed. D. C. Cotton & T. J. Wilde. Dubuque, IA: Kendell/Hunt Publishing Company.

Durand, C., & Bayle, E. (2002). Public assistance in spectator sport: A comparison between Europe and the United States. *European Journal of Sport Science, 2*(2), 1–19.

Eitzen, D. S., & Sage, G. H. (1997). *Sociology of North American sport* (6th ed.). Madison, WI: Brown & Benchmark Publishers, p. 317.

El Nasser, H. (1999, June 16). Commotion kicking up over space for soccer. *USA Today,* p. 17A.

Elliott, J. E. (1985). *Comparative economic systems* (2nd ed.). Delmont, CA: Wadsworth Publishing Company.

Entertainment Software Association. (2004). Facts and Research: Sales and Genre Data. Retrieved February 1, 2006, from http://www.theesa.com/facts/sales_genre_data.php

Estano, N. (2005, December 12). The (Fast) Evolution of Snowboarding. Retrieved January 22, 2006, from www.thewbalchannel.com/weather/5425475/detail.html

Fish, M. (2005, June 20). Tight public money forces teams to get creative with stadium finance plans. *Street & Smith's SportsBusiness Journal, 7,* 19.

Fisher, E. (2006, January 9). Next for iPod: NHL and NASCAR. *Street & Smith's SportsBusiness Journal,* 1.

Fisher, E. (2006, January 9).Google gets in the game with NBA. *Street & Smith's SportsBusiness Journal,* 1.

Fleming, W. R., & Toepper, L. (1990). Economic impact studies: Relating the positive and negative impacts to tourism development. *Journal of Travel Research, 29*(1), 35–42.

Florida Sports Foundation. (2004). About Us. Retrieved April 30, 2006, from http://www.flasports.com/page_aboutus.shtml

Folk, W. R., Jr., & Aggarwal, R. (1988). *International dimensions of financial management.* Boston, MA: PWS-Kent Publishing Company.

Frechtling, D. C. (1994). Assessing the economic impact of travel and tourism-measuring economic benefits. In J. R. B. Ritchie & C. R. Goeldner (Eds.), *Travel, tourism, and hospitality research: A handbook for managers and researchers* (2nd ed., pp. 368–391). New York: John Wiley and Sons.

Frey, J. H., & Johnson, A. T. (1985). Conclusion: Sports, regulation, and the public interest. In A. T. Johnson & J. H. Frey (Eds.), *Government and sport* (pp. 261–264). Totowa, NJ: Rowman & Allanheld Publishers.

Genest, S. (1994). Skating on thin ice? The international migration of Canadian ice hockey players. In J. Bale & J. Maguire (Eds.), *The global sports arena: athletic talent migration in an interdependent world* (pp. 125–131. London: Frank Cass & Co. Ltd.

Gilpin, K. (1996, November 29). Seven ski resorts merge. *New York Times,* p. D13.

Glier, R. (2003, May 14). NCAA tennis: Too many foreigners or not? *USA Today* [Online]. Retrieved December 15, 2005, from http://www.usatoday.com/sports/college/other/2003-05-14-ncaa-tennis-euros_x.htm

Go, F., & Christensen, J. (1989). Going global. *Cornell Hotel & Restaurant Administration Quarterly, 30*(3), 72–79.

Golf Research Group. (August, 1997). The US golf development report. Retrieved July 17, 1999, from http://www.golf-research.com/usgolf.htm

Gorman, J., & Calhoun, K. (1994). *The Name of the Game.* New York: John Wiley & Sons.

Graham, E., Ruggieri, C. A., Clements, P. J., & Cody, A. (1994). Introduction. *International Corporate Law/Mergers & Acquisitions Yearbook,* 2–5.

Gratton, C., & Taylor, P. (1985). *Sport and recreation: An economic analysis.* New York: E. and F. N. Spon.

Gratton, C., & Taylor, P. (1992). *Government and the economics of sport.* Essex, England: Longmon Group.

Gray, S. J., McDermott, M. C., & Walsh, E. J. (1990). *Handbook of international business and management*. Oxford, UK: Basil Blackwell Ltd.

Greer, D. (1992). *Industrial organization and public policy* (3rd ed.). New York: Macmillian Publishing Company.

Gruen, A. (1976). An inquiry into the economics of racetrack gambling. In D. Watson & M. Getz, *Price theory in action* (4th ed.). Boston, MA: Houghton Mifflin.

Guardian Newspapers. (2003, February 6). Sports Lobby Government for Olympic Cash.

Hall, J., & Mahony, D. (1997). Factors affecting methods used by annual giving programs: A qualitative study of NCAA Division I athletic departments. *Sports Marketing Quarterly, 6*(3), 21–30.

Hamilton, B. (2003). Class action in price-fixing litigation when the fixed price is a wage rate: Law et al. v. NCAA. *Antitrust Bulletin, 48*(2), 505–529.

Harris County-Houston Sports Authority. (2006). Government Documents. Retrieved February 12, 2006, from http://www.hchsa.org/legal/legal.html

Hawk, B. E. (1988). European Economic Community and United States antitrust law: Contrasts and convergences. *Australia Business Law Review, 16*(4), 282–325.

Hayes, J. P. (1993). International expansion: A four-point PR program. *Franchising World, 25*(5), 9–11.

Herzog, B. (2004, January). Vancouver, Wash.- Based exercise equipment firm sees quarterly sales drop again. *Knight Ridder Tribune Business News*. Retrieved February 28, 2006, from http://proquest.umi.com/pqdweb?did=533778661&sid=2&Fmt=3&clientId=2138&RQT=309&VName=PQD

Hirschey, M. (2003). *Managerial economics* (10th ed.). Cincinnati, OH: Southwestern College Publishing.

Hirschey, M., & Pappas, J. L. (1995). *Fundamentals of managerial economics* (5th ed.). Fort Worth, TX: The Dryden Press.

Hofacre, S., & Burman, T. (1992). Demographic changes in the U.S. into the 21st century: Their impact on sport marketing. *Sport Marketing Quarterly, 1*(1), 31–36.

Horovitz , B. (1999, August 5). Olympics chief looks to Web for solutions. *USA Today*, 3.

Horowitz, I. (1999). The reasonableness of horizontal restraints. In J. Kwoka & L. White (Eds.), *The antitrust revolution: Economics, competition, and policy* (2nd ed.). New York: Oxford University Press.

Howard, D. R., & Crompton, J. L. (1995). *Financing sport*. Morgantown, WV: Fitness Information Technology.

Hugh-Jones, S. (1992, July 25). A survey of sports businesses. *The Economist*, S3–17.

Humphreys, J. M., & Plummer, M. K. (1995). *The economic impact on the State of Georgia of hosting the 1996 Summer Olympic Games*. Report prepared for the Atlanta Committee for the Olympic Games.

Illinois Department of Professional Regulation. (2006). *Business requirements: Illinois department of professional regulation: Athletic trainer license*. Retrieved February 28, 2006, from http://spinotew1.commerce.state.il.us/dfsim.nsf/0/787342171755c79f8625663a0072178e?OpenDocument

International Health, Racquet and Sportsclub Association. (2005). About the Industry. Retrieved December 29, 2005, from http://cms.ihrsa.org/IHRSA/viewPage.cfm?pageId=804

International Working Group on Women and Sport. (2002). Women and Sport Progress Report 1998–2002. Retrieved December 16, 2005, from http://www.canada2002.org/e/progress/progress/chapter2_9.htm

Jacobs, J. A., & Portman, R. M. (1997). Risk of self-regulation. *Association Management, 49*(3), 89–90.

Jacobs, S. H. (1997). Regulatory reform: Times for action. *OECD Observer, 206*, 5–9.

Jensen, J. (1997). Sports, event marketing shops seeking mainstream alliance. *Advertising Age, 68*(31), 14–15.

Johnson, A. T., & Frey, J. H. (1985). *Government and sport*. Totowa, NJ: Rowman & Allanheld Publishers.

Johnson, W. O. (1991, July 22). Sport in the year 2001. *Sport Illustrated, 75*, 46.

Jones, K. (1999, July/August). The next generation of legislatures. *State Legislatures*, 38–41.

Jones, L. P., & Ergas, H. (1993). Appropriate regulatory technology: The interplay of economic and institutional conditions. *World Bank Research Observer*, 181–213.

Kanters, M. A. (1999). *The economic impact of the WRAL Southeastern Wake County athletic complex*. Technical Report. Department of Parks, Recreation, and Tourism Management, North Carolina State University, Raleigh, NC.

Kaplan, D. (1999). Going public makes company an open book. *Street & Smith's SportsBusiness Journal, 2*(7), 21–23.

Kaplan, D., & Mullen, L. (1999). Angry Ascent shareholders seek suitors. *Street & Smith's SportsBusiness Journal, 2*(8), 1, 47.

Kass, M. (1996, December 20). Score another victory for Jerry Jone's Dallas Cowboys. *The Business Journal: Serving Greater Milwaukee.* Retrieved May 12, 2004, from http://www.bizjournals.com/milwaukee/stories/1996/12/23/newscolumn2.html

Keat, P., & Young, P. K. Y. (1992). *Managerial economics.* New York: Macmillan.

Kelly, J. R. (1985). *Recreation business.* New York: John Wiley & Sons.

Kelly, J. R., & Godbey, G. (1992). *The sociology of leisure.* State College, PA: Venture Publishing.

King, B. (2002). *Street & Smith's SportsBusiness Journal, 4*(47), 25–39.

King, B. (2005, March 7). The 24/7 fan. *Street & Smith's SportsBusiness Journal,* 23.

King, B., & Warfield, S. (2005, February 14). Should you believe all you hear about NASCAR? *Street & Smith's SportsBusiness Journal,* 19.

Knowles, G., Sherony, K., & Haupert, M. (1992). The demand for Major League Baseball: A test of the uncertainty of outcome hypothesis. *The American Economist, 36*(2), 72–80.

Koch, J. V. (1984). Intercollegiate athletics: An economic explanation. *Social Science Quarterly.* 360–373.

Lachowetz, T. (2001). Regional Sports Alliances: A Conceptual Approach. *Conference Proceeding,* 16th Annual Conference of the North American Society for Sport Management, Virginia Beach, VA, 47.

Lambert, R., Larcker, D., & Weigelt, K. (1991). How sensitive is executive compensation to organizational size? *Strategic Management Journal, 12*(5), 395–402.

Leonard, W. M. (1998). *A sociological perspective of sport* (5th ed.). Boston, MA: Allyn and Bacon.

Leontief, W. W. (1985, March-April). Why economics needs input-output model? *Challenge,* 27–35.

Li, M., Hofacre, S., & Mahony, D. (2001). *Economics of sport.* Morgantown, WV: Fitness Information Technology.

Lieberman, P. (1994, April 11). For some golfers it's worse than a bogey. *Los Angeles Time,* p. A1.

Lipsey, R. G., Courant, P. N., & Ragan, C. T. S. (1999). *Economics* (12th ed.). Reading, MA: Addison-Wesley.

Lombardo, J. (2003, October 27). NBA season preview: Game plan calls for growth overseas. *Street & Smith's SportsBusiness Journal,* 25.

Lombardo, J. (2004, October 25). Global trade: NBA imports talent and exports the game. *Street & Smith's SportsBusiness Journal,* 21.

Love, W. D. (1995). Been there, done that. *LIMRA's MarketFacts, 14*(6), 38–40.

MaCarhty, L., & Wilcox, R. (1997). NAFTA and the North American sport industry. Paper presented at the 12th annual conference of the North American Society for Sport Management, San Antonio, TX.

Mahony, D., & Howard, D. (2001). Sport business in the next decades: A general overview of expected trends. *Journal of Sport Management, 15*(4), 275–296.

Mahtesian, C. (1997, October). Revenue in the rough. *Governing,* 42–44.

Mankiw, N. G. (2001). *Principles of microeconomics* (2nd ed.). Orlando FL: Harcourt Inc.

Mann, H. (1974). Advertising, concentration, and profitability: The state of knowledge and directions for public policy. In H. Goldschmid, H. Michael Mann, & J. Fred Weston (Eds.), *Industrial concentration: The new learning.* Boston, MA: Little, Brown & Company.

Masteralexis, L. (1997). Antitrust law and labor law: Professional sport. In D. C. Cotton & T. J. Wilde (Eds.), *Sport law for sport managers.* Dubuque, IA: Kendall/Hunt Publishing Company.

Maynard, R. (1995). Why franchisors look abroad. *Nation's Business, 83*(10), 65–67+.

McComick, R., & Tollison R (1990). Crime on the court. In B. Goff & R. Tollison (Eds.), *Sportsometrics.* College Station, TX: Texas A & M University Press.

McConnell, C., & Brue, S. (2005). *Economics* (16th ed.). New York: McGraw-Hill.

McEvoy, C. (1999a, July 16). The SGB interview: Tim Harrington. *Sporting Goods Business, 32*(11), 48–51.

McEvoy, C. (1999b, November 5). Batting around NCAA standards. *Sporting Goods Business, 32*(16), 39.

McGuigan, J., & Moyer, R. (1986). *Managerial economics* (4th ed.). St. Paul, MN: West Publishing Company.

Mcnow, G. (1989, May). From calamity to conglomerate. *Nation's Business,* 48–51.

Meek, A. (1997). An estimate of the size and supported economic activity of the sports industry in the United States. *Sport Marketing Quarterly, 6*(4), 15–21.

Metge, B., Nathanson, A., & Levin, M. (1996). *Strategic alliances under the antitrust laws.* Retrieved March 28, 2000, from http://www.mintz.com/newspubs/Antitrust/Antt1096.htm

Miller, F., & Redhead, S., 1994. In J. Bale & J. Maguire (Eds.), *The global sports arena: Athletic talent migration in an interdependent world* (p. 142). London: Frank Cass & Co. Ltd.

Miller, L., & Fielding, L. (1995). The battle between the for-profit health club and the "commercial" YMCA. *Journal of Sport and Social Issues, 19,* 76–107.

Mitnick, B. M. (1980). *The political economy of regulation: Creating, designing, and removing regulatory forms.* New York: Columbia University Press.

Mueller, C. E. (1996). Laissez-faire, monopoly and global income inequality: Law, economics, history and politics of antitrust law & economics. In C. E. Mueller (Ed.), *Antitrust overview:* Vero Beach, FL USA: Antitrust Law and Economics Review.

Mullin, B., Hardy, S., & Sutton, W. A. (2000). *Sport marketing* (2nd ed.). Champaign, IL: Human Kinetics.

Mullin, L. (1999). Churchill to bankroll spree with new stock offering. *Street & Smith's SportsBusiness Journal,* 1, 9.

Munsey, P., & Suppes, C. (2005). *Citizen ball park.* Retrieved December 19, 2005, from http://www.ballparks.com/baseball/national/phibpk.htm

Murphy, P. E., & Carmicheal, B. A. (1991). Assessing the tourism benefits of an open access sports tournament: The 1989 B.C. Winter Games. *Journal of Travel Research, 30,* 32–35.

Myers, K. J. (Ed.). (1998). *Sports market place.* Mesa, AZ: Custom Publishing Inc.

National Association of Intercollegiate Athletics. (2005). *Member institution.* Retrieved December 20, 2005, from http://naia.collegesports.com/member-services/about/members.htm

National Collegiate Athletic Association. (2004, March 22). *News release.* Retrieved April 30, 2006, from http://www.ncaa.org/wps/portal

National Collegiate Athletic Association. (2006, April 28). *The online resources for the National Collegiate Athletic Association.* Retrieved April 30, 2006, from http://www.ncaa.org/wps.portal

National Federation of State High School Associations. (2005). *About the NFHS.* Retrieved December 15, 2005, from http://www.nfsh.org/scriptcontent/va_custom/vimDisplays/contentpagedisplay.cfm? content_id=37

NCAA News, (2000, August 28). Demand again well above supply for tickets to Final Four. *National Collegiate Athletic Association.* Retrieved April 30, 2006, from http://www.ncaa/org/news/2000/20000828/active/3718n11.html

Nicolaides, P. (1989). Globalisation of services and developing countries. In R. O'Brien & T. Datta (Eds.), *International economics and financial markets* (pp. 172–194). New York: Oxford University Press.

Noll, R. G. (1974). Attendance and price setting. In R. G. Noll (Ed.), *Government and the sports business.* Washington, DC: Brookings Institution.

Office of Management and Budget. (1997). *North American Industry Classification System (NAICS) - 1997.* US Department of Commerce, Washington, DC.

Ozanian, M. K. (1997). Valuation scoreboard. *Financial World.* Retrieved August 18, 1999, from http://www.financialworld.com/archives/1997/June/sportsvalues.html

Pappas, J. L., & Hirschey, M. (1987). *Managerial economics* (5th ed.). Chicago, IL: The Dryden Press.

Park, S., & Celeste, R. F. (1996). Strategic alliances for innovation: Emerging models of technology-based twenty-first century economic development. *Economic Development Review, 14*(1), 4–11.

Parkin, M. (1993). *Economics* (2nd ed.). Reading, MA: Addison-Wesley Publishing Company.

Patino, M. J. (1999). *The sport summit/sport business directory* (5th ed.). Bethesda, MD: E. J. Krause & Associates, Inc.

Petersen, H., & Lewis, W. (1999). *Managerial economics* (4th ed.). Upper Saddle River, NJ: Prentice-Hall.

Pitts, B. G., Fielding, L. W., & Miller, L. K. (1994). Industry segmentation theory and the sport industry: Developing a sport industry segment model. *Sport Marketing Quarterly, 3*(1), 15–24.

Pitts, B. G., & Stotlar, D. K. (1996). *Fundamentals of sport marketing.* Morgantown, WV: Fitness Information Technology.

Pointer, M. (2005, December 16). International flavor in top basketball programs levels off. *IndyStar.com.* Retrieved February 2, 2006, from http://www.indystar.com/apps/pbcs.dll/section?Category=SPORTS

Quirk, J., & Fort, R. (1992). *Pay dirt: The business of professional team sports.* Princeton, NJ: Princeton University Press.

Reason, T. (2002, April). Diamonds in the rough: Minor league baseball is afraid of becoming a victim of its own success. *CFO, Magazine for Senior Financial Executives*. Retrieved February 28, 2006, from http://www.cfo.com/article.cfm/3004004?f=related

Recreation Executive Report. (1997). Number 9, The Sporting Goods Manufacturers Association. Washington, DC: Leisure Industry/Recreation News.

Regan, T. H. (1996). Financing sport. In B. L. Parkhouse (Ed.), *The management of sport*. St. Louis, MO: Mosby-Year Book.

Richardson, A. J., & McConomy, B. J. (1992). Three styles of rule. *CA Magazine, 125*(5), 40–44.

Robertson, G. (2003). Fighting the couch potato culture. *CRAEDO News*. Retrieved October 20, 2003, from http://www.craedo.com/view.aspx?T=N1AR&ID=11

Rogers, J. E., & Arriola, A. Z. (1997). Telecommunications: An international legal guide supplement (Mexico). *International Financial Law Review*, 48–50.

Rovell, D. (2003, June). McFarlane wins auction for historic Bonds ball. *ESPN sport business*. Retrieved February 28, 2006, from http://espn.go.com/sportsbusiness/news/2003/0625/1572871.html

Ruibal, S. (1999, June 28). Extreme sports make mark on line. *USA Today*, p. 8C.

Sack, A. (1988). College sport and the student athlete. *Journal of Sport and Social Issues, 11*, 31–48.

Sailes, G. (1999, April). Basketball at midnight. *The Unesco Courier*, pp. 25–26.

Salvatore, D. (2001). *Managerial economics in a global economy* (4th ed.). New York: McGraw-Hill.

Samuelson, P. A. (1970). *Economics* (8th ed.). New York: McGraw-Hill.

Sanderson, A., & Siegfried, J. (2003). Thinking about competitive balance. *Journal of Sports Economics, 4*(4), 255–279.

Sandomir, R. (1988, November 14). The $50-billion sports industry. *Sports Inc.,* 14–23.

Schaffer, W. A., & Davidson, L. S. (1975). The economic impact of professional football on Atlanta. In S. P. Ladany (Ed.), *Management science applications to leisure-time operations* (pp. 276–296). Amsterdam: North Holland.

Schifrin, M. (2001, May 21). Partner or perish. *Forbes*, 26–28.

Schiller, B. R. (1989). *The microeconomy today* (4th ed.). New York: McGraw-Hill.

Schoenfeld, B. (1999, January 4–10). Smartest in sports see new golden age. *Street & Smith's SportsBusiness Journal, 1*(37), 1, 34–39.

Scott, F., Long, J., & Somppi, K. (1991). Salary vs. marginal revenue product under monopsony and competition: The case of professional baseball. *Atlantic Economic Journal, 13*(3), 50–59.

Scully, G. (1974). Pay and performance in Major League Baseball. *American Economic Review, 64*, 915–930.

Scully, G. (1995). *The market structure of sports*. Chicago, IL: The University of Chicago Press.

Seeley, A. M. (1997). Bringing fitness to the masses. *Parks & Recreation, 32*(10), 72–76.

Shim, J. K., & Siegel, J. G. (1995). *Dictionary of economics*. New York: John Wiley & Sons, Inc.

Siegried, J. J., & Eisenberg, J. D. (1980). The demand for minor league baseball. *Atlantic Economic Journal, 82*(2), 59–69.

Sigelman, L., & Brookheimer, S. (1983) Is it whether you win or lose? Monetary contributions to big-time athletic programs. *Social Science Quarterly, 64*, 347–359.

Simon, H. (1959). Theories of decision making in economics. *American Economic Review, 49*, 253.

SMG World. (2005). *About SMG*. Retrieved December 28, 2005, from http://www.smgworld.com/

Smith, K. (1995, July 28). *Denver Business Journal, 46*, p. A4.

Southwick, L., Jr. (1985). *Managerial economics*. Plano, TX: Business Publications, Inc.

Spalding Sports Worldwide, Inc. (1999). *History*. Retrieved March 21, 2000, from http://www.spalding.com/history2.html

Spanberg, E. (1999, April 5–11). Retail sales leave stocks in the rough. *Sports Business Journal, 20*.

Spekman, R. E., & Isabella, L. A. (2000). *Alliance competence: Maximizing the value of your partnerships*. New York: John Wiley and Sons, Inc.

Sport Business. (1997, October 31). Nike to open 10m store in Melbourne. Retrieved October 29, 2000, from http://www.sportbusiness.com/dailynews/news007.htm

Sport Business. (1997, October 31). PGA sets scene for world tour. Retrieved October 28, 2000, from http://www.sportbusiness.com/dailynews/news007.htm

Sport Canada. (2005). *Mission*. Retrieved December 19, 2005, from http://www.pch.gc.ca/progs/sc/index_e.cfm

Sporting Goods Manufacturers Association International. (2005, January 17). *Press release*. Retrieved January 23, 2006, from http://www.sgma.com

Sporting Goods Manufacturers Association. (1997, January). *Press release*. Retrieved September 3, 1999, from http://www.sportlink.com/research/1998_research/industry/export98-01.html

Sporting Goods Manufacturers Association. (1997, March). *Press release.* Retrieved September 3, 1999, from http://www.sportlink.com/press_room/1997_releases/m97-3.html

Sporting Goods Manufacturers Association. (1998). *1998 state of the industry report.* Retrieved from http://www.sportlink.com/research/1998_research/industry/98soti.html

Sporting Goods Manufacturers Association. (2004, February). *U.S. sporting goods export resumes growth.* Retrieved December 29, 2005, from http://www.sgma.com

Sporting Goods Manufacturers Association. (2005, February). *Press release.* Retrieved December 29, 2005, from http://www.sgma.com

Sporting Goods Manufacturers Association International (2003, January 19). *Press release.* Retrieved January 23, 2006, from http://www.sgma.com

Statistics Canada. (2000). *Government revenues, expenditure and debt.* Retrieved August 5, 2000, from http://www.statcan.ca/english/Pgdb/State/govern.htm#rev

Staudohar, P. (1989). *The sports industry and collective bargaining* (2nd ed.). Ithaca, NY: ILR Press.

Staudohar, P. (1999). Labor relations in basketball: The lockout of 1998–99. *Monthly Labor Review, 122*(4), 3–9.

Staudohar, P. (2003). Why no baseball work stoppage? *Journal of Sports Economics 4*(4), 362–366.

Staudohar, P. (2005). The hockey lockout of 2004–05. *Monthly Labor Review, 128*(12), 23–29.

Stern, R. N. (1981). Competitive influences on the inter-organizational regulation of college athletics. *Administrative Science Quarterly, 26,* 15–31.

Stigler, G. (1964). A theory of oligopoly. *Journal of Political Economy, 72,* 44–61.

Street & Smith's SportsBusiness Journal. (2000). Special report: Internet sports sponsorships, *2*(46), 34.

Street & Smith's SportsBusiness Journal. (2000). Special report: Sponsorship, *2*(46), 25–38.

Street & Smith's SportsBusiness Journal. (2002). Sports related laws and legal cases through the years, 4, 18.

Street & Smith's SportsBusiness Journal. (2005, December 19). Sports sites on the Web, 14.

Stynes, D. J. (1999a). *Economic impact concepts.* Retrieved April 28, 2000, from http://www.msu.edu/course/prr/840/econimpact/

Stynes, D. J. (1999b). Economic impacts of tourism. *Bulletins on Concepts and Methods,* Department of Parks, Recreation, and Tourism Resources, Michigan State University.

Sullivan, L. (1977). *Antitrust.* St. Paul, MN: West Publishing Company.

Taylor, A. (1999, August 25). Tennis no match for net of full life. *Black World Today.* Retrieved February 27, 2000, from http://www.tbwt.com/views/andre

Team Marketing Report. (2006). *Resources.* Retrieved April 30, 2006, from http://www.team marketing.com/fci.cfm?page=fci_nfl_05.cfm

The Division of Research. (1990). *The economic impact of the MCI Heritage Classic on the economy of Hilton Head Island, SC.* College of Business Administration, the University of South Carolina, Columbia, South Carolina.

The economic and fiscal impact of aging retirees on a small rural region. (1999). *Gerontologist, 39*(5), 599–610.

Thoma, J. E., & Chalip, L. (1996). *Sport governance in the global community.* Morgantown, WV: Fitness Information Technology.

Thomas, C., & Maurice, S. (2005). *Managerial economics* (8th ed.). New York: McGraw Hill.

Turco, D. M. (1993). Assessing the economic impact and financial return on investment of a national sporting event. *Sport Marketing Quarterly, 2*(3), 17–22.

Turco, D. M. (1995). Measuring the Economic Impact of a Sporting Event. Paper presented at the 1995 North American Society for Sport Management Annual Conference. New Brunswick, Canada.

U.S. Bureau of Economic Analysis. (2005). *U.S. Economic Accounts.* Retrieved December 20, 2005, from www.bea.gov

U.S. Census Bureau. *Statistical Abstract of the United States, 1997.* Retrieved January 20, 2006, from http://www.census.gov/prod/www/statistical-abstract-1995_2000.html

U.S. Census Bureau. (1997). *Statistical Abstract of the United States (1997).* Washington, DC: Bureau of Economic Analysis.

U.S. Census Bureau. (1999). Retrieved May 6, 2000, from www.census.gov/statab/www/pop.html

U.S. Census Bureau. (2000). Retrieved December 15, 2005, from www.census.gov/population/projections/nation/summary/np-t4-a.txt

U.S. Census Bureau. (2002). *Statistical Abstract of the United States (2002).* Washington, DC: Bureau of Economic Analysis.

U.S. Census Bureau. (2002). *Statistical Abstract of the United States, 2002.* Retrieved January 26, 2006, from http://www.census.gov/prod/www/statistical-abstract-2001_2005.html

U.S. Census Bureau. (2003). *Statistical Abstract of the United States, 2003.* Retrieved January 26, 2006, from http://www.census.gov/prod/www/statistical-abstract-2001_2005.html

U.S. Census Bureau. (2004). *Fact Sheet.* Retrieved December 15, 2005, from http://factfinder.census.gov/servlet/SAFFFacts?_sse=on

U.S. Census Bureau. (2004). *2002 Economic Census: Arts, Entertainment and Recreation Industry Series.* Washington, DC: Bureau of Economic Analysis.

U.S. Census Bureau. (2005). *Federal, State, and Local Governments: State and Local Government Finances: 2002–03,* Washington, DC.

U.S. Census Bureau. (2005). *Statistical abstract of the United States, 2005.* Retrieved January 21, 2006, from http://www.census.gov/prod/www/statistical-abstract-2001_2005.html

United Soccer League. (2006, April). *About USL.* Retrieved April 30, 2006, from http://www.usisl.com/about/index.html

United States Census Bureau. (2006). *American fact finder: 2002 economic census.* Retrieved February 28, 2006, from http://factfinder.census.gov/servlet/IBQTable?_bm=y&-geo_id=&-fds_name=EC0200A1&-_skip=500&-ds_name=EC0244I4&-_lang=en

United States Department of Justice. (2003). *An antitrust primer for federal law enforcement personnel.* Retrieved February 28, 2006, from http://www.usdoj.gov/atr/public/guidelines/209114.pdf

Vitullo-Martin, J. (1998, May 20). The private sector shows how to run a city. *The Wall Street Journal,* p. A14.

Vrooman, J. (1997). Franchise free agency in professional sports leagues. *Southern Economic Journal, 64*(1), 191–219.

Walker, S. (1999, July 30). Country clubs get snubbed. *The Wall Street Journal,* pp. W1, W9.

Walsh, R. G. (1986). *Recreation economic decisions: Comparing benefits and costs.* State College, PA: Venture Publishing.

Wang, P., & Irwin, R. L. (1993) An assessment of economic impact techniques for small sporting events. *Sport Marketing Quarterly, 2*(3), 33–37.

Warfield, S. (2004, August 16). Addition of IRL road races paves way for dates in Mexico, Canada. *Street & Smith's SportsBusiness Journal,* 32.

Warren, M. (1992). *Government regulation and American business.* St. Louis, MO: Center for the Study of American Business, Washington University.

Weisbrod, B. A. (1977). *The voluntary nonprofit sector: An economic analysis.* Lexington, MA: Lexington Books.

Wikipedia. (2006, April 6). Major Professional Sports League. Retrieved April 30, 3006, from http://en.wikipedia.org/wiki/Major_professional_sports_league#The_North_American_Leagues

Wikipedia. (2006, April 6). Semi-professional. Retrieved April 30, 2006, from http://en.wikipedia.org/wiki/Semi-professional

Wilcox, R. C. (1994). Preface. In R. C. Wilcox (Ed.), *Sport in the Global Village.* Morgantown, WV: Fitness Information Technology.

Wotruba, T. R. (1997). Industry self-regulation: A review and extension to a global setting. *Journal of Public Policy and Marketing, 16*(1), 38–54.

Yeh, K. T. (1997). *The assessment of economic impact studies on sport-related events in North America: a content analysis.* Unpublished doctoral dissertation, University of Northern Colorado, Greeley, CO.

Yeh, K. T., & Li, M. (1998). Globalization of sport: What sport management professionals should know. *Journal of the International Council for Health, Physical Education, Recreation, Sport and Dance, 34*(2), 29–33.

Zabojnik, J. (1998). Sales maximization and specific human capital. *The Rand Journal of Economics, 29*(4), 790–802

Zikmund, W. G. (2005). *Business research methods* (5th ed.). Fort Worth, TX: The Dryden Press.

Index

net sport exports, 122–124
   personal sports consumption, 114–120
Gross National Sports Product (GNSP), 107
Gruen, A., 44

H
Hardy, S., 41
Harris County-Houston Sports Authority, 23
Hart-Scott-Rodino Antitrust Improvement Act (1976), 191
Haupert, M., 44
Hawk Sports Management, 21
Hecht v. Pro Football Inc. (1977), 200
Hofacre, S., 6–8, 12, 113
horizontal integration, 101

I
independent professional athletes, 11
independent sport activity producers, 11
Indiana Convention Center and RCA Dome, 18–19
industry, definition of, 1–2
Indy Racing League (IRL), 215
inequities, 171
input-output (I-O) model, 127–130
   See also multipliers
intercollegiate sports, 10
Intercollegiate Tennis Association, 215
international expansion, 238
   benefits of, 225
   facility issues, 224
   financial issues, 221–223
   forms of, 220–221
   legal issues, 223–224
   National Basketball Association's (NBA's) efforts in, 219–220, 224
   rationale for, 217–219
   steps and strategies for, 224–225
International Health, Racquet and Sportsclub Association (IHRSA), 117–118
International Management Group (IMG), 21, 221
Internet, the, 231, 232–234
Interpublic (IPG), 219
Interscholastic Sailing Association (ISSA), 16
interscholastic sports, 10
Irabu, Hideki, 216

J
Janoska, J. J., 229–230

Jennett, N., 44
joint ventures, 103
Jones, Jerry, 199

K
kinked demand curve, 78–79
Knowles, G., 44

L
labor
   demand for, 151–154
   labor markets, 156–158
   labor productivity, 154, 167
   labor supply, 154–156, 167
Ladies Professional Golf Association (LPGA), 194
law of comparative advantage, 211–213
   applications of, 213
   and the globalization of sport, 214–216
Law v. National Collegiate Athletic Association (1995), 201
Leiweke, Todd, 237
Li, M. 6–8, 12, 113
licensing (revenue) agreements, 182
Little League, 236
LOCI model, 140
Los Angeles Memorial Coliseum Commission v. the National Football League (1984), 183
luxury tax, 181

M
Mahony, D., 6–8, 12, 113
Major League Baseball (MLB), 12, 26, 97, 192, 198, 216, 231, 236
   and disparity in local support, 186
   and free agency, 161–162
   recruitment of foreign-born players, 215
   and the reserve clause, 158
Major League Baseball Players' Association (MLBPA), 161–162, 192
Major League Soccer (MLS), 12, 100, 231
   recruitment of foreign-born players, 215
Manchester United, 219
marginal revenue product (MRP), 151–154, 165–167
market allocation, 197
market failure, 170, 174, 176
market power, 171
market rivalries, 61–62

market structures, 64
McConomy, B. J., 176
McCray, Nikki, 160
McNally, Dave, 161–162
Meek, A., 4–5, 44, 107, 114, 115, 124
mergers, 101–103, 189, 191, 194–196, 220, 237
    conglomerate mergers, 195, 196
    horizontal mergers, 194–195, 196
    vertical mergers, 195, 196
Messersmith, Andy, 161–162
MIA v. NCAA (2004), 202
Milicic, Darko, 217
Miller, L. K., 5
Miller, Marvin, 161
Molinas, Jack, 194
Monaco, R. M., 229—230
monopoly, 69–70, 174–176, 177, 189, 196–197
    bilateral monopoly, 157–158, 167
    as an issue in the globalization of sport, 216
    natural monopoly, 171
    price and output in, 70–71, 174, 178
    and society, 71–73
monopsony, 156–157, 167
    in professional sports, 158–161
Mullin, B., 41
multipliers, 130, 138
    earning (income) multiplier, 131
    employment multiplier, 131–132
    and the multiplier effect, 132
    output (sales) multiplier, 131
    Type I multiplier, 132
    Type II multiplier, 132
municipal recreation departments, 10

N
NASCAR, 77, 193, 231
National Association for Intercollegiate Athletics (NAIA), 9
National Basketball Association (NBA), 12, 97, 194
    and the Bird Rule, 164
    efforts in international expansion, 215, 218, 219–220, 224
    and free agency, 163–164
    recruitment of foreign-born players, 215
National Basketball Players' Association (NBPA), 163–164, 165
National Collegiate Athletic Association (NCAA), 9, 10, 14–15, 26, 34–35, 234

acting as a cartel, 80–81, 184–185
and antitrust laws, 200–202
Division I, 9, 15, 215
Division II, 9
Division III, 9
Final Four basketball ticket lottery of, 48–49
problems facing, 185
self-regulation of, 184–185
National Collegiate Athletic Association v. Board of Regents of the University of Oklahoma and University of Georgia Athletic Assn. (1984), 201
National Federation of State High School Associations (NFHS), 16
National Football League (NFL), 12, 13, 192, 198, 199, 200
    acting as a cartel, 81
    acting as a monopsony, 157
    and free agency, 162–163
    as a monopoly, 69, 70
    and NFL Europe, 218, 220
National Football League Players' Association (NFPLA), 12, 192
National Hockey League (NHL), 12, 97, 99, 157, 199
    and free agency, 164–165
    recruitment of foreign-born players, 215
    and tax breaks in Canada, 90
National Hockey League Players' Association (NHLPA), 164–165
National Junior Collegiate Athletic Association (NJCAA), 9
National Labor Relations Act (1935), 157, 170, 173
National Sporting Goods Association, 57, 230, 233
Nautilus International, 62, 63, 70–71
"Network Sports Presidents Roundtable," 234
NFL Europe, 218, 220
Nike, 18, 62, 64, 99, 196, 218, 233
    "Code of Conduct," 30
    East Asian production of, 211
nonprofit sport organizations, 33
non-sport businesses, expenditures of (ENB—expenditures of non-sport businesses), 124–125
Norman, Greg, 219
North American Free Trade Agreement (NAFTA), 224
North American Industrial Classification System (NAICS), 1–4
Northern Securities Co. v. United States (1904), 189

jobs in, 125

See also sport industry delivery; sport industry self-regulation

sport industry delivery

by community, 93–95

by government, 85–93

by the private sector, 95–104

sport industry self-regulation, 169–170, 236

and collegiate athletics, 184–185

and competitive balance, 186–187

and government roles, 187

league-wide regulatory policies, 181–183

rationale for, 180–181

risk of, 185–186

syndicated (single-entity) ownership structure, 183–184

sport management firms, 21–22

Sport Marketing Quarterly, 21

sport participation, 115, 117–120

sport spectatorship/viewership, 115, 117

sporting boats, in the United States, 121

sporting goods, 17–18

sporting goods manufacturers, wholesalers, and retailers, 17–18

Sporting Goods Manufacturers Association, 119, 123, 124, 230

Sportmart, 221

Sports Authority, 18

Sports Broadcasting Act (1961), 81, 173, 179, 192, 198

Sports Business Journal, 21

sports facilities and buildings, 18–19

Sports Illustrated, 21

SportsLine USA, Inc., 98, 102

sports media, 19

sport broadcast media, 19–20

sport Internet media, 19, 21

sport print media, 19, 20–21

Stern, David, 220

Stigler, G., 80

Stotlar, D. K., 5–6

strategic alliances, 103–104, 237

supply, 44–47, 58

price elasticity of, 53–55

See also demand and supply

surplus

consumer surplus, 174

producer surplus, 175–176

surveys, 138–140

Sutton, W., 41

T

Tampa Sports Authority, 23, 24

Team Marketing Report, 41–42

television contracts, 182, 192, 200, 201

Toolson v. New York Yankees (1953), 192

Turco, D. M., 130, 143

two-part pricing, 75

U

United Soccer League (USL), 13–14

United States Football League (USFL), 160, 200

United States Olympic Committee (OSOC), 16–17

United States of America (USA) Volleyball, 12

United States v. E. C. Knight Co. (1895), 189

United States Football League v. National Football League (1986), 200

U.S. Department of Justice, Antitrust Division, 193

U.S. Travel Data Center, 138

V

vertical integration, 101–102

W

Wal-Mart, 196

Walsh, R. G., 87

Weisbrod, B. A., 94

Wheeler-Lea Act (1938), 191

Whitsitt, Bob, 237, 238

Wilson, 18

Women's National Basketball Association (WNBA), 12, 13, 200

Women's Sports Foundation, 16

World Golf Championship, 219

World Hockey Association, 164

World Hockey League (WHL), 199

Worldwide Basketball and Sports Tours, Inc. v. NCAA (2004), 202

Wotruba, T. R., 180

Y

Yahoo, 233

Yao Ming, 215, 217

Yew, Kay, 237

About the Authors

Mark Eschenfelder is an associate professor of economics at Robert Morris University. He received his BS degree in economics from Southern Illinois University—Edwardsville, his MA in economics from Western Illinois University, and his PhD in economics from the University of Missouri. His research focus is on economics education. He is co-director of the Annual Teaching Economics Conference and of the Center for Economic Education at Robert Morris University. The Annual Teaching Economics Conference addresses the interests of teachers of college-level economics. Participants at the first 16 conferences represented more than 100 colleges and universities from 35 states, the District of Columbia, and Canada. The Center for Economic Education at Robert Morris University is affiliated with the National Council on Economic Education and EconomicsPennsylvania. The Center promotes K–12 economic education in the local community. Eschenfelder has taught courses in the economics of professional sports and has conducted numerous workshops for K–12 teachers on the use of examples from the professional sports industry to teach economics. Eschenfelder is active in the Pennsylvania Economic Association and currently serves as its president.

Ming Li is the Director of the School of Recreation and Sport Sciences at Ohio University and a professor in Sports Administration. Before joining the faculty at Ohio University, he taught at Georgia Southern University for eleven years. During those years, he coordinated both the graduate and undergraduate sport management programs. Li's teaching and research interests are in financial and economic aspects of sport, and international sport management. He received his bachelor's degree in education from Guangzhou Institute of Physical Culture (PRC), his master's degree in education from Hangzhou University (PRC), and his Doctor of Education from the University of Kansas in Sport Administration. His professional affiliations include: American Alliance for Health, Physical Education, Recreation and Dance (AAHPERD), North American Society for Sport Management (NASSM), Sport Marketing Association, and International Council for Health, Physical Education, Recreation, Sport and Dance (ICHPER.SD). He used to hold offices as Member-at-Large on the Executive Council of NASSM, Chair of the Sport Management Council of the National Association for Sport and Physical Education (NASPE), and Director of the Sport Management & Administration Commission of ICHPER.SD. He was the recipient of the 1999 Taylor Dodson Award given by the Southern District American Alliance for Health, Physical Education, Recreation and Dance. The award is presented annually to a young professional who has demonstrated strong leadership qualities in the field of health, physical education, and dance. Li has actively participated in the NASPE-NASSM Sport Management Program Review process. In 2001, he finished his three-year term serving on the Sport Management Program Review Council (SMPRC). He has served as a consultant to several institutions in program evaluation and development in sport management. Li has memberships on the editorial boards of several professional journals, including *Journal of Sport Management*, *International Journal of Sport Management*, and *Sport Marketing Quarterly*. He was recently appointed the Assistant Editor for the *ICHPER.SD Journal*. In 1996, he worked for the Atlanta Committee for the Olympic Games (ACOG) as an Olympic Envoy. For the contribution he made to his profession, the institution, and the community, he was given the 2000–2001 Award for Excellence in Service by Georgia Southern University. Li has published more than 25 articles in refereed journals, two books (i.e., *Economics of Sport* and *Badminton Everyone*), and four book chapters, and made numerous refereed presentations at state, national, and international conferences. Li is an Honorary Guest Professor of the Guangzhou Institute of Physical Education, Guangzhou, China.